Public Relations on the Net

Public Relations on the Net

Winning Strategies to Inform and Influence the Media, the Investment Community, the Government, the Public, and More!

Shel Holtz

American Management Association

New York • Atlanta • Boston • Chicago • Kansas City • San Francisco • Washington, D.C.
Brussels • Mexico City • Tokyo • Toronto

This publication is designed to provide accurate and authoritative
information in regard to the subject matter covered. It is sold with
the understanding that the publisher is not engaged in rendering
legal, accounting, or other professional service. If legal advice or
other expert assistance is required, the services of a competent
professional person should be sought.

Library of Congress Cataloging-in-Publication Data

Holtz, Shel.
      Public relations on the net: winning strategies to inform and
influence the media, the investment community, the government, the
public, and more! / Shel Holtz.
          p.   cm.
      Includes index.
      ISBN 0-8144-7987-1
      1. Public relations—Computer networks.   2. Internet (Computer
network) I. Title.
      HD59.H596   1998
      659.2′09285′4678—dc21   98–8580
                                                                    CIP

Printing number

10 9 8 7 6 5 4 3 2

To my children, Benjamin and Rachel,
who think their Dad types on a computer for a living.
Their amusement always helps keep things in the proper perspective.

Contents

Acknowledgments

My appreciation for the Internet's capabilities as a tool for achieving two-way symmetrical public relations outcomes is the result of years of contact with others who share my passion for the Net's capabilities and potential. My continued admiration goes out to all of them, including:

My fellow members of NetGain, the first virtual consortium of electronic communications professionals: Craig Jolley of Online and Strategic Information Solutions, Peter Shinbach of The Birmingham Group, Tudor Williams of Tudor Williams Inc., and Charles Pizzo of P.R. PR.

Dan Janal, author of *The Online Marketing Handbook*, good friend, and regularly available conversationalist.

Jeffrey Hallett, principal of PresentFutures Group, whose insight into the synchronizing of the electronic media with the transformation of the business economy has been a revelation.

Don Middleberg, whose recognition of the Internet as a necessary component of communications planning has led the industry.

Katherine Paine, CEO of The Delahaye Group, and Angela Sinickas, principal with William M. Mercer, Inc., who have raised the measurement of Internet effectiveness to an art.

For their continued willingness to share ideas online and off, and in no particular order: Tom Geddie, Tim Hicks, Brian Kilgore, Ron Solberg, Mike Bayer, Ayelet Baron, Debra Goldentyer, Steve Crescenzo, David Murray, Dan Oswald, Jerry Bryan, and Peter Dean.

For the contribution it has made to my skills and abilities, the International Association of Business Communicators (IABC), with particular nods to President Elizabeth Allan and staff members Chris

Grossgart, Pam Arnold, Carole Sears, Natasha Spring, Jane Schenk, and the rest of the crew.

And of course, my wife Michele, who claims she isn't an Internet professional but uses it in her daily activities. That makes her a model of the Net's potential, not to mention increasing her tolerance for the amount of time I spend online, writing about being online, and talking about being online.

Introduction

The Internet represents one of the most important tools ever employed in the practice of public relations. Using it to its best advantage, however, requires strategic thinking about how to apply the Net to communications efforts. Communications professionals need to understand what the medium does best and what it doesn't do so well, then integrate it into comprehensive efforts that capitalize on the spectrum of possibilities it presents.

Much of the Net's potential remains to be established, but so far, the Internet *has* proven itself adept at a number of applications—applications with which the more traditional tools of public relations cannot compete.

Unfortunately, we haven't seen many of these capabilities applied to online public relations thus far. Rather, the Net has served as little more than an additional publishing vehicle. If someone justifies it as a communications tool, it's usually because it represents a cheap way to get material to a lot of people without the per-unit cost associated with printing or the production costs related to getting the message out via broadcast channels.

This is not a huge surprise, considering the technology-adoption curve. This curve suggests that the first uses to which any new technology are put duplicate the functions of existing technology. Only after we grow accustomed to using the new technology for these old uses do we begin to think outside the box and develop new applications that break through our previous limitations.

The Internet is experiencing the same phenomenon. A number of conditions need to be met before the Net becomes a tool for more than publishing and broadcasting—the two existing applications that have been applied to the Internet so far. Among these conditions are:

• *More people online.* Right now, only about 20 percent of the U.S. population is online, and significantly less of the worldwide community.

• *Ease of use.* You might think the point-and-click nature of the World Wide Web is simple enough, but it's still confusing for a lot of people. Besides, just *getting* onto the Web can present the average person with a technological challenge.

• *Speed.* The critics don't call it the World Wide Wait for nothing. Forget the fact that people used to wait until 6 P.M. for the evening news and an entire *day* for the newspaper to show up. The two or three minutes it takes for some Web pages to appear is more than many people can stand. Download times of several hours for files are intolerable.

• *Convergence.* OK, so you're on the Web. You find something interesting. You want to *act* on it. As often as not, you're required to jot down an 800-number and pick up a telephone. Sure, there's audio and video online, but the sound is tinny and the image is the size of a postage stamp and moves like a Keystone Cops movie. Before the Net can be fully utilized, all the media need to be available on a common interface with the degree of quality to which we have become accustomed on the separate channels.

Don't think that these factors are science fiction or even distant possibilities. They all are in development *now* and will most likely be taken for granted within five years. As they are happening, and more and more distinct and definable audiences take to the Net, organizations have the opportunity to begin applying the best strategic practices to communicating with those audiences online.

A Jump Start on the Twenty-First Century

This book is designed to help companies avoid the wait for the Internet to become a routine part of the landscape. But taking advantage of the principles and tactics outlined in these pages requires a fundamental, up-front understanding of what "public relations" means—at least in the context of how it can be applied effectively online. If your view of public relations is wrapped in notions of spin-doctoring and covering up problems, you won't find nifty new ways to accomplish these less-than-noble objectives here. Similarly, public relations is not a synonym for "marketing": This book is *not* about how to generate publicity for products or services. There are plenty of books that already adequately cover marketing and publicity tactics for the Internet.

So in order to be absolutely clear, let's establish a working definition of public relations right up front:

> ***Public relations is the strategic management of relations between an organization or institution and its various constituent audiences.***

Every organization has any number of strategic audiences, those audiences that can influence the company's ability to stay in business and succeed. These audiences include:

- Customers
- Consumers
- Employees
- The investment community
- The media
- Communities in which organizations do business
- Government
- Activist groups
- Academia

Each of these audiences can be divided into subaudiences. Included in the investment community, for example, are shareholders, investment analysts, and brokers. The subaudiences can be further broken down. Among shareholders, there are institutional owners (such as large pension funds), large individual shareholders, and mom-and-pop owners. Each audience has different interests and issues—and consequently, different informational needs and different reasons for engaging in a dialogue and interacting with the organization. The same subdivisions can be applied to any audience. Within the media segment, there are print and electronic media; consumer and trade media;

daily, weekly, monthly, and quarterly publications; large and small outlets; general and niche vehicles (the difference between, say, the *Los Angeles Times* and *The Wall Street Journal*).

Most companies are organized into functions that facilitate the day-to-day and long-term issues associated with getting the job done and putting money into the bank. Without an effective, strategic public relations function, these companies would encounter no end of trouble in managing all these varied and complex relationships. The representative of one department could say one thing to a regulatory agency while somebody from another department could offer a contradictory point of view to a newspaper reporter. When the inconsistency becomes a public issue, the company's credibility suffers. Further, few individuals in the company, no matter how admirable their motives, would present a view that balances *all* of the organization's interests with a thorough understanding of the implications of adopting a certain position.

The professional practice of public relations, then, is the effective management of relations with all of these audiences in a manner consistent with the best interests of the organization.

Under this definition, where do press kits come in? Press conferences? Press releases? These are just some of the *tactics* employed in a communications effort that has been developed to achieve specified measurable objectives. Campaigns that are limited to the distribution of materials and messages to audiences don't tend to work very well. These efforts are top-down, one-way communications efforts and don't address the very real need of the audiences to engage in an evolutionary discussion with the organization. There are even *two-way* communications processes that are ineffective, because the company holds all the cards. Sure, you may offer audiences an opportunity to submit input, but is it a real dialogue? The best public relations efforts are not only two-way but also *symmetrical*—that is, they afford both the company and the strategic audience equal opportunities to participate in the discussion and (even more important) equal opportunities to achieve an objective. This notion is the essence of the second overarching principle of public relations necessary to take advantage of the material in this book:

> *Effective public relations efforts are designed to result in a win-win for both the company and the audience with which it is communicating.*

For many, this approach to public relations may sound unfamiliar. After all, the very concept of public relations has been besmirched in recent years by a minority of practitioners who embody the worst tactics associated with the profession. These practices have led many in the public to associate public relations with redefining issues, twisting facts, and even outright lying. Of course, it's the unethical and unprincipled practitioners who grab the headlines. The vast majority of people engaged in public relations go about their work quietly and rarely draw any attention.

Enter the Internet

Still, even the best, most altruistic efforts to communicate with strategic audiences have been hampered by the triple limitations of time, money, and resources. There isn't enough money to staff a department to develop and implement comprehensive communications strategies with *every* audience whose activities could possibly have an impact on the organization. It is nigh impossible just to identify every one of those audiences, no less establish and maintain channels of communication with them that meet their needs and address their continually evolving issues. And what kind of tools are there that satisfy the demand for two-way, interactive, symmetrical communications?

The Internet and many of its associated technologies offer a solution to these challenges. When integrated into a strategic communications effort based on solid, business-oriented objectives, the Net can make it easier to achieve those most effective win-win scenarios. That's what this book is designed to help companies and other organizations do—apply the Internet to communications strategies that result in the achievement of measurable, bottom-line objectives.

About This Book

In *Public Relations on the Net,* I've taken an approach to the subject matter that is at once strategic *and* tactical. That is, the material addresses the means by which you can establish a return-on-investment for your online efforts, *and* it suggests the various tactical tools to use as you implement your strategy.

Structure

Part One: Communications on the Internet

Before we can understand where public relations is going on the Internet, we need to step back for a few minutes and assess where it has been and what its current state is. Part One begins with a report card on public relations efforts on the Internet, then covers in detail the considerations that must be included in any online communications activity. It looks at the ways in which electronic communications tools have changed the way audiences expect to get and use information.

A full understanding of the Internet and its components—e-mail, the World Wide Web, and discussion groups—is necessary, and that is presented here as well. Part One also discusses the principles of influencing audiences online and how to monitor activity online.

Part Two: Audiences and Measurement

Part Two, the heart of the book, dissects each of the key strategic audiences public relations professionals work with. These include:

- The media
- The financial and investment communities
- The government
- Communities
- Activist groups
- Audiences affected by organizational crises

Your company may well have audiences that are not covered in specific chapters. Customers and consumers are generally targets of marketing efforts as opposed to public relations campaigns, although they certainly become a strategic audience during a crisis or when an activist group makes an unanswered claim that garners significant attention. Employees are, by-and-large, an audience for intranets (i.e., private networks within organizations), which is too big a topic to tackle in these pages. However, this book ultimately addresses all audiences in the context of the various types of issues covered.

Part Two wraps up with a review of the various ways your organization can use the Internet to take its message directly to its smallest defined audience without relying on other media, as well as with methods by which you can measure the effectiveness of your online efforts.

Appendixes and Glossary

No Internet-based book would be complete without a set of Web sites and other online resources, so the Appendixes include these here. There is also a list of recommended readings—printed materials that can supplement the information presented in these chapters. Appendixes also cover how to establish a beneficial working relationship with your information technology* department, how to promote your online efforts, and writing for the computer screen. The book concludes with a Glossary of online terms.

Audience

This book is aimed primarily at public relations and organizational communications professionals trying to make sense of the Internet and how to use it effectively on behalf of their companies and clients. The reach of the material in these pages, however, goes well beyond the limits of the profession. I can think of two reasons nonpractitioners would want to understand how to communicate and wield influence on the Internet:

1. Every organization and institution has audiences with which it must communicate, but not every organization is large enough to retain a communications staff or pay a public relations agency to handle its efforts. In these cases, senior management—often the CEO—is responsible for coordinating communications efforts. Those individuals need to learn to use online tools to achieve their objectives in the absence of a communications professional to do it for them.

2. Sadly, there are public relations practitioners out there who just don't have a real interest in learning new tools. (Worse, there are those who prefer to practice propaganda and "spin" rather than effective, strategic public relations.) Frankly, CEOs don't care who manages the relations with constituent audiences, as long as the communication

---

*Information technology (IT) is the department name used throughout the book, although different companies have different names. Your company may call it information systems (IS), management information systems (MIS), or any of a host of other names.

gets done. In many organizations facing this dilemma, strategic communication falls to other departments, running the gamut from human resources to legal. The individuals in these jobs, facing the added responsibility of managing communication, can learn a lot from this book.

In short, every organization has audiences on which it relies to varying degrees to exist and thrive. If you are responsible in any way for managing your organization's relationship with one of those audiences, you'll find value in these pages.

Part One

Communications on the Internet

1

A Report Card on PR Use of the Internet

It would be charitable to characterize the use of the Internet for public relations as in its infancy. In fact, the profession's use of the Internet can be better described as embryonic. True, some advanced thinkers within the profession are using the Internet for crisis communications, issues identification and management, and interactive communications. Others are developing electronic newsletters, customizing the delivery of information to target audiences, and applying the Internet and the Web to one-to-one marketing and communication. Still, only a handful of practitioners have advanced to this stage, and even today's leading-edge applications barely scratch the surface of the Net's potential.

Most public relations activities on the Internet are limited to using it as yet another channel for the one-way, top-down publishing of information under the traditional formula of mass communication. And then there are the huge number of organizations and institutions that have not yet embraced the Internet at all as a communications tool.

The communications profession lags woefully behind much of the Internet community. However, we are not alone. Most of the professional uses of the Net are relatively primitive. The Internet is so new that businesses, unsure of what to do with it, are applying old uses to it. That's not uncommon, since the initial uses of *any* new technology are, in fact, the same things that were done with the *old* technology. Consider television, for example. In its infancy, television was used to do pretty much what was already being done with other, older technologies. Situation comedies (such as *The Jack Benny Show* and *The Burns and Allen Show*), dramas (such as *The Shadow, Inner Sanctum,* and *Playhouse 90*), and live broadcasts (including presidential speeches and boxing from the Los Angeles Olympic Auditorium) made the switch from radio to television. It took some time for the technology to become common enough for outside-the-box thinkers such as Rod Serling and Paddy Chayefsky to expand the scope of television's uses. Only after the technology was integrated into our culture were they able to apply new uses to television that had never been possible before.

Personal computers followed the same path. Most of us used our first computer for its word-processing capabilities. We replaced perfectly good typewriters with far more expensive PCs and went to training classes to learn how to use them. Later, desktop publishing replaced the tools of publication production: exacto knives, waxers, artboards, and typesetting machines. Now that the PC has been around for a while, we are more likely to take advantage of new applications that could never have existed without the computer: relational databases, brainstorming assistants, and photo manipulation programs.

And now we have the Internet, which has been part of the general landscape since only late 1993. As with every other technology, its early uses mimic those things we already were doing with existing tools:

- *It's based on document formatting, so it's a publishing medium.* This has led to a lot of Web sites that are treated precisely like magazines, newsletters, manuals, handbooks, and other print-based publications.
- *It's on a screen, so it's like television.* Treating the Internet like a new type of TV has led to efforts to apply entertainment principles to the Internet (such as the failed online soap opera *The Spot*).
- *It's like publishing and television wrapped up in one.* Since advertisers employ both media, the Internet must be a natural forum for luring customers.

The speed with which the general public has adopted the Internet, though, means that organizations do not have the luxury of time: We cannot wait for the natural evolution that carried other new technologies. Enough people are already using the Internet to compel us to begin applying sound principles of communication to the way we employ the technology on behalf of our organizations and clients. It took thirty years for radio to find its way into 40 million American homes, thirteen years for television, but only four years for the Web.

How Did We Get Here?

Communications professionals are on the cusp of a fourth stage of involvement on the Internet. This fourth stage will see online public relations evolve into strategic efforts that focus on results rather than on the tools of the technology. The first three stages didn't afford communicators much of an opportunity to make this transition. Let's look at the four stages.

Stage 1: Nerds in Charge

The Internet's history is well documented in a variety of books, articles, and online resources, so I won't spend a lot of time recounting it here. Suffice it to say that the Internet had its beginnings as a tool that allowed university-based scientists working in various government-funded programs to exchange information with one another despite their use of incompatible computer networks. Its popularity grew among the scientific, academic, and computer-science community, notably as a means of exchanging e-mail and participating in discussion groups.

The Internet did not appeal to audiences outside this limited group (sometimes referred to as computer nerds) for a variety of reasons. At first, computers were not widely available or widely used. Even after the introduction of the PC in the early 1980s, modems were seen as exotic tools with no practical business application. The growth of the bulletin board system (BBS) community initially did little to change that perception. BBSs were seen as the archaic, chaotic provinces of bedroom and garage hobbyists; there was little if anything of value to businesspeople online. It was still a difficult environment to learn to navigate even after larger commercial online services, led by Compu-Serve, began providing businesspeople with useful resources online. Configuring a modem was complex, the speed at which a modem worked was pitifully slow, and the text-based commands that users had to employ were far from intuitive. Only the most intrepid individuals from outside the scientist-academic-computer science community made the effort.

In 1989, while working at the Particle Physics Lab in Geneva, Tim Berners-Lee led a ninety-day development effort that resulted in the introduction of the World Wide Web as a new element of the Internet. Berners-Lee currently leads the World Wide Web Consortium. Prior to the introduction of the Web, the only way for an individual to view a document that resided on one of the computers constituting the network was to "telnet" into that computer. Using the telnet protocol* is a cumbersome and confusing process. You need to know how to get past the requirement for a login id and a password, and even then each computer features different navigation procedures. Plus, the entire operation is text-based. As a result of all this, the average person wanted nothing to do with the Internet. Berners-Lee wanted to create a protocol that allowed an individual reading an online document to be able to tab over to a highlighted word, hit the *enter* key, and have the protocol handle all the work that formerly required the telnet operation. The protocol would figure out on what computer the document resided, get into that computer, and retrieve the desired document.

The original World Wide Web was still a text-based system. The software that made it work resided on a server, not on a user's desktop computer. The user would have to logon to the server and activate the program (the most popular of which was called Lynx). Essentially, a user was turning his desktop computer into a dumb terminal (not unlike the Wang terminals common in office environments in the 1980s) while the server did all the work.

The Hypertext Transfer Protocol (developed by Berners-Lee) that makes the Web possible was (and still is) based on the concept of hyperlinks. It was the actualization of a concept that had been around for a long time: Visionary Ted Nelson popularized the concept with his never-completed Xanadu system, initially conceptualized in 1960. A hyperlink, in the Web's original incarnation, was a string of text characters accompanied by encoded information about the location of related information. That string of text would appear in a highlighted format; when invoked, the protocol would kick in, following the instructions in the code in order to retrieve the associated document. For instance,

---

*A *protocol* is a rule that governs how various elements of the Internet work. For details on the various protocols, see Chapter 3.

the following bit of code indicates that the acronym IABC (for the International Association of Business Communicators) would be a hyperlink:

```
<a href = "http://www.iabc.com/homepage.html">IABC</a>
```

When a user tabbed over to this highlighted text and hit the *enter* key, her computer would send out a request to the computer that contained the desired document (called the home page) and return the document so the user could view it on her screen.

Who would use such a system? At first, scientists, academics, and computer professionals. After all, generally, the only documents available on the Internet at the time were scientific in nature. Scientists at universities and research centers embedded the code in their papers, linking to documents referenced in their footnotes. Sometimes, they turned to members of their information technology staffs to help create the code. The system grew so popular with scientists and the few non-scientific members of the Internet community, though, that users began storing other hypertext-laden documents on their Internet-connected computers.

In 1993, a team from the National Center for Supercomputing Applications at the University of Illinois, led by a graduate student named Marc Andreesen, developed a graphical "front end" to the World Wide Web. They called the software a browser and named it Mosaic. This application ushered in several advances over the text-based version:

- Rather than tab over to a hyperlink, you could simply use your mouse to point your cursor at the link and click.
- The document that appeared on the screen could be formatted with headlines, bullet lists, and various other text treatments.
- The document could include graphics, such as photos or illustrations.
- The software resided on the user's computer rather than on a remote server.

Suddenly, the Web became a graphics-rich, easy-to-use environment. And the code that drove the Internet—the Hypertext Markup Language (HTML)—was so simple to learn that building a site on the

Web was practically child's play. Still, by and large, since it was the existing Internet community that knew about the Web, it was the Internet community that established Web sites.

The programmers, code writers, engineers, and computer scientists who made up this community weren't trying to market or sell anything. In fact, since they were the same people who had populated the Internet *before* Mosaic's introduction, they by and large held the same widespread belief that the Internet should never be commercialized. As recently as 1994, the common sentiment was: "Information should be free, the Internet is about people and community and exchange, and the very idea of business being done online is an abomination." As a result, the vast majority of Internet domains (i.e., addresses) ended in *edu*, the designation of an educational institution.

When these individuals built sites—even those that were housed on servers owned by the companies they worked for—the objective was simply to see what they could do, how far they could stretch the limitations of the browser. Once a site or a page was completed, the designer simply went into a Usenet discussion group and alerted others that the site was there. For a while, the World Wide Web was a sort of hyperlinked, global show-and-tell: "Come to my page and see what I did!" Also, serious academics produced their research on the Web and created sites designed to introduce their departments and the focus of their efforts. The notion that the power of the Internet and the World Wide Web might be brought to bear on commercial interests was not only viewed as inappropriate— it was actively resisted.

Stage 2: The Nerds Go Commercial

By now, the pool of systems professionals who were using the Internet had expanded beyond those based in universities and research centers and into the business world. Network specialists—responsible for their organizations' local area networks (LANs) and wide area networks (WANs)—initially began noodling with the Internet as a means of exchanging network-based information with their peers, using e-mail and Usenet newsgroups. As the Web exploded, they joined the fray, at first with pages that simply tested their ability to create HTML.

The startling growth of the Web's popularity (and consequently, the entire Internet) happened so quickly that the information technology specialists who were developing pages quickly developed audiences that transcended other systems professionals. Hobbyists began building personal home pages and sites dedicated to their personal obsessions—favorite movies, singers, conspiracy theories, and political and social points of view, to name a few. Others, less inspired or interested in creating content, merely spent time "surfing" around this new medium, looking to see what was there.

With so many people in cyberspace, many of the systems professionals thought it might not be a bad idea to develop a page or two that focused on the organization for which they worked. Thus, the Web saw its first commercial sites, which led to a rash of complaints and even of some activism designed to put an end to what many of the early inhabitants of cyberspace saw as a blatant violation of the online world's unwritten rules. Not that the early business-oriented pages were all that effective—many were merely online versions of existing print material, rewritten to adopt the wry, cynical tone employed by many early Web pages. It was not uncommon for early sites to make inappropriate use of logos, to misrepresent aspects of the business, and to convey inaccurate information. Often, sites went up and were never updated. And few business-oriented sites did more than announce, "Hey! Here we are!" They were nothing more than billboards in cyberspace.

Stage 3: Communicators Elbow In

Inevitably, communicators were among those who succumbed to media hype about the Internet, found service providers, logged on, and began to explore the contents of the Net. Many of them found that their companies had sites they hadn't known about. *Wait a minute*, they thought. *How come somebody's communicating about our company and it's not being supervised by the communications department?*

Of course, it wasn't only communicators who discovered the existence of "official" company material on the Internet. The organization's legal staff discovered inappropriate use of copyrighted material. And surprised executives were often informed of their company's online presence by their children. (*"Hey, Dad! I didn't know your company used four-letter words in your advertising."*)

The discovery of the company's Web site led communicators to knock on the systems department's door. (In some cases, it was the *lack* of a company site—the fact that a competitor had a site but theirs did not—that led communicators to approach the systems group.) The goal was the same: to apply fundamental communications principles to the company's online presence. "If we're going to have a Web site," the communicators figured, "we may as well make sure we're using approved copy to describe our products or services."

In some cases, the two departments worked together smoothly. In others, hostility erupted between the systems and communications departments. Communicators believed that the systems-based Webmaster was misusing the Web: Since it was a communications medium, it belonged in the jurisdiction of the communications department. The systems group felt that the communicators, who had heretofore expressed absolutely no interest in the Web, suddenly wanted to wrest it away from the department that had built it from scratch only because it had become popular. (Much of this hostility still exists. How communicators can deal with it is addressed in Appendix A.)

Stage 4: The Net as a Business Tool

Many organizations are starting to get beyond the question of who within an organization should own the Internet. Ultimately, the Internet and its various elements are business tools that need to be applied like any other business tool. Nobody within a typical organization argues over who owns the company's printing press or who has access to outside printing resources. Those departments that need to have something printed in order to address a sound business need simply do so (using appropriate organizational channels, of course, such as the purchasing department).

When it comes to the Internet, the role of each department in the company should be based on the department's area of expertise and the benefits it can bring to the use of the medium. The public relations department is charged with maintaining excellent relations with the company's various audiences. Thus, any use of the Net consistent with that mandate should be the province of the PR department. The marketing department is responsible for making the company's products and services more desirable. Consequently, any online efforts toward that end should be the responsibility of the marketing department. Communicating investment information online should be the province of the investor relations department.

Does that mean there is no longer a role for the systems professionals who introduced the Internet to the company? Of course not. The systems professionals should be responsible for the hardware, the connections, the configurations. No communicator in her right mind would try to set up and operate an offset press by herself, and likewise, none would try to set up a server by herself. Conversely, no printer would be expected to assume responsibility for the content of the publication she is going to print, and likewise, systems departments should not presume to be responsible for the company's online content.

Ultimately, no organization intentionally invests money that is not expected to provide some kind of return on the investment. Money budgeted for the Internet is no exception. This fourth stage of the Internet's business evolution is seeing an organization's various departments assume responsibility for the elements of the Internet that are related to the results for which they are responsible. When most organizations have entered this latest stage, outside-the-box thinking will become the norm. The Internet will be used to meet challenges and capitalize on opportunities in ways that were unthinkable before it was introduced to the business world.

Grading Public Relations on the Internet

Most public relations activities online currently rest squarely in Stages 2 or 3. They are not strategic (that is, they are not aligned with the company's bottom-line strategies). They are not measurable (that is, there is no mechanism for assessing their effectiveness). They are not targeted toward specific audiences or constituencies.

For the most part, organizations' online public relations efforts are limited to a small component of a larger, catchall company site on the World Wide Web. Most companies establish their outpost on the Web using the company name, such as *www.acme.com*. The home page is static—it never changes. On the page, the company proudly displays its logo and links to the various sections of the site. As a result, the one site needs to accommodate all possible audiences, from customers and consumers to newspaper reporters and investment analysts. One link points to product information, another to job opportunities. Click here for the latest annual report, or here for a listing of dealerships (or sales offices or medical networks and so on).

Under this scheme, the public relations activities usually are restricted to an archive of press releases, accessible by clicking on a link typically called something like "In the News." Some organizations include speeches. There is virtually nothing on the site that would draw a member of a specific defined constituency to a *particular* release, speech, etc. And there is even less that helps a representative of a constituent audience meet his specific needs. As a result, it is impossible to assess the impact of this type of online effort on the objectives that have been set for that audience.

Of course, some organizations are beginning to adopt next-generation approaches to the Internet. They are, for example, using the company's home page to communicate its current most important message or to address an emerging crisis. They are adding position papers to the archives of press releases and speeches. They are providing resources useful to specific audiences. But these companies remain a tiny minority.

When asked to assess the return on investment for these efforts, we proudly point to hits.* Katherine Paine, CEO of The Delahaye Group, suggests that hits is an acronym for How Idiots Track Success. She's exactly right. Hits don't tell us much of anything, beyond how busy the server is! (More on this in Chapter 13, when measurement and evaluation are discussed.) Some software allows us to count individual visits, but this is only a little better than counting hits. Counting visits won't tell us if the visitor to our site got the information she wanted, if she made a particular decision based on the visit, or if she was part of the audience we were trying to attract. Measuring the effectiveness of an online effort by counting visits is like limiting the assessment of how well a print campaign worked by counting the number of people who received the printed material!

For the most part, however, this is the state of online public relations. Many PR departments are leaving the online work to technical staff. Others outsource it. Some ignore it altogether. Nearly all see it as something separate and distinct from their day-to-day public relations work.

---

*Servers record a hit whenever a file is transferred as a result of a request somebody makes. For example, let's say you have a page on your Web site with two pictures on it. When somebody visits that page, the server transfers three files to the visitor's browser—the Web page file itself and the two pictures. The server then records three hits. This is not a very sound way to determine the popularity of a site.

The Need for Change

Given time, public relations professionals—and those who communicate on behalf of their companies—will embrace the Internet strategically. We have no choice. The Net will become an integrated part of our culture, a routine element of the landscape, and we will incorporate it into our thinking as easily as we do television and video, desktop publishing and audio teleconferencing.

Unfortunately, we don't have the time to wait for that natural evolution to sweep us up. Our audiences already are online. Just how many people are on the Internet? I hesitate to give a number, since it will be out of date before the pages of this book roll off the press. Estimates for the turn of the century are in the neighborhood of 200 million. A few other statistics are significant enough to rate attention:

• The demographic makeup of the Internet community is leveling. Based on a number of studies looking at the demographics of Internet users, there no longer is an "average" online user. The ratio of men to women is almost equal, all ages are represented (with senior citizens constituting the fastest growing segment), and income and education are no indicators of who uses the Net.

• Popular mythology suggests that most of the people on the Internet are looking at pornography, engaging in mindless chat, and inhabiting juvenile discussion groups. In fact, the single greatest use of the Internet is research, according to a Price-Waterhouse study.

The Internet's egalitarian nature means that many members of our audiences have already developed an innate understanding of how to use the Net to communicate and to influence. They have cultivated this ability without joining professional associations or earning communication degrees, and without accumulating professional experience. It is simply part of a culture that is unfolding at lightspeed. This has significant implications for public relations people. On the Internet, where anybody can become a publisher, customers can and do organize campaigns to influence company behaviors. Online protests can achieve previously unheard-of results. Boycotts can be undertaken overnight. Products and services can be disparaged in open forums populated by people who share common interests. Concerned audiences may assume that lies and misrepresentations are accurate, and those lies can spread like the Ebola virus. Crises can be created online, and crises generated elsewhere can be exacerbated. We must learn to use the Internet to address these issues on behalf of our organizations.

But we also must learn to use it proactively, as a means of reaching our audiences with the most effective tools, of engaging them, and of listening to them. And if we wait? Then we deserve our fate. We put our organizations at risk and we leave communication to those who do not fully comprehend the process of managing institutional relationships in support of the organization's key strategies.

Conclusion

Excellent communications and public relations are those that serve to facilitate the relationship between an organization and its strategic publics. The Internet can play a significant role in this kind of public relations, but generally it has not yet been used to that end. The balance of this book focuses on just how to begin applying the Internet to strategic communications.

2

How Communication Has Been Forever Changed

The Internet has changed communication forever.

A lot of public relations professionals who started out as newspaper reporters and are firmly grounded in the principles of one-to-many, top-down communication don't want to hear it, but there's no hiding from it: The principles that have guided communication no longer work. They have been replaced by a new set of principles that must be clearly understood before we can begin to take real advantage of the best tool for communicating in this new age.

Communicating in the Information Economy

Make no mistake: It *is* a new age—or, to be more accurate, a new *economy*. In his book *The Third Wave,* Alvin Toffler defined the new economy as an *information economy,* a term fraught with potential for misinterpretation, notably because the information economy is the successor of the *industrial* economy. It's all too easy for the executives of a "big iron" company—one that is firmly rooted in manufacturing—to dismiss the information economy as a phenomenon that affects only businesses that deal in information.

That is a dangerous mistake. When defining an *economy,* one of the key factors is the primary element of production.* The first econ-

---

*Another key factor is the currency used in the economy. Whereas money is the currency of the industrial economy, some suggest that *attention* will be the currency of the information economy. We can argue how realistic this suggestion is, but there is no doubt that getting the attention of our audiences will be a challenge of monumental importance—another reason to learn how to use the Internet strategically. This issue is addressed further in Appendix C.

omy of significance in human history was the agricultural economy, whose key production elements were land and labor. When machines began replacing the work of humans a few hundred years ago, the industrial economy was born and capital was added to land and labor to create a triumvirate of primary production elements.

Today, however, all three primary elements of production—land, labor, and capital—have been supplanted by information. That is not to say that land, labor, and capital no longer play a part in the process of production. Without them, how could Levi Strauss & Company stitch together pants to sell in retail stores? However, information today has become more *important*. It is information that helps determine the markets for the company's various products, establish the fashion trends to pursue, and identify the fabric needed by each manufacturing site based on forecasted volumes. Information suggests the approach to advertising to different markets. Without systems that provide this information—and a host of other data—and open access to it by any Levi Strauss employee who needs it, the company would founder. The best factories, the most qualified workers, the strongest capitalization—none of it would matter. The days are gone when somebody like Henry Ford could just introduce a car to the marketplace and everybody would buy it.

Characteristics of Communication in the Two Economies

The industrial economy was distinguished by a series of characteristics, protocols for behavior that governed how industrial organizations were managed. The way we communicated in the industrial economy was entirely consistent with those characteristics, which have been turned on their head in the information economy.

Industrial Economy	Information Economy
• Top-down	• Networked
• Based on quantity	• Based on quality
• Batch-processed	• Customized
• Producer-driven	• Customer-driven

Let's explore each of these characteristics and how communicating with constituent audiences is changing as a result of the changing nature of business at large.

Top-Down vs. Networked

Industrial economy companies were organized around a command-and-control structure, exemplified by the organization chart. The typical organization chart had one box at the top, occupied by the top dog (whose title might be president, chief executive officer, chairman, or principal). Below him were a few boxes occupied by the top dog's direct reports. Each had responsibility for a specific part of the organization's operation, and the cascading set of boxes beneath each of those direct reports worked to produce results associated with that aspect of the business. The function of the organization chart is to control information.* Decisions in this environment are made at the levels where authority has been assigned. The more important the decision, the higher up the chart you have to go, since that's where the information required to make an informed decision resides.

Communication worked the same way. As communicators, we occupied boxes near the top of the chart. (In the box at the very top resided the top dog, whether a CEO or a client, whose strategies we were working to support.) From this lofty position, we set objectives. We identified audiences, segmenting them based on the research and demographics. We picked the issues to communicate based on our objectives. We selected the tools to use (press releases, video news releases, story placements, press conferences). We selected the channels to use. Audiences had little to say, despite their needs. Of course, we might have used focus groups and other techniques to obtain audience feedback, but those still were on our terms. We selected the focus group participants, the venue, the facilitator, and the subject matter.

Everything is different in the information economy. In the information economy, control of information gives way to open access to information. The hierarchical organization chart—an effective tool in the industrial economy—is a liability in an environment in which success depends upon moving quickly and being flexible and adaptive. In place of the organization chart, successful companies are developing

---

*That's not surprising when you consider that the organization chart has its genesis in the military command-and-control structure, also designed to control information. The commander in chief, in the solitary box at the top of the chart, possesses all information, while the foot soldier at the bottom of the chart—the most likely to be captured—is in possession of only what he needs to know in order to accomplish his objectives for the day.

networks of people and information, all readily accessible by any employee who needs them to make an informed decision, solve a problem, or capitalize on an opportunity. Similarly, the way we communicate with our audiences needs to become more networked, with information accessible to those who need it when they need it. The more people who join the network, the more valuable it becomes. These networks continue to expand at mind-boggling speeds, both inside our organizations and among our audiences—on the Internet.

Based on Quantity vs. Based on Quality

Companies earned wealth in the industrial economy by selling as many units of their products as they could. The front office cried, "More, more, more!" and it reverberated through the marketing department (which created the need) to the sales department (which filled the orders) to the factory floor (where the output had to keep up with demand). All efforts were geared toward producing and selling as many widgets as possible.

Public relations efforts mimicked the quantity imperative. If we had a press release to distribute, it had to go to as many media outlets as possible, so we would rack up as many column inches of print and minutes of air time as we could. If we identified a spokesperson to represent a product, we worked our tails off to make sure that as many writers and reporters interviewed her as we could scare up. If she appeared on *Good Morning New York,* she also had to be on *Good Morning Detroit, AM Toronto,* and *Regis and Kathie Lee.* When we published an annual report, we crammed it with all the messages we wanted all our audiences to absorb, and we printed scores of them. The prevailing belief was that the more opportunity there was for our target audiences to see the message, the more likely it was that they *would* see it. We measured our effectiveness primarily by the number of pairs of eyeballs that had potentially seen the message.

The information economy turns the quantity imperative on its head. The number of items an organization sells depends entirely on the *quality* of the item. People pay for quality, but they won't pay even a deeply discounted price for something that falls below their quality standards. Ever since the Japanese began to beat U.S. businesses by offering better products, thousands of American companies have made quality a focus. While quality also has become a hollow cliché in many organizations—and a source of income for an army of consultants and authors—products and services truly must meet the requirements they promise to meet. Raising the bar on its ability to meet requirements gives a company a competitive edge; hence, the push to continually improve quality—that is, to come closer to achieving the Holy Grail of zero defects.

The same concept holds true of communication in the information economy. Successfully placing a billion impressions is counterproductive, to say the least, if the quality of the message is substandard. Quality communications are those that meet the requirements—the *expectations*—of the audience for which they are intended. Public relations practitioners can achieve quality with a single well-placed message in an Internet discussion group, a powerful dialogue in an e-mail discussion list, or a meticulously researched position statement on a targeted Web site.

Batch-Processed vs. Customized

If quantity was an imperative of the industrial economy, then economics demanded that each of the widgets produced be exactly like all the others. Making a widget that was *different* would mean increased costs, even though a customer or two would have benefited from a revised configuration. Henry Ford, when introducing the Model A to the public, wryly noted that the car was available in any color a customer might want—as long as it was black! If a customer wanted a Model A, black was the only option.

No longer. Now, a driver expects to be able to order a customized car that meets her specific and unique desires. She can specify not just the color but the type of stereo, power equipment, moon roof, spoiler, wood paneling, and transmission. Customization is the key to market share in the information economy, based on knowing what various classes or categories of customers want. Just try to tell a homemaker that she can obtain a product one way and one way only. She doesn't have to acquiesce: Competitors are ready to satisfy her needs with different sizes, strengths, scents, ingredients, and packaging, designed to address different situations. (If you think there's only one way to buy Tide laundry detergent, for instance, it's probably been a while since you've moseyed up and down the aisles of a grocery store.)

Still, public relations efforts generally result in the production of

one kind of information to accommodate all members of an audience—
and these communications are sometimes meant to accommodate all
audiences. Consider the example of an annual report, usually considered the organization's premier communications tool. It is crafted to
deliver key messages to investment analysts, brokers, institutional
shareholders, mom-and-pop shareholders, prospective investors, financial media, public media, trade media, current and potential strategic partners, government, and every other conceivable audience. The
reason? It would be outrageously expensive to produce customized versions of the annual report to address the specific information needs of
each audience—and that doesn't even account for the cost of developing and maintaining the mailing lists for each audience segment. Instead, it is incumbent upon cost-conscious communicators to keep the
per-unit cost of the annual report (the cost of each printed copy) as low
as possible. Crafting a report that suits as many audiences as possible
makes it possible to achieve that cost target.

Thanks to the critical nature of information, however, one-size-
fits-all no longer cuts it. Each individual expects to get just the information he needs, information that answers the question he has *right
now*. Providing that information requires organizations to find a way to
allow audiences to customize the information made available to them.

Producer-Driven vs. Customer-Driven

Industrial economy companies made their decisions at the top of the
organization chart, determined by what those at the top believed would
sell. How did they arrive at the conclusion that this or that product or
service would be a success? Some relied on market research. Others
looked to internal research and development departments. Some took
cues from their spouses (and not always unsuccessfully: Lillian Disney
suggested to Walt that Mickey was a better name for his new animated
mouse than Mortimer). A lot of executives pursued new technologies
developed in-house, regardless of how useful the public might find
them. The point is that the decisions were made by a core group of
high-ranking executives acting in virtual autonomy.

But customers call the shots in the information economy. Improved customer satisfaction is the new rallying cry at many organizations, and consultants are garnering high prices teaching companies
how to be more customer-driven. In most cases, the answer is simple:

Listen to what customers say they want, and make sure you provide it. Companies such as Matrix Marketing, Inc., are earning big returns providing phone-based customer service on behalf of clients, by listening and cataloging the information customers provide in sophisticated databases. They feed that information back to their clients, who use it to make product and service decisions.

Companies engage in communication with strategic audiences by counting on their public relations departments to establish key messages and push them down to their audiences. Generally, the company dictates the theme of these discussions. In the information economy, the dialogue has to be two-way, with the company engaging in discussions in which the agenda can be set as easily by either the audience or the company.

Four New Communications Models

The shift from an industrial to an information economy would not have been possible without the development of the technologies to facilitate the flow of the information that is the economy's engine. The Internet and other online forums (such as America Online, CompuServe, and independent bulletin board systems) have hastened the changing expectations of audiences about how they get and use information. Four models of communication that public relations practitioners have taken for granted since the inception of the profession have undergone irrevocable changes as a result of the introduction and rapid assimilation of online technology—changes entirely consistent with (and in fact, partly driven by) the shifting characteristics of successful information age businesses. Let's analyze the four models.

From Few-to-Many to Many-to-Many

A. J. Leibling, a media critic with *The New Yorker,* wrote, "Freedom of the press belongs to those who own one." Since the advent of modern mass communications (heralded by the invention of the printing press), most formal communication has been a one-way, top-down affair. A media elite, made up of the few organizations and institutions with the wherewithal to publish and distribute to the masses, communicates to audiences. The audiences are limited to playing the role of information consumers. For the vast majority of people, the ability to publish our opinions, thoughts, or positions is beyond the realm of possibility. The cost of a page in *The Wall Street Journal* or a minute of advertising time on *ER* is simply more than the average person—even some institutions—can afford.

In the old, traditional, few-to-many communications model, the organization set the agenda and exercised control over the nature of the information published. The objective of the communication was in the hands of the organization that paid for it. The audience could be targeted through tried-and-true demographic segmenting. Once identified, the organization then selected the publications the target audience read, placed billboards in the neighborhood the target audience populated, and bought airtime on the television and radio shows to which the target audience tuned in.

Once the members of the audience received the information, their opportunities to engage the publishing organization in any kind of substantive dialogue were limited. They could write letters to the editor or call the organization's offices. But the organization had no compelling reason to respond (although it often aggregated the results of feedback in order to assess the effectiveness of the communication). In fact, organizations—even those with the budgets and staff resources to engage in the initial communication—did not have the *ability* to respond to individuals, at least, not outside the scope of day-to-day customer service activities.

Further, audience members had limited opportunities to engage other audience members in a discussion of the company's message. How could you go about finding somebody who viewed the same material you read and was sympathetic to your point of view?

The introduction of computer-mediated communication has turned the few-to-many communications model on its head. The Internet provides a platform for publication that anyone can afford and helps individuals target their audiences. The exclusive ability to publish, once held by organizations, has been redistributed to the masses, and the consequences are staggering. No matter how much money an organization spends on its communications efforts, in the wired world, it is now just one voice among many. Many of the Web sites ranked among those getting the top 5 percent of traffic are individual—not institutional—efforts.

Businesses need to recognize the many implications of the new many-to-many model:

• People who share an interest in your organization, its products, the environment in which it operates, or the issues with which it grapples can talk freely with one another in public forums.

• People who are fans of the organization or its products or services can publish Web sites that glorify the subjects of their interest. Barbie doll collectors, for example, craft pages dedicated to the Mattel product; *Star Trek* fans build *Star Trek* sites.

• Those who have a problem with an organization can craft sites that criticize or denigrate the company and its reputation. These "attack" or "rogue" sites have been launched against companies like NutraSweet (by activists), Disneyland (by a disgruntled fan), Exxon (by environmentalists), and Allstate Insurance (by a customer whose claim was rejected). More information on how to handle attack sites is available in Chapter 10.

My first exposure to the power of the many-to-many communications model did not involve business but did spotlight the power of the networked community to diminish the power of—and the need for—traditional, institution-driven communication. My son, Benjamin, who was about ten years old at the time, had fixated on an animated Japanese movie called *Lensman.* The name of the movie rang a bell; I had several friends who read science fiction novels while I was in high school, and I thought one of them had mentioned a book by the same name. Since my wife and I were trying to entice Ben to read more, I thought finding the book on which his favorite movie was based would motivate him to read it. The local library did not have the book in its card catalog, and I couldn't find it in *Books in Print.* I drove to a bookstore specializing in science fiction and fantasy, but the youngster behind the counter had never heard of it.

At this point, most of us would be inclined to believe we were mistaken (it wasn't *Lensman,* it must have been something like *Cameraman.*) But I wasn't ready to give up. Since I was a relatively new subscriber to the CompuServe information service, I spent a few minutes rummaging through the list of discussion forums before finding the Science Fiction and Fantasy Literature group. I posted a message there explaining my plight, then checked back about four hours later to see if anybody had responded.

I found fourteen replies waiting. Each one identified E. E. "Doc" Smith as the author, and each one pointed out that Smith had written an entire series of Lensman books. Several of the replies listed the titles of all the books in the series. A few of the messages offered synopses of each book's plot. Two reviewed each book in the series. My favorite reply came from a U.S. serviceman stationed in Germany who explained that he was a big fan of the books, and he knew they were out of print in the United States. However, he said, they *were* in print in English in Germany, and if I failed to find the books at home, I could send him a check and he would ship the books to me from Europe.

Let me reiterate: It took only *four hours* to learn from ordinary people who shared a common interest in science fiction what I was unable to learn from the official sources of information.

On the WELL, one of the early virtual communities based in San Francisco, a discussion group carries this concept to a new height. "Ask the Experts" is a forum for people with questions, populated by people with answers. Thousands of WELL subscribers (known as WELLbeings) review the questions that are raised, looking for one consistent with their areas of expertise so they can provide an answer and look smart.

I encountered another instance of many-to-many communication after I submitted a letter to the editor to *FastCompany* magazine. I was disturbed that a series of articles on change management failed to recognize the importance of a strategic communications effort. My letter appeared in the magazine along with my name and e-mail address. Within a few days, I received an e-mail message from a *FastCompany* reader who thought the whole issue of change management warranted continued discussion. She had sent her message to every author of a letter to the editor that had been printed in the magazine, establishing a de facto Internet mailing list. The discussion among that group of letter writers continued for several weeks.

In the many-to-many environment, an individual's or institution's credibility is based on the value of the information posted. That credibility is assessed by the individuals who read it, but it is tested in discussions in which those individuals can engage with one another.

Media covering cyberspace have reported hundreds of instances of many-to-many communication influencing participant behavior. A few include:

- Senior citizens, who form communities in order to engage in social activities in the evening, when many are reluctant to go out (seniors, in fact, represent the fastest growing online audience)
- Medical patients, who uncover treatments their doctors were unaware of
- Caregivers of Alzheimer's patients, chained night and day to their loved ones, who form an online support group
- Investors, who create an online club to share successes, tips, and advice
- Employees, who visit a "sound off" discussion group in order to get anger or frustration off their chests

Note that none of these examples has anything to do with computers, computer users, the online world itself, computer games, or anything related to the digital world. Rather, they are real-world subjects: The audience has simply found a forum using the new tool of cyberspace.

Case Study: *Time* Magazine

Time magazine's technology editor thought he had uncovered a sensational scoop. An undergraduate at Cornell University had reportedly conducted a thorough study of the Internet and determined the exact extent of pornography online—and it was *huge. Time,* Cornell, and the student entered into a secrecy agreement: The study would not be discussed until the *Time* cover story appeared. However, the technology editor sought opinions about the issue from the online community, which let people know that *Time* was planning on publishing *something.* At the time, the online community was very sensitive to the subject of pornography on the Internet, since members of Congress were crafting legislation that would effectively censor the Net, which heretofore had been a sort of wide-open frontier where the members of the population were creating the rules without interference from outside powers.

Alerted that *Time* was going to publish the results of a study, members of media-related discussion groups—notably on the WELL—prepared to dig into the study the instant it was released. Volunteers agreed to dissect various elements of the study. For example, Donna Hoffman, a research professor at Vanderbilt University's Owens Graduate School of Management, would explore the methodology used. Also involved was Mike Godwin, staff counsel for the Electronic Frontier Foundation, an advocacy group dedicated to the retention of liberties in cyberspace. The group coalesced virtually overnight, made up of people who never would have met without the Internet's community-building attributes.

Time released the article with a sensational cover, an illustration of an impressionable child being seduced by a computer screen. The online activists instantly went to work. Within a matter of days, they had dismantled the study, casting serious doubt about its methodology, results, and conclusions. One member of the group investigated the undergraduate who wrote the study, and found that he had contracted with a publisher to write a handbook about how to make money in the pornography business. The results of the study would reinforce the market for the manual.

Time's technology editor struggled in online forums to defend the article, but ultimately, about two weeks after the story ran, *Time* published a full-page retraction, essentially agreeing with the conclusions of the online activists that the results of the study were fraudulent.

How might those who disagreed with the results of the study have voiced their beliefs in the absence of the Internet and its many-to-many nature? Certainly they never would have been able to form an *ad hoc* task force. Individually, they might have written letters to the editor, which *Time* may or may not have opted to print. Individually, they never would have led a publishing giant like *Time* to retract so visible and prominent a story. The many-to-many model made it possible.

Receiver-Driven Communications

Before the Internet, communications were essentially producer-driven (as noted earlier in this chapter) and linear. That is, material was presented in a logical, sequential order. As gatekeepers, the authors and editors gathered the facts and information they would use in the document, then culled the elements that would make it into print, making judgments about the importance and relevance of each bit of information. Then they arranged the information in a sequence that began at the beginning and proceeded through a logical progression. The objective was ultimately to bring the reader along to the publishing organization's point of view or compel the reader to undertake an action consistent with the company's goals.

The order in which the material was presented was based on the perspective of the author and the institution for which the author worked. For example, an insurance company might present its information to prospective and existing customers based on its different plans: "We have health and welfare plans, disability plans, life insurance plans, and property and casualty plans. Under health and welfare, we offer medical, dental, and vision insurance plans. In the category of medical insurance, we offer an indemnity plan, a Health Maintenance Organization, and a Preferred Provider Organization." Within each section, there would be descending levels of information. Also, each section would be written in such a way that the reader was taken by the hand and led through the information. Anybody trying to start in the middle would be confounded, because the context of the material was set in the beginning. In the linear environment of communication before the Internet, readers had no choice but to start at the beginning and read from start to finish, the way the author intended.

Such a presentation would be fine if a consumer wanted an overview of an insurance company's lines of business. Most of the time when we dive into this kind of information, though, it is because we already *know* what we need to know: *I already have a life insurance policy. We are about to have a baby, and I'd like to be a responsible parent. I would like to increase the level of life insurance I'm carrying. How many levels of insurance can I increase from my current level before I am required to take a physical and get a doctor's approval?* In a linear document, it can take a fair amount of time to dig up that information, particularly if the way you come at the information is inconsistent with the structure used to present it. Even more frustrating to a consumer might be this scenario: *I carry your medical insurance. My kid just fell off his bike and broke his arm. What do I do?* Flipping through a long document designed to provide detailed information on all kinds of plans would simply be too time-consuming.

The Stress of Information Overload

In fact, most people are crushed for time these days. We live in an era that is suffering the consequences of the downsizing/rightsizing/capsizing binge of the 1980s and early 1990s. Downsizing rarely is accompanied by a reduction in work requirements. Instead, the tasks performed by those who have been let go shift to those who remain. Eight-hour workdays are nothing more than a joke in many organizations. We work ten-, twelve-, fourteen-hour days. We work Saturdays. We bring work home with us.

Part of the blame for the amount of time we spend at work is the amount of information with which we must cope. *Information overload* is the term most often associated with this flood of information that constantly overwhelms us. Through various traditional and emerging media, we are blasted with messages day and night, and from this barrage we must find those nuggets of information that meet our individual needs. The amount of time we spend sifting through the irrelevant material in order to identify that which is relevant is a source of frustration.

There are many reasons for the increased volume of information. Publishing technology has allowed publishers to create cost-effective special-interest magazines that target small audiences. (Imagine visiting a newsstand twenty years ago and finding magazines like *Ferret World*!) Desktop publishing has made it easy for everybody to produce her own material. Companies that once produced a single employee publication now distribute dozens of separate departmental newsletters, bulletins, magazines, and other communications. We live in a world where information is delivered through a fire hose, but our individual capacity is about the size of a thimble.

A study sponsored by Pitney Bowes reveals that information technology is largely to blame for information overload. The study—"Managing Corporate Communications in the Information Age"—was conducted by the Institute for the Future, Gallup, and San Jose State University. It concluded that the average *Fortune* 1000 worker sends and receives 178 messages *per day*—and the increasing number of message-delivery technologies is responsible. New technologies, such as e-mail and groupware, do not replace older, more traditional methods of communication (e.g., faxes, telephone, voice mail). Instead, they are *additive,* making it harder and harder to get the attention of an individual to whom you need to communicate. Individuals with access to multiple communications vehicles *use* multiple vehicles. People mix and match methods in order to make sure their message gets through: "Hi, Mark. I'm leaving this voice mail to confirm you got the e-mail that followed up on the fax to remind you about the overnight delivery that you should have received yesterday."

The information overload our society experiences has led to a fundamental shift in audience requirements. It once was perfectly acceptable to adopt the communications attitude that said, "You'll get what we've got when we get it to you." That accommodated delivery of scheduled communications like annual reports, the distribution of press releases, the production of institutional material. But it does *not* accommodate the new paradigm, in which the audience demands, "I want what I want when I want it." (This new requirement is, of course, consistent with the customization characteristic of an information economy.)

Many of those who fear the Internet and its associated technologies (such as corporate intranets—networks set up with companies for employees) are concerned about key messages getting lost in the tidal wave of material that a many-to-many environment can produce. How do the most important messages stand out when they ultimately are just one more drop in the sea?

In accommodating the "I-want-what-I-want-when-I-want-it" model, though, it becomes easier to distinguish between messages that are *"pushed"* at audiences because of their importance and those that are just made available to satisfy the information needs of individual audience members. You can employ strategies that ensure that important top-down messages get the attention they deserve, and leave everything else in an environment where individuals only *"pull"* it if they need it, rather than having it thrust upon them whether or not it's relevant.

Case Study: California Franchise Tax Board

In early 1997, my accountant called and informed me he needed my 1994 California state tax form. Having moved from Los Angeles to the Bay Area, and having changed jobs twice since 1994, I had no idea where that paperwork was. In a box in the garage, to be sure, but which one? I was not inclined to start rummaging through dusty old boxes in the hopes of finding a couple of sheets of paper.

"You'll need to call the Tax Board to have them send you the form to request a photocopy," my accountant said.

Dynamite. I could look forward to about half an hour on the phone, trying to get through to the appropriate department to send me the form, then wait a week before it actually arrived in my mailbox. Of course, the form *might* be available at the local post office, but since it wasn't quite the heart of tax season yet, the odds were only about fifty-fifty that I would find it there. Still, it seemed like a better idea than making a lengthy, long-distance call to Sacramento.

Then the thought flashed through my mind: Maybe the Tax Board had a Web site. I called up a search engine and entered my search query: "California Franchise Tax Board." The agency's site was listed at the very top of the list of search results. I clicked on the link and found myself on the Tax Board's home page, where a listing of available forms was one of the first links available. I clicked on it and found a link to the form I needed. I clicked on that, and (like magic) the form appeared on my screen. I printed it out. Four minutes after my accountant's call, I had the form in my hands. *I want what I want when I want it.*

Influencing Audiences Through Pull Mechanisms

Making information available through "pull" mechanisms such as that described in the Tax Board case is helpful to audiences. But how does it help companies achieve their communications objectives? Part of the answer rests with the idea of targeting your audience. If you know who they are, and (demographically speaking) they have access to the Internet, they will find you. In early 1998, the U.S. presidency seemed to be in crisis, the result of allegations of sexual misconduct and related improprieties. The public hungered for information about the issue, so much so that visits to news-related Web sites reportedly surged to historic levels. It's an extreme example, but those who have an interest in a particular topic gravitate to those sites where there is related valuable information. And they tell others who share the same interests about the site, resulting in even more visits.

Even more important, though, is the need to integrate so-called push and pull strategies. As I drove through Napa Valley, I saw a billboard that featured an enticing photograph: a hunk of butter melting over an ear of corn. The only text on the billboard: *www.realbutter. com*. I had no interest and dismissed it. My wife, though, who is an outstanding cook, *had* to go see what the site had to offer. Similarly, Disney advertises its Web site at the end of movie trailers, Toyota adds its Web site to its television commercials, and Pentel includes its site in its print advertisements. At US West, the Denver-based baby bell, managers and supervisors receive an e-mail bulletin that provides them with links to detailed information on issues their employees may ask questions about.

Network World magazine, a trade publication, includes links to resource pages on its Web site related to articles appearing in print. A recent issue, for example, featured an interview with an industry executive. It filled a full page of the magazine, but the link offered readers who were interested the opportunity to read the *entire* interview, including all the questions and answers that didn't make the print version.

It is equally important to recognize that people are picking and choosing the information they want (consistent with the customization characteristic of an information economy and the receiver-driven model of communication). The technology is making it possible to ignore news and information of no interest. People can subscribe to services that customize their news delivery so information that matches their profile is the *only* information they see. Thus, if you plan to deliver a key message through mass distribution—say, through the successful distribution of a press release resulting in placement of your story in the top twenty-five newspapers in the country—you have no guarantee that your target audience will even see it. As customization technology continues to improve and becomes available to more and more people, this hard fact will become even more critical. (ABC News already is experimenting with the means by which individuals can assemble a newscast to meet their personal interests by selecting only those stories that appeal to them.)

Planning Template: Web-Based Receiver-Driven Communications

Far too many companies employ the "shovelware" principle, tossing whatever information they already have in other formats onto a Web site and claiming they have established a presence in cyberspace. If you are going to achieve measurable results, you need to plan the kind of material that will satisfy the needs of your audience. Follow these steps to ensure success:

1. *Identify the target.* Who is the audience?
2. *State your objectives.* Why is your organization communicating with this audience? What do you want to achieve? How will you know that you have achieved it?
3. *Determine the key messages that must be pushed to the audience.* Clarify top-down messages and identify distribution methods for delivering them (e.g., advertising, direct mail).
4. *Figure out what information audience members are likely to want.* Based on your key messages, and factoring in your knowledge about the audience's interests, list the kinds of questions individuals may ask or additional information they may want.
5. *Determine how audience members are likely to seek additional information.* What path could individuals follow to get to the information they want?
6. *Integrate your communications.* Make sure that your initial top-down communication includes information about how to obtain additional information and how to engage the organization and/or other audience members in providing feedback or discussing the issue.

Access-Driven Communications

If someone wants what she wants when she wants it, the institution had better make sure she has access to the vehicle used to make what she wants available. After all, making the information available through means to which the customer does *not* have access won't do her any good!

This is a difficult concept for public relations practitioners to accept, since part of communications training—and one of the most fun parts of doing the job—is selecting media. Of course, the traditional approach to media selection has not been entirely arbitrary. Each medium selected must be appropriate to both the audience and the message. But when you were *pushing* the message to the audience, in the old industrial economy, the range of options was greater. You could send a printed brochure or a videotape or a solar-powered calculator with your message imprinted on it. You could produce billboards, stage a media event that results in television and newspaper coverage, place an article in a magazine, sponsor a promotion, or buy advertising. As long as the audience tuned into the news, opened a newspaper, read the magazine the demographics suggest they read, or got their mail, they saw your message.

When individuals *pull* the information they want, though, they are discarding the bulk of the communications tools thrust at them so that they can dispense with the superfluous data that constitute overload. Today, you need to make the information available *specifically* in the media they are most likely to use when they pull information.

Until recently, the telephone was the best tool to accommodate individuals who pulled information. Interactive Voice Response (IVR) empowered individuals to follow recorded prompts in search of information. While IVR can be a source of tremendous aggravation when it is not well designed, when implemented effectively, it can facilitate quick retrieval of desired data. Examples of IVR satisfying individual information needs include:

• *Bank balances.* When was the last time you waited until a monthly statement arrived in the mail to find out how much money you had in your account? Even the most technophobic people pick up the phone and punch one or two keys in order to obtain their balance as of yesterday's bank closing time.

• *Movies.* 777-FILM has become a huge success in major motion picture markets by helping people get information on the films they want to see. They can even purchase advance tickets using the system.

• *Technical support.* Why wait half an hour to get a live technical support staffer on the phone when you can use a series of prompts to get the answer to your computer problem yourself? Usually, these support lines start with some broad questions, the answers to which help narrow the field of problems to yours, and then provide the answer.

Fax-on-demand is another tool that meets the need for information-on-demand. These systems provide users with a menu of documents. When you dial into the fax-on-demand IVR system, the voice prompt asks you to enter the number of the document you want and your fax number. The document is then automatically faxed to you. Fax-on-demand has been a success in some quarters because of the predominance of fax machines. In the cases of both telephone IVR and fax-on-demand, the popularity of the tool among the general public (and, by extension, within targeted audiences) has made them desirable pull communications tools.

Today, the World Wide Web is fast becoming the tool of choice for individuals seeking to retrieve specific information. Accessibility is getting to be less and less of a problem, as Web and e-mail kiosks pop up in airport terminals and hotel lobbies, to say nothing of Internet cafés. In addition, the Web is now a resource common to both businesses (which provide access to the World Wide Web as well as intranets, which take advantage of the same interface) and the public at large (in homes, schools, libraries, housing projects, nursing homes, and other residences). People are getting Web-based information from their computers, from their network PCs, even from television sets and telephones.

As the number of people who routinely use the Web skyrockets, the case for making information available on the Web grows stronger.

Tip: Be Redundant . . . and Repetitive . . . and Redundant
While many members of your target audience may be on the Web, it's highly unlikely that *all* of them are. It pays to make sure you send your message through multiple media to increase the odds that as many members of your audience see it as possible. Offer the information on the Web *and* via fax-on-demand or IVR. Go ahead and get the media placements and hold the special events. It always has been a rule of communication that redundancy is a good thing, and the existence of the Web doesn't change that!

Attracting a Market Sample of One

Under the traditional communications models that evolved while the industrial economy was in full swing, we learned to target our audiences through the use of demographics. Whole businesses prospered by establishing those demographic groups, identifying, say, that people who voted one way were likely to be in a certain income category, with certain academic credentials and certain buying patterns. The ability to cross-reference trends and patterns against demographic niches was vital. How else would we know which newspapers to target with our press releases, which magazines to seek article placements in, and which cities to hold special events in?

In the information economy, however, demographics mean less and less—particularly when pushing information in media you have no guarantee your audience will see! The environment that encourages individuals to pull the information they want requires a new approach, one in which you need to ensure that information is waiting where individuals are likely to go looking for it.

Demographics still play a part in this approach, known as *a market sample of one.* If you are promoting a wine-tasting event, you need to know the types of Web sites the high-income members of your target audience are likely to visit. You may want to buy banner ads on travel and gourmet sites. If you are seeking support for a new initiative to ease export regulations, you may want to lure people from appropriate trade publications, business journals, and Web sites that address international trade.

In any event, your goal is not to distribute the material to every possible member of the target audience but rather to entice each individual, one at a time, to your site. The same principle applies to the use of other online resources to direct individuals to your business, your cause, or your product—*even if you don't have a Web site.*

The public relations task of targeting audiences—and even much of the other work involved—will go through a significant transition as a result of this new model. "We won't need people who churn out press releases or design ads," according to Marian Salzman, corporate director of emerging media for advertising giant Chiat/Day. "The challenge will be to spread branded information so that it gets to the targeted individual. That requires understanding the consumer on a niche level."

Case Study: The Pediatric Crohn's and Colitis Association

Michael Thatcher, a graduate student at Brown University's School of Communications, had a problem. One of his school assignments was to create a public relations program for the Pediatric Crohn's and Colitis Association (PCCA), a six-year-old nonprofit organization for children suffering from bowel and colon diseases. Creating the campaign was not the problem; the problem was the PCCA's limited budget, which prohibited any expenditure for publicity.

The PCCA had never before engaged in any publicity. Nevertheless, as the only organization dedicated to helping these children and their families, the group wanted to create greater awareness and increase membership. Its member base was predominantly local, and the organization aspired to become a national resource for its target audience. The PCCA had never before engaged in any publicity. "Nobody knew who they are or what they do," Thatcher says. Changing that was his assignment.

One of Thatcher's other activities was his work at the Boston University Macintosh Lab, where he noodled around on the Internet. "I picked up on the idea of using the Internet to let people know the PCCA exists," he says. He first probed the World Wide Web, using search tools to find sites that featured the words "Crohn's" and "colitis." He found one page dedicated to the topic that provided links to other resources. "Funny thing was, the Web page was maintained by somebody here at Boston University. I went looking for global resources and found someone down the street!"

Thatcher spoke with the keeper of that page, who agreed to include information about the PCCA among the resources he shared with the world through his site. "That was very encouraging," Thatcher says. "The page gets activity from hundreds of people every day—that's hundreds of people who already have an interest in the topic." Thatcher also found four Usenet newsgroups that discussed his topic, along with a listserv mailing list and discussion forums on CompuServe, Prodigy, and America Online.

A strategy developed around Thatcher's discoveries. "By communicating with these various online groups, we get free exposure to a pretargeted audience," he says. "We communicate directly with the individuals we're interested in." Posting consistent messages about the PCCA to each of these groups, and participating actively as an association in the discussions, would create a lot of nationwide and even global publicity in very short order.

What about budget? How could the PCCA establish all those connections? Simple. Thatcher started phoning existing members and asking what kind of online services they used. His first success was a member with a Prodigy account who volunteered to feed PCCA communications to the Prodigy discussion group. More phone calls led to more volunteers.

How It Works

How does a market sample of one work? Using the PCCA's experience, let's imagine a scenario with a woman—let's call her Sally—whose two-year-old daughter was just diagnosed with one of the potentially terminal illnesses the PCCA addresses. Sally is frightened and confused. But she has access to the Internet through an account with a local Internet Service Provider. (It doesn't matter *why* she has the account—it could be to communicate with her brother by e-mail, visit cooking-oriented Web sites, or get tips on taxes. The only thing that matters is that there is *information* out there, and she knows how to find it.)

Sally searches the World Wide Web and does some research on her daughter's illness. The Web sites not only refer to the PCCA but also link to Usenet discussion groups where the illnesses are discussed—groups like *alt.support.crohns-colitis*. She visits that group and posts a message explaining her situation and her fears. Checking back the next day, she finds several responses, including one that reads, "Hi, Sally. My name is Dave. My heart goes out to you. My son suffered from exactly the same illness as your daughter. Thank God I found the PCCA. Here's how they were able to help me."

In contrast, how would a public relations effort find Sally using traditional methods? You could try to place an article in parenting magazines, then hope that the infinitesimally small percentage of parents who read the magazine *and* have children who contract one of the illnesses actually *remember* reading the article when the illness occurs. You could undertake a direct mail campaign, using mailing lists of new parents sold by hospitals. You could target pediatricians, heightening their awareness. All of these options are expensive and offer uncertain results.

The method described above—having the information waiting when Sally came looking for it—did not try to identify the target audience, because fundamentally there *was* no target audience. There was only Sally and her quest for information.

Is this approach effective? Consider that the PCCA, using only the Internet and other online services as a means of attracting a market sample of one, quadrupled its membership in a matter of only a few months.

Conclusion

Some communicators seem to believe there is a place for those who use the new tools of online communication and a place for those who hold to the traditional tools. Nothing could be further from the truth. Communicators will be expected to integrate *all* of the tools in order to achieve measurable results. That integration requires a solid, complete understanding of the new communications models and of how to use them in tandem with the traditional tools in order to achieve the measurable results of the communications effort.

3

Public Relations Tools of the Internet

To understand how to use the Internet as part of your public relations tool kit, you need to have a fundamental understanding of what the Internet is, how it works, and what its capabilities are. I don't propose to offer an in-depth technical explanation of the Net—there are plenty of texts available for anyone interested in learning more about it. Rather, this brief overview is designed to give you just enough information to be able to assimilate the Internet into your thinking about public relations strategies.

What Is the Internet?

The Internet is, at its core, a network comprised of smaller computer networks. Each of the networks—and each of the computers on those networks—can retrieve information that is made available on any of the other networks and their computers. In other words, when you are on the Internet, the information available to you expands beyond what is on your own hard drive or your own local network. You have access to all the information that others make available from their systems throughout the Internet.

All this is made possible by a series of protocols, which are rules that govern how computers handle certain types of information. The family of protocols that govern the Internet is called TCP/IP (which stands for Transmission Control Protocol/Internet Protocol). The Internet is nonplatform-specific; that is, it works on any kind of computer—PCs running DOS, PCs running Windows, Macintoshes, Unix, anything. As long as the network and its computers are configured to address TCP/IP protocols, they can function as a component part of the Internet.

TCP/IP tells computers how to locate the source of information and how to manage the delivery and receipt of information. Specifically, the Transmission Control Protocol manages the packaging of data into small packets. Each packet is sent over the Internet via the route that is fastest at the instant it leaves its point of origin. When all the packets arrive at their destination, they are reassembled so the recipient can see the data in their original form. The Internet Protocol handles the address that is associated with each packet to make sure it goes where it was intended. Every node on the Internet is assigned an IP "address," a series of numbers separated by dots (or periods). For example, IBM's IP address looks like this:

```
129.34.139.30
```

Of course, while numbers are easy for computers to deal with, nobody could remember such a string of numbers, no less memorize dozens or even hundreds of them! To make it easier, the Internet makes it possible to assign a name to each IP address. When you type *www. ibm.com* in your Web browser, your request is routed to a piece of hardware called a name server. The name server looks to see if *ibm.- com* is a legitimate name. Once the name is found, the server sends your request to the related IP address.

Client-server is another term you hear as you work with network specialists to implement Internet communications plans. It refers to a type of computing activity in which information resides on a computer known as a server. Servers are configured with appropriate software that incorporates the right set of TCP/IP protocols to do what they are supposed to do. Your computer is the "client"—that is, it is the individual workstation that is going to make a request of the server. When you retrieve your e-mail, for instance, your client computer sends a request to the e-mail server, which makes sure you are authorized to get your e-mail (i.e., you entered the appropriate password), then responds to your request by delivering the messages it has collected to your desktop.*

---

*The terms *client* and *server* can get confusing, since a client computer can also be a server and vice versa. For example, you can use your computer as a client when you retrieve your e-mail, but it also can be configured as a Web server, distributing Web pages to other client computers that request them.

While TCP/IP consists of these two protocols, it also includes a suite of secondary protocols that rely on TCP/IP to work. These include:

- *HTTP—Hypertext Transfer Protocol,* which manages information configured for the World Wide Web.
- *FTP—File Transfer Protocol,* which manages the transfer of whole files (such as word-processor documents) from somewhere on the network to your computer.
- *SMTP—Simple Mail Transfer Protocol,* which manages the sending of e-mail.
- *NNTP—Network News Transfer Protocol,* which manages Usenet discussion groups.

Note that there is a host of other protocols as well, which are more technical in nature and are not important to the understanding of the Internet as a public relations tool. Your systems or network administrator should handle these protocols; you should never have to worry about them.

It is the protocols that function as a part of TCP/IP—e-mail, the Web, discussion groups, and file transfer—that make the Internet useful and provide organizations with new tools to deliver their messages and engage their audiences in dynamic multidirectional communication. We'll explore each of these four sets of tools and how they can be employed in organizational communications efforts.

E-Mail

The Internet has become a part of our culture as a result of the introduction and rapid assimilation of the World Wide Web into popular consciousness. However, e-mail—not the Web—remains the Internet's most widely used feature. In fact, *four times* the number of people with access to the Web use Internet-based e-mail. These include people in a work or academic environment whose computers are configured for e-mail but not Web access, as well as those with older computers that cannot handle the memory requirements of modern Web browsers.

E-mail takes many forms, but at its core it is a message that one individual sends to another individual or group of people at a particular address (associated with the IP address of the recipient). In general, you create an e-mail message using an e-mail client—that is, a software application designed to manage your e-mail needs. These include:

- Creating and sending messages.

- Retrieving messages waiting for you on your server (usually known as a POP3 server).

- Assigning actions to messages, such as automatically forwarding all messages from a designated address to a list of other people who should see all correspondence from that individual.

- Managing messages, including establishing categories of incoming mail, such as "products," "legal," "personal," and "media." Messages that meet the criteria you select are automatically routed into the appropriate category. For instance, if you get mail from *Los Angeles Times* reporters and you know the paper's e-mail domain is *lat.com,* you can set up your e-mail client to automatically store all mail from *lat.com* in the "media" folder.

E-mail clients are available in a variety of configurations. You can spend a lot of money on one or none at all. Some e-mail clients can be downloaded free, including Eudora Lite (from *www.eudora.com/ eudoralight*) and Pegasus Mail (from *www.pegasus.usa.com*). Other programs can run about $100.

Tip: See if You Can Use Internal E-mail to Get on the Net
If you work in an office environment and already have e-mail associated with your company's internal network, it won't necessarily work with the Internet. First, Internet e-mail must be POP3-compliant—that is, it must be able to talk with an Internet server. Second, it needs to be connected to the Net itself. Check with your company's systems administrator to find out if and how you can use your internal mail system for Internet e-mail.

Each e-mail message you receive or send contains a "header." It is made up of all the information the Internet needs to route the message to the correct place and contains a wealth of data you may need. A typical header looks something like this one, part of an actual e-mail message I received from a public relations-oriented Web site (the National PR Network):

```
Received: from julia.siinternet.com [208.225.225.13]
From: swynkoop@usprnet.com (National PR Network
  Community)
To: <shel@holtz.com>
Date: Sat, 24 Jan 1998 14:44:44
Reply-To: swynkoop@usprnet.com
Errors-To: swynkoop@diac.com
X-URL: http://www.usprnet.com
X-Mailer: NetMailer v1.04B [D.R-D2F27392415261104]
Subject: National PR Network—New, Free InfoExchange
```

Let's look at each line of the header to see what we can learn:

- *Line 1:*   Lists the server from which the mail was sent. This generally refers to the Internet service provider somebody is using to provide e-mail services to him.
- *Line 2:*   Tells us who sent the mail. In this case, it was Steve Wynkoop, one of the founders of the National PR Network.
- *Line 3:*   Specifies the recipient of the message.
- *Line 4:*   Gives the date and time the message was sent.
- *Line 5:*   Tells the e-mail address you should use to reply to the message. If you simply click the *reply* button on your e-mail client, this is the address to which your reply will be sent.
- *Line 6:*   Specifies the e-mail address that will be notified if the message can't get through for some reason (say, if your mail server is down or the recipient's address was incorrectly entered).
- *Line 7:*   Gives the address of the Web site associated with the sender of the message.
- *Line 8:*   Specifies what kind of software was used to send the message.
- *Line 9:*   Tells the subject line Steve entered so I would know what the message was about.

Additional lines can appear on an e-mail header, many of which are highly technical in nature.

Most e-mail is limited to ASCII characters.* Newer e-mail clients also allow you to incorporate World Wide Web markup, so you can add boldface, italic, text sizes, background images, and other elements to your e-mail. You also can attach files to your e-mail, allowing you to send along a word-processor file or a graphic image with your basic text.

Using E-Mail

Since so many people have Internet e-mail addresses and use e-mail on a daily basis, it becomes one of your most powerful Internet-based tools for a public relations effort. You can use e-mail to send messages and engage in conversations with:

- Individuals, in a one-on-one format
- Groups of people whose addresses you list on a single message (a distribution list)
- Subscribers to a mailing list

One-on-One

There are countless uses of e-mail for one-to-one communication, from nurturing a relationship with a reporter to engaging in a delicate negotiation with a designated representative of an activist group. In fact, e-mail has become so efficient as a means of contact that it has replaced the telephone as the principal method of communication for many public relations counselors working in the agency environment.

E-mail becomes the best choice for communicating under the following circumstances:

- The individual with whom you are communicating prefers to use e-mail.
- You need to have a chronological, word-for-word record of the entire communications process.
- You need to include other documentation in your correspondence, such as reports or graphic images, that can be sent as e-mail attachments.

---

*American Standard Code for Information Interchange. These are basically the characters you can see on your keyboard.

• You need to be able to communicate in as close to real-time as possible but cannot be assured of real-time availability for a phone call.

> ***Under no circumstances should you* ever *send e-mail to somebody who has not indicated she is willing to communicate with you via e-mail!***

Distribution Lists

E-mail clients provide three methods you can send use to a single message simultaneously to multiple people. You can (1) add them all to the recipient line, usually separated by commas or semicolons; (2) include them in a "CC" listing, which sends a complete copy of the message but indicates that the recipient is being copied and is not part of the primary distribution list; or (3) add them as a "BCC," a blind copy, which allows you to send a copy to a third party without the primary recipients seeing that anybody was copied.

You can use distribution lists to:

• Make sure all parties involved in a negotiation are able to participate in various discussions.
• Conduct focus groups.
• Specify participants for intensive discussions.
• Share research findings with key audience members.
• Provide regular updates on particular issues to targeted audience members.

Subscription Mailing Lists

Subscription mailing lists are facilitated by software that resides on a server. The software manages subscriptions to the list. When you send a message to the software, it automatically distributes your message to all other subscribers. Mailing lists can be interactive (that is, any subscriber can send a message) or one-way (allowing you to distribute messages to subscribed individuals, but restricting their ability to respond or to initiate their own original messages).

The subscription mailing lists can be set up by allowing individuals to subscribe or by physically adding new names to the list. Rather than send e-mail to individual recipients, the e-mail is sent to the list, which automatically distributes the message to all subscribers.

Some of the software programs that facilitate such lists reside on the e-mail server and are known generically as listservs. (Listserv is also the name of one of the proprietary software programs that manages e-mail lists. Others include Majordomo and Listproc.) Another class of software is a database configured to perform list management functions. When a reporter visiting the Bell Atlantic media relations Web site signs up to receive certain types of press releases (see Chapter 6), the information is recorded in a database that ensures that press releases are distributed via e-mail only to those reporters who asked for them.

In addition to allowing audience members to request receipt of certain types of documents by e-mail, you can use a list to provide regular updates to targeted audiences and to encourage a discussion among audience members about specific topics.

Rules for E-Mail

E-mail can be a powerful tool but it also can get you in trouble if you don't use it correctly. As with any other form of communication, standards have emerged for the proper construction of e-mail messages. Ignoring any of these guidelines can result in a perception that you are not a competent user of the Net or that you do not care about how you are perceived. Both have an ultimate impact on your credibility. Here are the e-mail rules:

1. Write in complete sentences.

2. Use appropriate capitalization and punctuation.

3. Avoid excessive use of abbreviations.

4. Sign your message. Include your name, organization, and pertinent contact information (notably your e-mail address).

5. Use a descriptive subject line.

6. Keep your message short and to the point.

7. Don't attach anything to your e-mail message unless the recipient knows it's coming. (Nothing frustrates people more than waiting for a two-meg file attachment to download before they can read any of their e-mail.)

8. Reply promptly to messages you receive that warrant a reply. Do not send replies that simply say "Thanks" or some other nonsubstantive message.

9. Quote the part of a previous message to which you are responding, so that readers of the e-mail know what you're talking about. However, never quote the entire message to which you are responding. If your e-mail client automatically inserts the entire message, be sure to edit it down to just the part you need to enhance understanding.

E-Mail Newsletters

E-mail newsletters are growing in popularity because of their flexibility and the ease with which they can be produced. They can be used for just about any purpose and rarely raise hackles among Internet users because they almost always *ask* to receive it! For example, I offer four newsletters from my Web site. Visitors who are interested in topics like "Measuring Online Effectiveness" or "What's Working on the World Wide Web" simply enter their name and e-mail address and check the newsletter or newsletters they want to receive. If they ever want to stop receiving the newsletter, they simply e-mail me; the instructions on how to cancel a subscription are clearly articulated in each issue of each newsletter.

Producing an e-mail newsletter is generally a matter of typing a message in ASCII, although there are alternatives. You can produce a newsletter in any word processor or desktop publishing format and then save it using a product like Adobe Acrobat, which saves any document in a format that can be viewed on any computer by anybody who installs the free "reader" software (which is easily obtainable). Some companies have developed proprietary electronic newsletter software (the best example is E*News from Ion Systems). But ASCII-based newsletters are the most utilitarian because your audience does not require *any* special software; if people can receive e-mail, they can read your newsletter.

While electronic newsletters can take on any number of appearances, they should follow a basic standard format.

Template: E-Mail Newsletter
Title: What the newsletter is called
Date: The date the newsletter was distributed
Contents listing: The articles in the newsletter, listed in order

Graphical separator: Equal signs, asterisks, percent signs, or some other graphical indicator that one section of the newsletter or article has ended and another is about to begin
Headline: Preferably in all capital letters to make it easier to identify
Item: The actual text
Graphical separator: Same as above (you can use another set of characters) to separate the next item
Contact, copyright, and subscription information: Necessary for any publication

An Example of an E-Mail Newsletter

The following is one of the e-mail newsletters I distribute to those who subscribe from my Web site.

```
From: Holtz Communication + Technology
Subject: ONLINE PR & MEDIA UPDATE

August 1, 1997

<><><><><><><><><><><><><><><> <><><><><><><><>
In This Issue:

o A New Model for Press Releases?
o Are Press Releases for the Web Different?
o Media Relations Site: USC
o Boilerplate and Subscription Information
<><><><><><><><><><><><><><><> <><><><><><><><>

*******************************
A New Model for Press Releases?
*******************************
```

Can you fill in a few fields, click a submit button, pay twenty bucks, and get a "polished press release"? That's the promise from Adrian & Peterson, a Michigan-based public relations agency that has just launched PRWEB at www.prweb.com. One key element of the site is the Press Release Factory, which provides you with forms for fifteen different categories of press releases.

Let's say you want to issue a press release on a community activity. You type in such information as the host community, the name of the activity, a general description of the activity, where and when it will be held, who the beneficiaries are, and choice comments from your CEO and a community leader or two. Then fill in your payment information, and click the "Process Release" button. A program on the server will generate the press release from

the information you have submitted and display a first
draft on the screen. You can make some changes, click on the
"Finish" button, and your press release is done.

Not only can you send it to the media, but it automatically
is posted to one of PRWEB's fifty-one business categories,
where it's available for any reporter or editor who may
wander by looking to see what's new in, say,
"Telecommunications." Since anybody can post any press
release at no charge, there's no telling what you might
find. For instance, I found a release with the compelling
headline "ODS NETWORKS (TM) HELPS BT DEVELOP THE UK'S FIRST
METROPOLITAN AREA ATM SERVICE FOR MAJOR BANK."

There's no arguing that Adrian & Peterson have found some
clever uses for the Web. The question comes down to the
value of these tricks. Does anybody really believe he/she
can generate a solid, professional press release for $20
using a fill-in-the-blanks approach? Will any reporters or
editors actually bookmark something like PRWEB as a means
of staying on top of their beats?

Don't bet on either. At least the site is well-designed.

****
Are Press Releases for the Web Different?
****

A colleague suggested to me recently that a press release
is a press release, whether it's written for the Web, the
fax, or the U.S. mail. If your goal is to have a reporter
print out your press release, I would agree. However, if you
want a reporter to read the release on the screen, the
writing of the release needs to be approached differently.
It needs to be written for the screen.

The way people read computer screens—and Web pages in
particular—is different from the way they read paper.
Consider just a few of the differences:

    o You hold paper in your hand and adjust the distance
from your eyes; when you read, your eyes track along the
paper. A computer monitor, on the other hand, remains a
fixed distance from your eyes, and when you read, your eyes
remain fixed and the text moves as you scroll.
    o There is no three-dimensional nature to the
information on a computer screen. You cannot easily thumb
through the material to see how long it is or how it is
structured.
    o People tend to scan information on a screen for key

information rather than read each word as they do with paper.

 o Readers expect printed material to be linear, while they expect online material to be nonlinear, with information reduced to its smallest component "chunks" so they can read only those chunks in which they are most interested.

I'd like to point you to a Web site where you can see examples of good online press releases. Unfortunately, I haven't found any. Here's how I would approach a release:

 1. Under the descriptive headline, include internal links to the key elements of the release so a reporter can jump right to it and make a judgment about the value of the material. This quick listing, appearing at the top of the page, also serves as a quick-and-dirty summary of the release's substance.

 2. Keep extraneous information out of the release, even if you would attach it to a printed version. Earnings reports are a great example. Don't make the consolidated statement of earnings part of the release. Instead, make it a link a reporter can follow if she chooses.

 3. Offer links to related information a reporter is likely to find online anyway, including competitor sites, analyst sites, related articles from online media, and discussion groups where people are likely to be talking about the subject of your release.

 4. Include a link to your own company's Web site where the information is covered for public consumption.

 5. Include thumbnails of any photos or illustrations on a separate link.

 6. Offer contact information, including a hyperlink to the media relations contact's e-mail address.

With this kind of direction, a reporter only needs to receive a one- or two-line e-mail message advising him that the release is online. The e-mail message can, of course, include a hyperlink directly to the release.

Have you seen any Web-based press releases that have adopted these concepts? Let me know, because I sure haven't seen them!

```
**************************
```
Media Relations Site: USC
```
**************************
```

Many of the media relations sites available on the Web are nothing more than press release archives. The University of Southern California takes it several steps further.

They even give their Press Center a different name:
Services for Journalists. It's a title that embraces
everything an online media center should be. Here, a
reporter covering the university's 1997 commencement can
watch streaming video clips of any segment of the event,
from the color guard and the invocation to Jack Kemp's
commencement address. There's an "Experts Directory,"
listing the expertise of "more than 1,000 USC scientists,
scholars, administrators, and physicians who are both able
and willing to comment on issues and topics in the news."
The university's faculty/staff newsletter goes online in
the media center the evening before it is delivered on
campus. Presidential speeches are archived here as well,
along with press releases and information on the school and
its media representatives. Corporations that repurpose
their releases in HTML and call it a media center could take
a lesson from the home of the Trojans.

USC's "Services for Journalists" site is at:
http://www.usc.edu/dept/News_Service/
media_services.html

****
Boilerplate and Subscription Information
****

You received this newsletter either because you asked for
it or somebody who likes you forwarded it to you. Please
feel free to forward it to someone =you= like!

ONLINE MEDIA RELATIONS UPDATE is published by Holtz
Communication + Technology whenever we have accumulated
enough information to justify another issue. You can
subscribe by visiting the HC+T site on the World Wide Web
at http://www.holtz.com and selecting the SIGN UP page.
HC+T produces eight e-mail newsletters on a variety of
communication-related topics.

Holtz Communication + Technology helps organizations
apply online technology to strategic communications
efforts.

(C) 1997, Holtz Communication + Technology. All rights
reserved.

For help with this newsletter, send e-mail to
HELP-PR@UM1.UNITYMAIL.COM
To submit an item for this newsletter, send e-mail to
PR-SUBMIT@HOLTZ.COM
To comment on this newsletter, send e-mail to

```
PR-COMMENT@HOLTZ.COM
To unsubscribe from this newsletter, send e-mail to
SIGNOFF-PR@UM1.UNITYMAIL.COM
```

Other E-Mail Newsletter Guidelines

1. Force line breaks about sixty characters so the text does not wrap inappropriately depending on the e-mail program, screen resolution, and other user factors over which you have no control.
2. Keep the articles short and the number of articles to just a few. People do not commit a lot of time to reading a newsletter that comes via e-mail. They scan the article and then dispose of it. If they print it out, you have no guarantee they get around to reading it.
3. If appropriate, provide access to additional information. Even though the articles are short, your readers may want more details. One of the best ways to provide the access is by creating a hyperlink to details you have provided on the World Wide Web.

The World Wide Web

If e-mail remains the most pervasive application on the Internet, the World Wide Web is the feature that opened the Internet to the rest of the world. It also represents the most influential and useful new tool available in many years to organizations trying to manage their constituent relationships.

Before the Web (as we know it today) hit the scene late in 1993, all access to the Internet was made using archaic and nonintuitive text commands and over remote systems (that is, your computer linked up to another computer that was connected to the Internet). Even the World Wide Web, introduced to the Internet community in 1989, was at first a text-driven vehicle. As noted in Chapter 1, when the Web was introduced as a new method for navigating the Internet, the author of a document destined for the Internet attached special code to text that associated it with another document somewhere else on the Net. You would use the *tab* key of your computer to jump to any highlighted text that intrigued you. Once your cursor was over the highlighted text, you pressed the *enter* key in order to activate the hyperlink, which would automatically retrieve the new document, regardless of where on the Internet it was housed.

In late 1993, however, a team of students from the National Center for Supercomputing Applications at the University of Illinois introduced Mosaic, a utility for using the World Wide Web that was dubbed a browser. The browser retrieved a Web page and then "parsed" it— that is, it interpreted various bits of script embedded in the page, then displayed the text accordingly. Because Mosaic was a graphical interface—affecting type, colors, and other graphical elements—it also could display images, such as photos and illustrations. And rather than tab over to a hyperlink and press *enter* to activate it, you could simply point your mouse at the hyperlink (which now appeared as a blue, underlined word or phrase) and click on it. The process worked on exactly the same Hypertext Transfer Protocol (HTTP) as the original text-based Web.

This graphical, point-and-click approach to navigating the Internet was so simple that suddenly, the Internet became accessible to the average computer user. At the same time, developments allowed users to install TCP/IP software directly on their own computers; they could now establish a direct connection to the Internet. As more and more people signed up and installed Mosaic on their computers, more and more individuals and institutions created sites and pages to which people could navigate. Commercial versions of the Mosaic browser cropped up. Internet service providers (ISPs), the boom business of the mid-1990s, began giving browsers away free to anybody who signed up for their service.

Today, two browsers vie for market dominance. The Netscape Navigator is the direct descendent of Mosaic. The Microsoft Internet Explorer was a late entry into the browser market, but Microsoft's strategy of bundling the browser with its operating system quickly brought it to prominence. While the two browsers regularly introduce new features designed to outshine the competition, they work essentially the same way and display the vast majority of Web page elements in exactly the same way. That represents one of the great advantages of the Web: its platform independence. Regardless of what kind of computer you work on, which operating system you have, what kind of network you're connected to, or which browser you have, you can view most of the material posted on the World Wide Web.*

Demographics of the Web

For a long time, it was difficult to pinpoint the number of Americans with Internet access. Lately, however, different studies have provided some of the following statistics:

• Three of the major companies researching demographics on the Internet peg the number of Americans online at between 40 million and 47 million. Between 40 and 45 percent of those are women, and the rest of the demographic mix is leveling. Worldwide, it is estimated that there are 100 million users.

• Projections for 1998 anticipate 75 million total adult Internet users, 25 million child users, and 28 million user households.

• A mid-1997 study by Price Waterhouse showed that the Web is being used at the expense of television. A third of Web users who responded to the study said they used the Web instead of television, and just under a third said surfing the Web had replaced reading a book, magazine, or newspaper.

• The Graphics Visualization and Usability (GVU) Center at Georgia Tech, in its eighth annual World Wide Web user survey, determined that 85 percent of those who have access to the Web visit it daily, 24 percent use it more than twenty hours per week, and 32 percent are on the Web between ten and twenty hours per week. In addition, 82 percent consider the Web an "indispensable" technology.

• The GVU study revealed that 72 percent of the respondents use the Web primarily to gather information for personal needs. Only 6 percent of respondents say they have never used the Web to research information about products they were thinking of buying.

• According to the *Internet Advertising Report,* every $1 expended on Internet advertising in 1997 generated $7 in sales.

All of this makes the Web a pretty compelling place to deliver your messages. Add to the equation the fact that people *"pull"* infor-

---

*As Netscape and Microsoft vie for dominance, they create proprietary elements of HTML that work only on their respective browsers. This competition affects only a fraction of Web-based content, however.

mation from the Web—it is receiver-driven information, as discussed in Chapter 2—and the Web not only provides access to your audiences, it gives you the potential to provide your audiences with material they will come and get.

What the Web Can Do

The Web's popularity led to a rush to create new applications and capabilities. After all, the nonproprietary nature of the Web made it possible for anybody with a good idea and some code-writing skills to build a new application and release it directly to the Web-surfing community from a Web site. As a result, the Web can now allow users to perform all sorts of feats. On a Web page, you can:

• View animations or listen to audio files, including *live* broadcasts.

• Complete forms and submit data.

• Manipulate data. For instance, you can perform a calculation such as assessing how much money you need to put aside in a stock fund in order to achieve a proper salary replacement ratio for your retirement.

• View data visually. On ESPNet's SportsZone, for example, you can review a baseball player's hitting by looking at an interactive map of a baseball park. Different color dots represent different types of hits (flies, line drives, etc.). You can manipulate data that enable you to see such things as how many ground balls resulted in hits when the player was hitting against a left-handed pitcher and was behind on the count. This is an exciting advance, since it allows communicators to present information in a manner that is both visual and customizeable.

• Engage in discussions with other visitors to a site, using Web-based discussion forums.

• View information in non-Web systems, such as inventories maintained in databases on mainframe computers.

In addition to these technical capabilities, the Web offers some heady advantages to organizations needing to communicate with their constituent audiences:

• *It is fast.* As soon as you have new information to share, it can be posted. There is no lag in the time it takes to distribute the information. Instead, it is waiting for those who come looking for it the instant you post it.

• *It is not constrained by space limitations.* When you print something, you need to limit the size for a variety of reasons (the expense of printing and distributing the material, measured against the likelihood that the individual members of your various audiences will read a lot of detail that might not be pertinent to them). On the Web, you can provide the basic information up front, then provide links to all manner of related details, allowing those who visit the site to select the information they want to see and discard the rest. Since the space required to store these volumes of information is ridiculously cheap, you can archive as much information as you want. The more information you store, the more likely your audiences will be able to find what they're looking for (assuming, of course, that you provide intuitive navigation tools they can use to find the information quickly).

• *It allows you to accommodate the receiver-driven nature of information-economy communications.* A typical home page on the Web—the top-level page of an organization's site—can be designed to help visitors pull the information they need. It can include the day's top news items, the company's current stock price, a news archive (containing speeches, press releases, and the like), and links to different categories of information (the company's position on various issues, product information, investor information, etc.). Figure 3-1 shows how the Xerox home page on the World Wide Web performs a variety of tasks. On it, the company displays its current promotion (for its optical character recognition software, TextBridge), news headlines, and links to everything from the annual report to product specifications. A visitor to the site can probably find the information she's looking for within a matter of minutes by selecting the link that most closely matches her needs.

• *It opens the opportunity to engage in one-to-one communication and marketing.* One-to-one marketing is the antithesis of mass media, where we saturate a targeted audience with the same message, giving no consideration to the specific experiences, concerns, or needs of each individual. The Web allows you to gather information about people who visit your site (among other alternatives) by including a form that

Figure 3-1. Xerox's home page on the World Wide Web.
(Copyright © Xerox Corporation 1996, 1997, and 1998. All rights reserved. Xerox®, The Document Company®, and the stylized X are trademarks of XEROX CORPORATION. Products and service names profiled herein are trademarks of Xerox Corporation.)

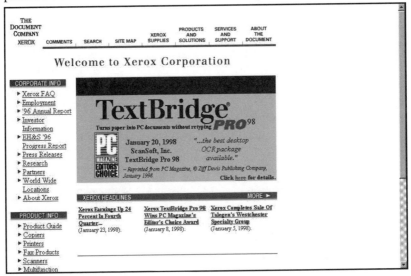

they can complete. Based on the information you obtain about an individual, you can begin to tailor the information you make available to him through the Web and other means (e.g., e-mail). The more you engage with the individual, the more you can refine your relationship with him to ensure that he receives *just* what he wants. Consider, for example, an investment adviser who is particularly interested in one aspect of your operations. You can make sure he receives timely updates on that aspect, along with related investment information.

Thanks to the World Wide Web, you need to consider several new angles on the task of planning a business communication. For example, is there something more effective than words and pictures to get the point across? Does interactivity have a place in the effort? What other information is available on the Web that either supports or conflicts with your message? How many different distinct audiences are likely to visit the site, and for how many of them should you provide distinct pathways to the site's resources?

Discussion Groups

Discussion groups (also known as forums, newsgroups, or bulletin boards) were introduced in the early days of the Internet through a system called Usenet.* Usenet newsgroups are established under a hierarchy of category names, such as *rec* (for recreation and hobbies), *soc* (social issues), *sci* (scientific discussions), or *comp* (computer-related discussions). (Many of the more popular newsgroups appear under the top-level hierarchy "alt," which, contrary to popular belief, does not stand for "alternative." Rather, it is an acronym for "anarchists, lunatics, and terrorists." It is the one part of Usenet where anyone can start a newsgroup without a consenting vote from other users.) Descending levels of the hierarchy help define the focus of the newsgroup. For example, *sci.chem.organic.synthesis* is a forum for chemists working on or interested in the process of synethesizing organic chemicals. Similarly, *talk.politics.guns* is the place for debate about gun control, and *alt.consumers.experiences* is the place where consumers can discuss their experiences with products and services.

Discussion groups exist in other venues as well. The commercial online services (e.g., CompuServe, America Online) maintain discussion forums. Private bulletin board systems are centered around such discussion groups. Web sites are building point-and-click discussions right into their structure. Even e-mail-based mailing lists are, ultimately, forums for discussion among people about a subject of common interest.

Discussion groups are of utmost importance to organizations seeking to communicate with and influence audiences—perhaps even more important than the World Wide Web, in the long run. This is the global conversation, the actualization of the many-to-many communications model. It is in discussion groups that individuals who previously never would have found like-minded souls now can gather an

---

*The Usenet system actually incorporates newsgroups that are hosted on servers outside the Internet. Those that are accessible to the Internet community, however, are hosted on Internet-connected servers.

activist group comprised of individuals from around the world in a matter of days, even hours. In newsgroups, individuals seek information from one another, bypassing the mass media they are growing to distrust more and more. By participating in a newsgroup, an individual is declaring her personal demographic. She is announcing the market of which she is a part.

As a result, newsgroups can be an excellent source for identifying and monitoring issues (discussed in more detail in Chapter 5). They also can be used as a sort of ongoing focus group, where you bounce ideas off participants or get reactions to current company actions or issues. It's also possible to target messages to members of discussion groups in order to influence them, which is precisely the strategy employed by Slocan Forest Products, Ltd., a Canadian forestry company that is the subject of the following case study.

Case Study: Slocan Forest Products

Slocan was the target of a hostile takeover bid by Canfor, a larger Canadian forestry company. Slocan opted to fight the takeover and took its campaign to the Internet, relying mostly on Usenet newsgroups. The company's seventy-two-year-old chairman, working with a public relations agency, posted messages on discussion groups that dealt with business as well as those that focused on Canadian political and environmental issues. The chairman gave out his e-mail address and included it on every takeover-related document the company issued.

The chairman received a flood of responses from each of the company's constituent publics. Shareholders commented that they appreciated the company's presence on the Internet and that information was available directly from the company rather than through the filter of the news media or other sources. Members of the community at large noted that the company's Internet presence suggested that Slocan was a progressive company—more so than Canfor, the company trying to take it over. The discussions heightened awareness of Slocan and its products. The chairman's involvement with the Internet earned some additional publicity in print publications. And employees found their lines of communication opened wider as a result of the publication of the chairman's e-mail address.

But nowhere was the impact felt more greatly than in the company's government relations efforts. In British Columbia, provincial government approval is required for one forest company to take over another. By stating its position in government and environmental discussion groups, Slocan was able to convince many readers that the takeover would be detrimental to the public interest. That message spread, in time influencing the provincial regulatory authorities and the cabinet minister responsible for making the decision. Ultimately, they produced a position paper on corporate concentration and takeovers that helped end the takeover threat.

File Transfer

Any kind of computerized file can be transferred from one computer to another. Word-processor files, spreadsheets, databases, audio files, video clips, animations, illustrations, photos—all can be moved easily from computer to computer or stored on a server where they are available for retrieval by anyone who needs them (and to whom you provide access).

Until recently, the process of transferring a file from a server to your computer required that you learn how to operate a separate utility known as an FTP client. The development of Web browsers, however, has led to the integration of FTP into the Web, making the process a simple matter of clicking on text hyperlinked to the file. The browser recognizes that the file type is not supported directly by the browser—that is, it is not a graphics or text file that can be displayed directly within the browser window—and then asks if you would like to save the file. These files do not even need to be stored in special directories designated for FTP.

There are no limits to the kinds of files you can store for retrieval by your audiences. You can, for example:

• Provide access to text files or word-processor documents that support a point of view.

• Upload spreadsheets that serve as starting points for calculations, budgeting, or other formula-based activities.

• Build executable applications. For example, businesses that manage employee savings plans distribute software that allows employees in client companies to calculate how much they should invest in the plan in order to achieve a certain level of retirement income security. You can distribute software with games and animations that reinforce your brand identity and with estimators and calculators that allow individuals to arrive at conclusions that support your product.

• Make print-quality images available for editors to download for inclusion in publications. These can run the gamut from mug shots of executives and product shots to packaging images and logos.

Conclusion

The Internet consists of tactical tools that allow us to do things like send e-mail, surf the Web, and participate in discussions with anybody who shares our interests. But if we are to engage in excellent communications—those that are two-way and symmetrical—then we cannot view these tools in a vacuum. Instead, we need to begin with our audiences, our strategies, and our objectives, then determine which of these tools can be brought to bear in an orchestrated effort to meet our objectives. Then, we must be able to measure just what the impact of those efforts was.

4

The Principles of Influencing Audiences Online

Public relations, as I have already suggested, is all about influence. Why would a company or client pay good money to communicate if it didn't expect to obtain some sort of return on the investment? Organizations are not like the public media; they cannot communicate out of a sense of altruism, then profit by selling space in their communications vehicles to advertisers who want to reach the same audience. Organizations communicate because they want something from the audience. What they want depends on the audience. They want consumers to buy their products, they want activist groups to leave them alone, they want voters to elect candidates who endorse the company's point of view. They want community members to support the construction of a new plant in their backyard. It all comes down to the same thing: Organizations want to influence the opinions, attitudes, or behaviors of their audiences.

(I want to reiterate that influence does not mean tricking, conniving, bullying, lying, spinning, twisting, or distorting. The best public relations practitioners exercise influence through a thoughtful, candid, accurate, honest engagement in a two-way dialogue with audiences designed to result in an outcome in which the organization *and* the audience both win. Often, the influence comes by convincing the audience to alter a viewpoint under which the company would come out a loser.)

The Internet represents a new approach to wielding that influence.

Since the Internet is a new medium, it requires a new mindset about how to approach it as a public relations tool. In this chapter, we'll explore the following critical communications aspects of the Internet:

- Differences from paper communications
- Narrowcasting
- Integration
- Netiquette
- Push versus pull
- Virtual communities

Differences From Paper Communications

When you read something on a computer screen—an online newspaper, an entertainment-oriented Web site, an electronic bulletin, an e-mail message—you are reading light, not paper. The item you are reading has no physical properties, no substance. It is merely a configuration of light displayed by a computer monitor. There are profound differences between material that is printed on paper and that which is viewed as light on a screen, particularly in terms of how they affect the way people absorb and react to the messages you are trying to deliver.

Understanding these differences is the price of admission to engage in successful Internet-based communications. So let's explore the key differences between reading text on paper and on a monitor, and how these differences can influence your communications effort.

Nonlinear

Paper is linear. When you get a memo, you automatically begin reading it in the upper left-hand corner, word by word. If it's a multipage memo, you *still* start at the beginning, on page one. Books begin at the beginning as well. You cannot generally open a book to a random page and begin reading—it won't make sense.

But information housed on an Internet server is nonlinear. There is no telling how somebody got to a particular chunk of information, where he started, or what he already knows. The whole notion of hyperlinking (see the section on the World Wide Web in Chapter 3) suggests that I can create a link that anyone can follow from my page to one of yours. The context of your page will change from what you intended as a result of the nature of the page where the link was provided. And all of the pages you crafted to set the stage of the information on that page will have gone unseen by your reader.

When writing material that will appear on the screen, then, you need to trust that the reader will take away what she needs from your site. That's quite a change from the traditional approach of giving her the information *you* want. You must write for the reader who has dropped in from parts unknown. You must anticipate why that individual has come visiting your site and make sure that what she sees has an established context, appropriate navigation to related information, and ultimately satisfies her.

Two-Dimensional

What you see on a computer screen is not three-dimensional. Of course, computer applications can render objects in three dimensions, but it's an illusion. The image twists and turns on a flat screen. Print, on the other hand, is *three*-dimensional. You can pick up a book, hold it in your hands, heft it. You can thumb through it, getting a sense of how many pages it has, how small the type is, whether there are any pictures, how the material is structured. And you can do all that in a matter of mere *seconds*.

Online, what you see is what you get. If it is not on the screen *right now*, you cannot see it. As a result, browsing the structure is not an option, short of laboriously clicking through every page of text. And that defeats the purpose of putting material online in the first place!

When a visitor comes to your site, she needs to be able to understand immediately where she is and where she can go from there. Her options and the means by which she will navigate through them need to be clear.

Interactive

Reading is passive. About the most we interact with text is the physical act of holding a book and turning pages. We interact even less with television screens. With the computer screen, though, we *expect* to interact, and well beyond the action required to scroll through text that appears below the bottom of the screen. In fact, interactivity now almost has a minimum standard. Online content—particularly Web content—that does not provide the minimum standard of interactivity is of less use to the reader, inhibiting comprehension of the message.

Interactivity takes many forms on the Web. It could be access to a database in order to assemble information in a meaningful way. It could be a calculation, such as a financial planning tool. Many Web sites feature surveys or the ability to provide feedback to the owners of the site. Almost all Web sites provide choices about what to look at next, about which path to follow.

Discussion forums have their own built-in interactivity. The whole idea behind a discussion group or bulletin board is the interaction among the participants of a group narrowly focused on its topic of interest. Even e-mail can incorporate interactivity. You can encourage replies, build your e-mail so it looks and acts like a Web page, even generate discussions among a list of people receiving the e-mail.

There also are levels of interactivity over which we have no control, and as a result, people who communicate on behalf of companies are going to need to learn how to engage directly with their audiences. Once somebody has reviewed information we make available, he can visit a discussion group and initiate a conversation about what we have written. Suddenly, large groups of people who share a common interest in our work can discuss it together—and perhaps choose to take action! (All companies should monitor online discussions about them; how to do so is the focus of Chapter 5.) Further, readers can respond directly to authors.*

Multimedia

In print, you are limited to words and pictures. Online, the options available to you expand to include audio, video, animation, user-controlled three-dimensional environments, and all forms of interactivity. Communicators need to explore these new tools in order to determine which best meet the objectives of the communications plan and the needs of the audience.

*This happened not too long ago when readers of a public relations journal took umbrage with an article that portrayed communicators in a less than favorable light. The discussion erupted in the Public Relations and Marketing Forum on CompuServe. The anger displayed by some of the participants prompted others to read the article. As the conversation intensified, the author joined the discussion by attempting to defend his approach. Ultimately, the discussion degenerated into some name-calling and heated disputes.

Physiology

Reading light affects the human body differently than reading paper. One of the most obvious ways our body reacts to reading light is for our eyes to blink less. The reduced rate leads to a higher incidence of eyestrain and headaches.

The size of type on the screen doesn't help. When you read paper, you unconsciously move the book or magazine closer or farther away, depending on your eyesight, in order to get just the right distance between you and the print. Computer monitors are fairly well fixed, though, as is the distance from the monitor to your chair. Thus, your eyes are forced to adjust to the type, rather than the other way around.

As if that isn't enough, scrolling text induces nausea. It's the same phenomenon as carsickness. Your eyes capture images in frames, not unlike the individual frames of a 35-millimeter film. Your brain assembles the images and creates the sense of fluid motion. A car speeding around curves or going over bumps causes your eye to snap more frames than the brain can assimilate. The overload of visual information is the cause of the nausea. Rapidly scrolling text through a window on a computer screen is no different.

Implications of the Differences

So information on a computer screen is a nonlinear, two-dimensional, interactive, multimedia-laden source of eyestrain that can make you feel nauseated. What does all this mean to you, trying to get a message across to an audience using the Internet?

First of all, it means that you can be pretty sure that people don't read what they see on a computer screen. Their eyes bounce all over the screen, looking here, looking there, in no particular order, trying to find the information they came for. In fact, a study conducted in 1997 by Sun Microsystems revealed 79 percent of people who visit Web sites scan them instead of read them. As a result, if you want to get your message across to people online, you need to make sure they can find the message during the process of scanning.

> *People scan text on computer screens.*
> *They do **not** read it word for word.*

We also can surmise that when people do read online, they read more slowly. The Sun Microsystems study bears that out: People read 25 percent slower on a computer screen. By necessity, then, copy prepared for the screen needs to be about 50 percent shorter than that which is written for paper.

The fact is, we can ensure that our online messages are absorbed by recognizing how differently people approach and use the medium. To treat the computer screen as a newfangled magazine page or television screen is to make a tactical error that could result in your messages getting lost or never getting read at all. (Tips on how to write for the computer screen are covered in Appendix C.)

Narrowcasting

Most business sites on the World Wide Web represent the greatest mistake companies make on the Internet. "It's called the *World Wide Web*," comes the cry from the corporate boardroom. "Therefore, it has to accommodate everybody in the whole wide world!" Nothing could be further from the truth. In an environment in which individuals *pull* information based on their unique information needs, the World Wide Web represents the greatest opportunity in the history of media to target audiences without the need for mailing lists or demographic breakouts.

Heretofore, narrowcasting required you to know that your target market is comprised largely of, say, affluent women, age 18 to 32. Then you had to know details about the habits of that audience, such as which publications they read. Armed with that knowledge, you would buy advertisements in those magazines and place articles in those newspapers. On the World Wide Web, conversely, all you need to do is make sure your site contains material that would interest your target market. *They* will now be able to find *you*.* Knowing your target market, and establishing objectives for that market, means your site can be configured to address their needs.

Most sites on the Internet, however, are designed to serve a one-

---

*Of course, you also need to promote your site appropriately, a subject covered in Appendix B. Even if you do not undertake a comprehensive promotion, though, if your site contains worthwhile material, the word would get around among members of your target audience.

site-fits-all function. The home page proudly displays the company logo and links to material that is so broad in nature that it doesn't really meet the specific needs of any one group. Companies that recognize the Internet's narrowcasting capabilities can establish any number of independent sites, each addressing a specific audience with a specific set of objectives.

The Walt Disney Company has figured this out. You can, of course, visit *www.disney.com* and use it as a launching point to get to sites of interest. But in 1996, when the company reissued its animated classic *The Little Mermaid,* advertising did not point audiences to the umbrella corporate site. Instead, it directed them to *www.thelittle mermaid.com*, a site specifically designed to appeal to fans of the movie. How else might Disney have reached the members of this audience directly? The diverse audience consisted of older children who saw the movie when it was first released, younger children seeing it on the big screen for the first time, parents looking for wholesome entertainment, and adult fans of Disney animation. What mailing list might the company have acquired to cover that varied collection of people? What publications might all of them read?

Mattel, Inc., has taken the same approach to collectors of its famous Barbie doll. These collectors take their hobby seriously and hunger for all the official information they can get from the company about upcoming collectible releases. In order to satisfy that need, Mattel offers *www.barbie.com*, a site designed to appeal to collectors. (See Figure 4-1 for the site's home page.) Mattel does, in fact, maintain mailing lists of the Barbie collector clubs about which it knows, but the Web site affords the company the opportunity to communicate with individual collectors and those who belong to clubs it has not yet identified.

Chrysler and Bell Atlantic both have set up sites on the World Wide Web for media relations—sites that are distinct from their consumer-oriented pages. Bell Atlantic carries its narrowcasting capabilities even further, allowing reporters to select exactly the types of press releases, speeches, and government filings they would like to receive by e-mail. (More about Chrysler and Bell Atlantic is in Chapter 6.)

Tip: Establish Different Corporate Web Sites for Different Audiences
You don't have just one corporate brochure so why would you have just one company Web site? Establish different

sites to meet the needs of different audiences. You can provide links to your various sites from a corporate umbrella site, but make sure the members of each of your strategic audiences can find what they're looking for on a site crafted just for them.

Figure 4-1. Mattel's home page for its Web site for Barbie collectors. (BARBIE and associated trademarks are owned by and used with permission by Mattel, Inc. © 1999 Mattel, Inc. All rights reserved.)

Case Study: CSIRO

The Australian Commonwealth Scientific and Industrial Research Organisation (CSIRO) is an independent statutory authority constituted and operating under the provisions of Australia's 1949 Science and Industry Research Act. Australia's largest scientific research agency, CSIRO made its first use of the Web to communicate a hot issue in October 1995, when rabbit calicivirus disease (RCD) escaped from a CSIRO testing area. The agency had been using a facility on an island to test the virus as a potential biological control method to reduce plague-level populations of rabbits, when scientists discovered that RCD was killing rabbits on the nearby mainland.

"All hell broke loose with accusations flying about how and who let it get out," says Jennifer North, senior communicator in the CSIRO National Awareness Group. She adds, "We now think native bush flies and strong winds were the culprit." In the meantime, though, various constituent audiences expressed concerns about the effects of the virus, particularly in light of the fact that CSIRO's testing had not been completed.

North learned that the media, federal and state government officials, and rabbit owners in search of information were deluging one of her colleagues, Niall Byrne, with phone calls and faxes. Byrne, communications manager for the CSIRO Division of Animal Health, was under such pressure that he had to fly several staff members in from other states to help out. "Within two weeks, CSIRO staff from all around Australia were being pestered by relatives, friends, and neighbors who expected them to be able to answer their questions about RCD," North recalls. "There was a danger that if CSIRO employees weren't correctly informed, they could increase worries among the general population. I saw a need to satisfy both internal and external demands for information."

In her job, North was responsible for the CSIRO Web site (*www.csiro.au*). Working with Byrne, within about a week of the outbreak she established a "Rabbit News" page on the agency's site (located at *www.csiro.au/communication/rabbits/rabbits.htm*). Soon after the site was launched, Byrne noted a drop in the number of phone and fax queries about RCD; in addition, callers who had read information on the Web site before seeking additional information were more informed.

"Over the next nine months, as RCD made erratic progress through all the mainland states, Niall acted as a focus for information," North says. "Every month, Niall would send me an update that went up on the Web. News releases went up as soon as I became aware of them." By late February 1996, North knew the rabbit site was working. "I would get complaints from people because there was no monthly update to post on the Web during summer holiday," she says (the annual vacation period occurs during January in Australia). "By mid-1996, as the virus reached all corners of Australia, the panic subsided and the updates became less frequent."

But the Rabbit News page remained a part of the CSIRO site for another year, North says, "because of the importance of the issue in Australia and because our monitoring shows it is still a very popular part of our Web site." The site will continue to undergo revision as circumstances change. And since the rabbit success, the site also has been used to address diseases in bats that can be passed to humans, as well as some penguin diseases.

North says feedback indicates journalists in particular have appreciated access to information available twenty-four hours a day on the Web site. While the Web has not penetrated deeply into Australian media yet—"In my experience, more freelancers seem to have it than those employed by major media organizations," North says—the site did have some impact on coverage of the rabbit virus. "The CSIRO staff that answered a flood of media inquiries noticed that a fair proportion of them had already checked the Web site, so they were starting from a reasonably informed base," she says. "We also noticed the accuracy of the media stories improved and our viewpoint was used more often— which is, after all, one of the aims of our public relations efforts."

Leveraging Other Online Media

The World Wide Web is not your only Internet opportunity to reach narrowly defined audiences. You can reach targeted groups using the following tools, discussed in detail in Chapter 3:

• *E-mail lists.* People subscribe to mailing lists when they are so interested in a topic that they are willing to receive a flood of e-mail about it from others who share their passion. You can participate in existing e-mail lists or start one of your own that targets your audience.*

• *Discussion groups.* The Usenet community alone is made up of more than 30,000 newsgroups, and that doesn't even begin to account for those forums that exist on CompuServe, America Online, and other proprietary services. Undoubtedly, a discussion group exists that already hosts members of your target audience. You can easily tap into that existing forum in order to begin engaging the group's members in a dialogue designed to achieve your communications objectives.

Integration

Companies seeking to achieve specific communications objectives rarely rely on a single tactic or a lone medium. The effort begins with the objective. For the sake of argument, let's make one up. Let's say our fictitious company, Amalgamated Magnets, is trying to convince an offshore government to continue providing us with a tax break for our two manufacturing facilities located in their country. The public relations objective might read like this: *"Communicate the benefits Amalgamated has brought to the country directly to the tax authority, as well as to legislators, the media, and the public at large, and clarify the company's plans for future enhancements."* The idea would be to make clear that the company is bringing the country far more than the measly tax dollars it might collect if the special status were to be revoked, and that more such advantages are on the way. (Of course, we

---

*E-mail lists and discussion groups fall into the category of virtual communities, and participating in them requires special care. Read the section later in this chapter about virtual communities.

also would be willing to negotiate additional actions in order to retain our current tax status.)

Once the objective is in place, we can begin to outline a public relations strategy. A traditional approach might include:

• Meetings between the plant management (well briefed by the public relations department) and representatives of the tax authority.

• Meetings between our government relations representatives (equally well briefed) and key influential legislators.

• An open house at one or both of the plants highlighting the programs the company has undertaken to educate local employees in high-tech skills (rather than bringing U.S. expatriates into the plant). The open house also highlights new investments in equipment and facilities. It results in a video news release for local television news broadcasts, press releases, and copies of executive speeches.

• Press releases on the company's total investment in the local community and its indirect impact on the local economy.

• Institutional advertisements in the local business press announcing the company's latest investment plans.

The Internet should be applied to this campaign in an integrated manner; that is, it should be treated as one of the media employed in order to achieve the advantages to which it is best suited. The Internet could be used for:

• Announcement of open house activities on the company's home page.

• Establishment of a special-purpose Web site dedicated to the company's positive image within the country, in both English and the country's native language. The site would feature an archive of all press releases and speeches, photos from the open house, and facts and figures about the company's investment and impact in the local economy. It could include testimonials from employees who have received the kind of training and opportunities that allowed them to dramatically improve their overall prospects. There could be details about the various plants and operations, including interactive maps of the plant floors and details about products made there. A survey could query locals about the value of the company's participation in the local economy and the most appealing enhancements to Amalgamated's current operations.

- Banner ads promoting Amalgamated's special-purpose site on selected World Wide Web sites that deal with the culture of the country.

- Participation in selected discussion groups dedicated to the conversations about the country.

Further integration could be achieved by including the address of the special-purpose Web site on all printed material and by issuing a press release that introduces the site. Any graphic identities, such as a logo, should be used on all materials, including the Web site.

Ultimately, this integrated approach establishes a consistent impression, a *brand identity*. Each element of the campaign reinforces the others, with each taking advantage of the strength of the medium that it employs:

- *Press releases* establish a record and inform key media of the primary messages we want to convey.

- *One-on-one meetings* allow us to position our messages based on the interests of each influential government representative. They also give government representatives an opportunity to voice their concerns and issues, which we can assimilate and address in subsequent stages of the campaign.

- *The open house* is a visible display of our commitment, and an opportunity for senior management to be seen.

- *The video news release* means that members of the public at large have an opportunity to hear key messages and see for themselves what Amalgamated is doing inside the walls of an otherwise anonymous manufacturing facility.

- *Institutional advertisements* seek the support of the local business community.

- The *Web site* in general provides all interested parties with an archive of all materials, including levels of detail that could not realistically be incorporated into press releases and other print vehicles. Interested parties would *pull* those elements in which they are interested.

- The *Web-based survey* can be used as proof that the population believes the company is contributing to the local economy. It also can

generate relevant ideas for new efforts that would further stimulate the
economy or otherwise benefit the local population.

• *Discussion groups* provide us with direct feedback from interested members of the general population, which we can incorporate
into our thinking. We also can try out various suggestions for compro-
mise before broaching them with decision makers.

This approach represents only one type of integration. Amalgamated could take a completely different integrated approach, this time
to a different problem. This second approach is more sequential: Amalgamated Magnets advertises its magnets in a full-page display ad in
Magnets Today and invites readers to visit the company's product-
oriented Web site to get more information. Visitors to the site get the
information they need to make a purchase decision, then type their zip
code into an interactive locator program to find the closest independent
dealer with the right magnet in stock. The program produces not just
the name of the dealer, but an address, a map showing how to get to
the dealer's location, and a phone number. The dealer has been instructed to ask customers who buy an Amalgamated magnet, "How
did you hear about us?" and make a hash mark on a special form for
each customer who answers, "I found you on Amalgamated's Web
site." Now Amalgamated can measure how many magnets it sells
thanks to its Web site.

Tip: Build the Internet Into Your Plans
Too often, the people responsible for crafting the Web site
are not part of the same group generating the total public
relations campaign strategy. Build the elements of the Internet into the overall strategy, then work with the Web design team the same way you would work with a printer, a
video producer, or any other vendor—as part of the team
working toward the same set of objectives.

The integration of the Internet into a public relations effort produces far greater results than isolated online campaigns that are unrelated to the company's other communications efforts. Take Ragu
spaghetti sauce, for example. The site (at *www.ragu.com* or *www.eat.*

com) is unquestionably great, featuring good information, interactivity, entertainment value—everything that makes a site compelling. There's just one problem: The brand that is promoted on the site is the fictitious Mama Ragu. Mama's personality infuses the site; you can even opt to receive an occasional e-mail from Mama, alerting you to coupon offers or advising you of a new product introduction. But Mama is an element *only* of the Web site; she appears in no other aspect of Ragu's advertising or communications effort. If you went to the grocery store after visiting the site, you might look for Mama on the shelf, but you would be disappointed: She's not there. Ragu's Internet public relations effort is *not* integrated with its other communications; it is isolated, and therefore it misses its potential for significant influence.

Netiquette

It is dangerous to think of the Internet as a technology. True, technology enables the Internet, and a certain amount of technological know-how is required to take advantage of it. But all that technology without people using it would represent a huge global network of nothing. The Internet is people connecting with people. Each member of the growing community of Internet users is an individual who, to varying degrees, has accepted the cultural standards that have emerged as part of the Net's social fabric.

The *Jargon Dictionary* defines *netiquette* as "the conventions of politeness used on Usenet, such as avoidance of cross-posting to inappropriate groups and refraining from commercial pluggery outside the biz groups."* The *Webopaedia* offers this explanation:

> The etiquette guidelines for posting messages to online services, and particularly Internet newsgroups. Netiquette covers not only rules to maintain civility in discussions, but also special guidelines unique to the electronic nature of forum messages. For example, netiquette advises users to use simple formats because complex formatting may not appear correctly for all readers. In most cases, netiquette is en-

---

*www.netmag.net/jargon.

forced by fellow users who will vociferously object if you
break a rule of netiquette.*

The definition of netiquette has, in fact, expanded beyond newsgroups and discussion forums, because the introduction of Web-based
discussion and chat capabilities has blurred the lines between discussion groups and Web sites. Fundamentally, netiquette suggests that you
had better behave in a manner consistent with the accepted standards
of behavior in any given online locale, or you will suffer the consequences.

For organizations seeking to curry favor with a particular audience, it is particularly important to understand the netiquette that has
evolved among the members of that audience in each of the online
locales they populate. Committing an online *faux pas* can have dire
consequences among members of a strategic constituency already sus-
picious of your organization's motives and inclined to expect the worst.

Of course, the traditional practice of public relations is one in
which those doing the communicating need to mind what they say.
Online, though, the situation is even more hazardous. It's not just what
you say that can hurt you; it's where you say it, how you say it, the
format in which you present it, and to whom you say it. Unfortunately,
there are no specific, detailed guidelines for engaging in appropriate
netiquette, because each online venue has its own set of values. However, there are some steps you can take to ensure that your message
is not lost as the result of inadvertently offending members of your
audience.

Netiquette Guidelines

For Discussion Forums

• "Lurk" before you participate. This means you should read
what other people are saying before you make your own contribution
to the discussion. Getting the lay of the land helps you develop a sense
of what is and is not appropriate.

• Read the FAQs (Frequently Asked Questions). Most Usenet
newsgroups have developed FAQs based on the questions most new-

www.pcwebopaedia.com.

comers to the groups routinely ask so discussion group regulars don't have to repeatedly answer them. New participants are encouraged to read the FAQs. Many other discussion venues have adopted the same concept.

• Behave as an equal participant in the discussions—a member of the community, rather than as an authoritative figure. Nothing turns off an online audience faster than somebody invading their turf in order to set them all straight.

• Be honest about who you are—a representative of your client or organization. Make it clear that you are there to make positive contributions. For instance, tell other forum participants that you are looking for feedback or that you would like to offer solutions to their problems.

• When you reply to something somebody else has posted, quote the relevant part of the post to which you are responding so that readers know what you're talking about. However, you should never post the entire previous message, which takes up too much space and makes your message difficult to read.

For E-Mail

- Do not send mass e-mail messages to people who have not given you specific permission to contact them. Mass e-mail solicitations are known as *spam*. Little that occurs on the Internet raises the ire of the online community as much as unsolicited e-mail.
- Make sure the subject line of your e-mail clearly articulates what the message is about.
- If you are responding to a message, do not include the entire original message. Instead, just quote the specific part of the message to which you are responding.
- Don't send an e-mail if you have nothing substantive to say.

For E-Mail Mailing Lists

• Follow all the rules given above for discussion forums and e-mail.

• Do not attach any files to your e-mail. Since the message is going to multiple recipients, including people you do not know, you cannot be sure that they all have software that is compatible with the file you are sending. Also, people subscribe to e-mail mailing lists in order to engage in discussions. They could well resent receiving a large file attached to a message.

For Web Sites

• Know your target audience. A site that is designed to encourage institutional investment in an organization's stock should not adopt the flip, sarcastic tone of many noncommercial sites aimed at younger audiences. A site aimed at children should not make blatant sales pitches.

• If your site features a feedback button (e.g., "Contact Us"), you must set up a mechanism to ensure that a response will be sent to anybody who takes advantage of the offer.

• Do not provide links to other Web sites to which your audience might take offense. If your site supports a point of view about a controversial political issue such as gun control, avoid linking to sites that address other unrelated issues, such as abortion. Your target audience came to the site based on a common interest in gun control and may well not share your organization's point of view on other topics. In fact, some people may be so incensed by your position on the unrelated issue that you could lose their support for your primary issue.

By following the rules of netiquette, you ensure that your communications efforts will not be undermined by an inadvertent slip of the keyboard!

Push vs. Pull

In Chapter 2, we spent some time examining the receiver-driven model of communications that has become pervasive online. The allure of the World Wide Web is based on its accommodation of the receiver-driven model. People don't sit staring at their computer monitors waiting to receive whatever information you have to deliver. The Web allows them to engage in the new activity of "pulling" the information they want, based on what they need, when they need it.

The Web is such a media phenomenon that the need for a Web site has become a given for many organizations. And many organizations are looking at the Web's potential for cost savings as a means of assessing its return on investment. "Our catalog is online," the thinking goes, "so we don't have to print it any more. That'll save us a bundle!"

The problem with this thinking is that not every message or every component of a public relations effort is best suited to a "pull" environment—notably those that you want to be sure people see, regardless of whether they think they are interested in what you have to say. You cannot influence an individual or an audience if they never see your message!

The simple answer to this dilemma is to assess the effectiveness of each element of your communications effort in both a "push" and "pull" environment. The Web does not suffice for those messages that simply must be seen by the target audience. However, once a member of the audience has seen the key message, she can visit a referenced Web site for additional levels of information.

A host of companies have emerged in the last couple of years promoting the ability of their proprietary technologies to push content over the World Wide Web. The first and most successful of these is PointCast. People who download and install the PointCast software receive a regular stream of news and information, which they can view on their Web browsers or the PointCast interface. Moreover, when their computers are idle for a set amount of time, PointCast headlines automatically appear as screen savers on their monitors. Clicking on an interesting headline launches that particular item. Most of the other entries in the push marketplace are spins on the same idea.

These technologies do not represent a solution for the communicator intent on getting his message to a targeted audience. No single push technology has become pervasive enough that it can be relied upon as a channel for distributing your message. More important, though, is that few of these mechanisms truly represent a pure push to the audience. Instead, the user configures the tool to receive only material in categories that are of interest. The user can configure PointCast, for instance, so that he receives winning lottery numbers only for the state of California, a horoscope only for Sagittarius, and sports items only about the Washington Redskins. Distributing your message over such a channel no more guarantees that your audience will see it than storing it on a Web site.

Rather than actually push messages, these technologies allow audiences to engage in what might be called "intelligent pull." Most people know where their interests lie, and once they have found a site on the World Wide Web that suits their needs, they return frequently to see if new information has been added to the site. Programs that incorporate intelligent pull notify users when the site has been updated so that the user no longer has to pull the page in order to check. Different programs take different approaches to this notification, but the end result is the same: Users learn automatically that a chosen site has new material and is worth checking.

Tip: Add Intelligent Pull to Your Site
The most current releases of both Microsoft's Internet Explorer and Netscape's Navigator—the two Web browsers that dominate the market—have intelligent pull features built in. The Microsoft version is called the Channel Definition Format, while Netscape's is called Netcaster. Configuring your site so visitors can take advantage of these features is as simple as adding the appropriate text-based code. One page can offer intelligent pull features to users of both Explorer and Navigator.

Still, intelligent pull does not ensure that those who are unaware of your site's existence ever get your message. You need to be able to push information at those audiences, even if the information is nothing more than a compelling reference to the location of your Web site. You can push using traditional communications tools, such as print or video, depending on who and how sophisticated your audience is. If you are going to use electronic tools as the cornerstone of your plan, though, there is only one true push technology available: e-mail.

E-mail has been the most effective form of push on the Internet since its inception, and there are a number of strategies you can employ to take advantage of its push nature in a manner consistent with proper netiquette. Some of these approaches include:

- Enabling visitors to your Web site to sign up to receive various categories of e-mail that interest them.
- Inviting members of an audience to subscribe to a mailing list, through which you distribute messages consistent with the theme of the list.

- Giving visitors to your online publication the option of receiving an e-mail digest of each issue's table of contents. They can click on individual headlines to go directly to that story, bypassing the rest of the content that may be of less interest.

As previously stated, your e-mail messages should be short and succinct. Your e-mail should state just the facts, then provide links to Web sites where people can select the information they want. It also can point them to other non-Internet resources, such as 800-telephone numbers, publications, television programs, or upcoming meetings.

E-mail messages distributed to lists of people who have given you tacit permission to send messages to them should contain some common elements.

Common Elements of Mass-Distributed E-Mail Messages

- The name of the individual or institution that sent the message
- The date the message was distributed
- A listing of the contents of the message in the same order in which the items appear
- Information on how to contact the author of the message
- Information on how to be removed from the mailing list

Submit It!, Inc., an online service for promoting Web sites, issues an e-mail newsletter to its paying customers that embraces all of these concepts. A sample issue appears below.

```
Submit It! News
October 8, 1997

Submit It! News is designed to keep Submit It! members
current on changes and updates to our service. We welcome
your comments and suggestions.

If you want TO UNSUBSCRIBE from Submit It! News, please
follow these instructions:
 -------------------------------------------------------
1. Send an e-mail to submit-it-mgr@submit-it.com
2. Leave the Subject line blank
3. Type "UNSUBSCRIBE submit-it-news" in the Body area of
the message
4. (Remember to turn off your signature)
```

==========
IMPORTANT NOTE
==========
Please do not reply to this newsletter as it is
automatically deployed via a mail server. If you have any
questions pertaining to information in this newsletter or
concerning one of the Submit It! services, see the contact
information below or go to our Contact page online at
http://www.submit-it.com/subcon.htm.

THIS ISSUE
This issue covers the following topics:
⇨ Discount on Search Engine Ranking Service Extended to
   Submit It! Members
⇨ Discount on Web Site Development Tool Extended to Submit
   It! Members
⇨ Automatic verfication feature added to Submit It!
   Online

SUBMIT IT! POSITIONAGENT (25% OFF)
====================
PositionAgent automatically monitors where your Web site ranks
in the top 10 search engines. Using your keywords, it generates
reports showing where your site is listed by page and position
within each of the search engines. These e-mail reports are sent
to you on a weekly basis. In addition, online graphic reports
and Web presence scores will help you measure the effectiveness
of your listings over time. Pricing starts at $60 for 6 months
of weekly reports on 5 URL/keyword pairs. Submit It! Members can
purchase the service for $45.

For more details on service features and volume pricing, see the
PositionAgent brochure at http://www.positionagent.com/.

GIF WIZARD (30% OFF)
============

Save time and money by shrinking your graphics file size up to
90%. This online utility will help you reduce the file size of
your image files so that they load faster. This will make your
customers happier and more likely to return to your site. For
further details about the service and discount pricing, see
http://www.gifwizard.com/cgi-bin/nph-gifwizsi.

Stay tuned for MORE DISCOUNTED TRAFFIC BUILDING PRODUCTS &
SERVICES. Your Submit It! Membership will become even more
valuable as we establish similar relationships with other top
Internet marketing companies.

AUTO-VERIFICATION ADDED TO SUBMIT IT! ONLINE
=========================
Submit It! is pleased to announce a verification service

available free to all members. We are the first and only company to integrate search engine verification into a Web site announcement service. This service enables customers to confirm their Web page listings on the Internet search engines and Yahoo! with one click.

After the verification service automatically checks the Internet search engines and Yahoo! for your Web page, you can view the results within your account via your browser. Or, at your option, you can enter your e-mail address and Submit It! will send you the report via e-mail and automatically reverify your listings every month.

Further, since this feature is integrated with your Web site information that already exists on the Submit It! system, you can easily and quickly resubmit any listings that do not appear after an appropriate lag time.

The verification feature is available now to customers using Submit It! Online. It will be integrated into Submit It! Desktop in its next version to be released in mid-October.

CONTACT INFORMATION
= = = = = = = = = = = = =
You can contact Submit It! at any time through the following methods:

E-mail

Support or suggestions for new features: support@submit-it
Questions about your existing license or a new license:
sales@submit-it.com
General comments: submit-it@submit-it.com

Phone and Fax

Phone: 617-275-0930
Fax: 617-275-0931

Mail

Submit It!, Inc.
23 Crosby Drive
Bedford, MA 01730

Virtual Communities

The successful practice of public relations depends upon knowing which publics—which strategic audiences—can have an impact on the organization's ability to meet its objectives, and what kind of dialogue will result in bringing the organization and the audience closer together. The idea is to manage the relationship so that ultimately, the organization's objectives are not inconsistent with those of the strategic audience.

Traditionally, audiences come in all kinds of configurations. Local communities are bound by a common geography and can be identified pretty easily. Journalists with an interest in your organization can be harder to peg. Some might cover your industry, others might cover a beat that is tangentially related to one of your company's products; and still others may report on business in a broader sense and are interested in your company only when you engage in a certain type of activity, such as a merger, a proxy battle, or a recall. Activist groups can present a special challenge, particularly if they are not members of an organized group (such as People for the Ethical Treatment of Animals, Greenpeace, or Mothers Against Drunk Driving).

Online, however, it can be much easier to find these audiences, since they tend to congregate in virtual communities that have emerged as an online center for people who share a common interest. Knowing how to find and tap into the power of these virtual communities can be a powerful public relations tool.

Until recently, virtual communities were limited to discussion groups. It was in these groups that people with common interests but located in diverse geographic locations were able to congregate in order to share their ideas, ask questions, seek solutions, and engage in debate. Discussion groups were initially developed so that research scientists and academics from distant universities could take advantage of the intellectual capacity of the entire community, but their subject matter soon expanded to address all manner of issues and themes. (On Usenet alone, you can find discussion groups on such things as *Star Trek*, dolphins, Appalachian literature, Toyotas, bass fishing, evangelical Christianity, conspiracy theories, nuclear engineering, and Jodie Foster.)

Certainly, all of the individuals who possessed an interest in or a passion for these topics existed before online newsgroups were introduced. But their sphere of peers then often was limited to a few friends or members of a local club. With the introduction of discussion groups, however, it became possible to expand the realm of peers to hundreds or thousands of others just like them, regardless of where they lived or what time zone they were in.

Suddenly, the members of these discussion groups became influential communities in their own right, and worthy of the attention of organizations. Consider, for example, the following excerpt from an actual posting to the Usenet newsgroup *alt.consumers.experiences.* The message is in response to a complaint posted by another newsgroup participant. (The name of the computer company and its product have been changed.)

```
I returned my Computer Model 8888 because the technician
(that was promised) never showed up. I called Acme on
December 21st—and the technician must have gotten lost. I
haven't even received a call from Acme. . . . I will NEVER
buy another Acme computer.
```

Thousands of people who participate in the *alt.consumers.experiences* newsgroup read that post, and it unquestionably influenced their opinion about the computer manufacturer. Each of them can express that opinion to dozens of other potential computer buyers, including many who are not online participants. (Information on how to monitor discussion groups, along with more details about how newsgroups influence public opinion, appears in Chapter 5.) The computer company (which apparently does not monitor these forums since it did not participate in the discussion) could exercise its own influence by participating in the discussion or by contacting the dissatisfied customers directly.

As more and more people populate discussion groups, they get to know one another and rely on each other for information based on their areas of expertise. Certain participants obtain varied levels of status because of the value of their contributions. The informal groups grow into full-blown communities, with all the properties that are inherent in community structures. There are cultural norms, standards of behavior, internal disputes, struggles for control, cooperative community-building efforts, and, in times of crisis, a coming together of members to protect their common interests. As these structures grow, so do the communities' influence.

The growing power of this actualization of the many-to-many environment, discussed in Chapter 2, opened new possibilities for organizations beyond monitoring the discussions in order to identify issues and looming crises.

Case Study: SPSS

"There are several newsgroups that are dedicated to our products, and others address related areas," says Mark Battaglia, vice-president of corporate marketing for Chicago-based SPSS, which produces and sells computer software for statistical analysis. "Monitoring the discussion in these groups is not only a way to take the pulse of our customers. It also serves as two-way communication." Most of the SPSS executive team members monitor several newsgroups every day.

The focus of most of the discussion in the product-specific newsgroups is on how-to issues, according to SPSS President Jack Noonan. "The communication goes on between multiple people in the group. What I look for is anything that seems to be broken when people ask how to do something. Is there something wrong in the implementation of the user interface? Is something wrong in the documentation?" These kinds of issues provide Noonan and his team with pointers to problems that can be addressed before they become major issues.

Battaglia notes that the newsgroups also help the company identify changes in the marketplace. "People ask about the ability to get a certain kind of file format exported from our products. That kind of feedback allows us to stay on top of product planning. It's a place to identify new opportunities."

There are additional benefits to monitoring the newsgroups, each of which generates about twenty to thirty messages per day, according to Noonan. "They can be a leading indicator of customer sentiment," he says, pointing to a recent example. The company had released an upgrade to one of its products, distributing a notice by postal mail that the upgrade would be available at a discount for a limited time. On a Usenet newsgroup, one customer noted the deadline was too soon; he didn't have enough time to process the paperwork. Others said they needed more time to evaluate their need for the upgrade. "We could hear these concerns, and as a result we extended the deadline, making it possible for people to have a smooth transition," Noonan says. For several days, Noonan received e-mail directly from customers who thanked him for listening to their concerns. "That kind of response goes a long way toward improving customer satisfaction," he says. It also establishes the company's reputation as one that listens and responds—a reputation it couldn't buy with the most bloated publicity budget. The end result was probably better than if the company had offered a longer deadline in the first place.

Participating in the discussion groups also builds customer loyalty. Once, a competitor joined an SPSS-specific newsgroup and began bad-mouthing the company, violating newsgroup netiquette. The regular participants took offense, noting that they used the newsgroup for specific reasons and didn't want to get distracted by commercial issues.

While the SPSS executives mostly just lurk in newsgroups, they do participate several times a week, "particularly when the participants are talking about our policies or asking about the status of various products," Battaglia says. "I'll jump in and let them know what we're thinking or point them to a part of our Web site where they can get some answers." Often, the messages to which SPSS executives respond begin with words like, "Is anyone from SPSS aware of. . . ."

This means the participants in the newsgroups *know* the SPSS staff is listening in. "They'll even advise us when there's a discussion in another newsgroup that we ought to be aware of," Noonan says. Often, SPSS executives meet the Usenet newsgroup participants face-to-face at conferences or other gatherings. "The relationship we've established online can be very beneficial," Noonan says. "You never know; they could turn into beta testers for us."

Web-Based Communities

The greatest obstacle to a real explosion in online communities was the fact that participants had to learn how to use special software or pay proprietary services in order to participate. Participating in CompuServe's highly lauded business-oriented forums, for instance, requires payment of the CompuServe monthly membership fee. To take advantage of Usenet, most people had to learn how to operate a piece of software called a news reader.* Those who made the effort liked learning new software and were serious enough about the field in which they were interested to make the effort. Those with modest interests tended to stay away.

As the World Wide Web continued its evolution, enterprising software developers crafted the means by which discussion groups could be facilitated directly on a Web page. Now, people can participate in discussion groups without ever leaving the simple point-and-click Web interface. Web authoring programs like Microsoft FrontPage have taken the Web-based discussion group to another level, in which anybody can create a discussion forum with no programming and no special software that needs to be installed on the Web server. Suddenly, anybody can develop a newsgroup on any subject without having to go through the bureaucratic rigmarole required to establish a new Usenet, CompuServe, or America Online discussion forum.

As a result, the kinds of communities that have flourished in the text-only environments of Usenet are now emerging on the World Wide Web. By making these discussion groups integrated elements of the sites, the site owners are building loyalty to the site since people develop a sense of belonging to a community. Consider, for example, *Intranet Design Magazine* (at *www.innergy.com*), a biweekly online

---

*Agent, from Forte, is one of the better commercial readers; a freeware version, called FreeAgent, is available from the Forte Web site at *www.forteinc.com*. Both Microsoft Internet Explorer and Netscape Navigator come with news readers built into them, but they still function as utilities separate from the Web browser.

publication that includes eXchange, a Web-based discussion group. Participants in eXchange include several knowledgeable experts who have become regulars, and upon whom other community members rely for ideas and the benefit of their experience. Given a limited amount of time to read online publications, the audience for *Intranet Design Magazine* would be unlikely to begin reading a new competing magazine because they would not be able to take advantage of those community members upon whom they have come to rely.

The same concept applies to just about any kind of venture, even professional associations. The International Association of Business Communicators, for example, includes a messaging section as part of its Web site at *www.iabc.com.* Here, members and others can discuss whatever public relations or communications issues are on their minds. A recent review of the site revealed discussions on how to communicate employee compensation programs, what to pay freelance editors, banking public relations, and event planning.

Case Study: Parent Soup

Parent Soup (at *www.parentsoup.com*, as shown in Figure 4-2) is a community of parents that is supported by advertising provided mostly by companies that have products to sell to parents and families. Discussion groups known as

Figure 4-2. The Parent Soup Web site.

communities are at the heart of the site. In these communities, parents with specific issues can find information, read features, subscribe to a newsletter, and participate in various activities. One of these groups, for parents of teens, is shown in Figure 4-3. Among the most popular features in these communities are the chat rooms, where parents can engage in scheduled real-time discussions with experts and other parents. Also popular are the forums, where they can discuss various issues in ongoing newsgrouplike exchanges. One of these discussion groups, for parents of children with attention deficit disorder (ADD), is shown in Figure 4-4. This is a "threaded" discussion group, which allows readers to follow the thread of a discussion from the initial message to all levels of responses. Indented messages indicate that they are responses to the message above.

The Future of Commerce

The convergence of Web sites and discussion groups is likely to herald a new forum for commerce. This new electronic marketplace already exists in some online outposts, such as Agriculture Online (at *www.agriculture.com*). Here, farmers and others involved in the agriculture business can get up-to-the-minute information on such issues as the markets, weather, and farming trends. They can interact with one another in discussion forums, such as one on livestock or another on the

Figure 4-3. The Parent Soup community for parents of teens.

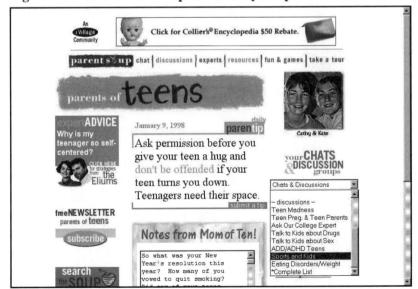

Figure 4-4. The Parent Soup discussion group for parents of children with attention deficit disorder.

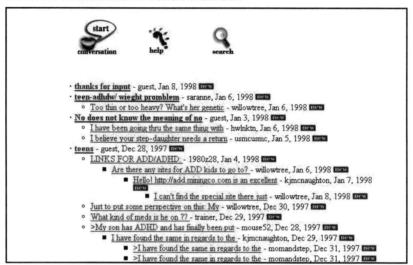

farming business. Finally, the site includes a transaction section, which features a marketplace, a listing of companies that pay to appear on the site. A paid classifieds section also appears (a recent ad for a 1991 John Deere front fold planter read, "Well maintained and stored inside," with a phone number and e-mail address included). There is even an online auction center.

The site effectively establishes a community of people *and* vendors, creating the potential for synergies that cannot exist in any other kind of environment. For example, a farmer having problems with a particular crop can get advice from an experienced community member about increasing yield by using a particular brand of fertilizer, which can be obtained directly from the vendor, which maintains a link in the site's marketplace.

According to John Hagel and Arthur Armstrong, online commerce specialists with the management consulting firm McKinsey & Company, this convergence ultimately will lead to a seminal shift in power from vendors to consumers. The owners of the communities, with their databases of members and the ability to target information to genuinely interested participants, will be able to command significant prices from vendors. Vendors would then bid on opportunities to sell to community members seeking certain products or services. (In the Agriculture Online example, a farmer requiring fertilizer with certain characteristics would announce his intent to buy 10,000 pounds of a product that meets his requirements. Suppliers that carry products that match those requirements would offer it to the farmer, who would be able to select the product offered at the lowest price.) The site owner would profit by taking a fee for each transaction completed on the site.

The Public Relations Role

Each of the virtual communities out there in cyberspace—on Usenet, on proprietary services like CompuServe, or on Web sites—represents a potential strategic constituency for your organization. These audiences can be current customers or prospective customers, critics, members of activist groups, representatives of the media, or members of just about any other strategic audience.

Thus, the principles of public relations apply to these new communities. Each needs to be assessed in terms of its potential impact on the organization, and a strategy must be mapped out that directs the company's relationship with the group. Once the nature of the organization's level of participation in the group has been defined, the individuals within the organization who will be responsible for that relationship need to learn the nuances of participating in discussion groups, adhering to netiquette guidelines.

Conclusion

You can toss Web pages up, engage in discussions, and blast hundreds of thousands of e-mail messages across the Internet. It all will be for naught if it does not conform to the principles of how audiences and individuals use the Internet and how the Net is affecting the very building blocks of communication. One of the best ways to assess how well your organization is perceived online is to monitor references to the company. How to engage in such monitoring is the focus of Chapter 5.

5

Monitoring Your Company or Client Online

In 1997, somebody posted a message to several Usenet newsgroups that criticized fashion designer Tommy Hilfiger. The post claimed that Hilfiger had appeared on the *Oprah Winfrey Show,* where he used racially charged language and said that had he known members of certain racial groups would like his clothing so much, he would not have made them so nice. The message went on to report that Winfrey subsequently threw Hilfiger off the show.

Outraged participants in the newsgroups copied the message, cross-posting it to other groups and e-mailing it to lists of friends. In short order, the story became accepted as fact.* The only problem was that it was not true. Not only had Hilfiger not used the offensive words, he had never even appeared on the *Oprah Winfrey Show.*

But it was too late: The damage was done as soon as the story became part of the lore of the Net. Months after Hilfiger's organization undertook efforts to disabuse the public of the story, you could find Web sites exhorting visitors to boycott Hilfiger products.

This story illustrates the power of the Internet and the need to incorporate monitoring activities into your online public relations plan. (How to respond to a crisis on the Internet is discussed in Chapter 11.) It is not enough to proactively use the Internet as a component of your

*A message that spreads through cyberspace and becomes accepted as truth is known as a meme.

coordinated communications efforts. You need to monitor activity initiated by others that could have an impact on your company, your markets, or your ability to do business. If the Internet is a digital, modern-day equivalent of the telephone party line, it is important to listen to *all* the conversations, not just those in which you are engaged.

There are two basic varieties of material that can be posted to the Internet about your organization:

1. That which is a direct response to your communications efforts
2. That which is posted by individuals or institutions with their own agendas

And there are two fundamental means by which the global Internet audience can create material to influence others about your institution and its activities:

1. By posting "rogue" or "attack" sites to the World Wide Web
2. By engaging in discussions on Usenet newsgroups or listserv mailing lists

Monitoring these discussions can play an important role in how online audiences (and ultimately, all audiences) perceive your company. You can respond to accusations, reinforce positive messages, and correct misconceptions. More important, though, is the ability to identify looming crises and develop plans to address them before they transcend the Internet and begin making headlines in traditional media. Indeed, most companies become aware of the significance of the Internet as a communications medium when an issue that began online finds its way into the newspapers and onto television news.

What to Monitor

The idea of monitoring the Internet for references to a company, an issue, a market, or some other topic makes a lot of public relations people nervous. The volume of material is daunting, and trying to find relevant information often appears like the proverbial search for a needle in a haystack. However, by using some of the tools available and by making such monitoring part of your organization's routine environmental scanning process, the task of finding important or substantive material becomes much easier.

Presumably, your organization already is making some effort to detect what is being said in public. The most common means of making this type of assessment is through a clipping service that scans newspapers and magazines for reference to your organization, then sends you the clippings on a regular basis. You (or someone in your company) then go through the clips to find those that meet the criteria for your attention. To this and any other scanning methods you employ, you need to add the two primary sources of information on the Internet: (1) the global conversation of many-to-many discussion groups, and (2) pages posted to the World Wide Web.

The Global Conversation of Discussion Groups

As previously discussed, Usenet newsgroups are discussion forums that individuals access using the Internet depending on their key areas of interest. More than 30,000 Usenet newsgroups are currently available, although not all newsgroups are available to all Internet users. (Each Internet service provider (ISP) decides which newsgroups are offered to its users.) However, a core group of about 18,000 newsgroups tend to be available to all users. People use Usenet newsgroups by posting "articles" to the groups, which can be read by anybody else visiting the newsgroup at a later time. Individuals reading an article can respond directly to the author of the original article or to the author of a follow-up article, or by creating a follow-up article that is, in turn, posted to the newsgroup.

As discussed in Chapter 3, newsgroups are identified using a hierarchy of words. The top-level hierarchy designates the broadest nature of the newsgroup. For example, *rec* signifies a recreation-oriented topic; *talk* suggests a debate. Subsequent levels narrow the discussion, so that *talk.politics.animals* suggests that the newsgroup is a forum for a political debate over animal rights. Figure 5-1 shows a "thread" on the *alt.autos.gm* Usenet newsgroup, dedicated to the discussion of General Motors cars. The thread began with one participant asking a question about the Chevy Cavalier; two other participants then offered their thoughts. Presumably, GM is aware of the newsgroup and monitors it regularly.

Usenet newsgroups have become popular with the new generation

Figure 5-1. A "thread" on the Usenet newsgroup *alt.autos.gm.*

Subject	From	Sent	Size
Cavlaier cutting-off problem	Ermina Britt	1/23/98 9:59 AM	1KB
Re: Cavlaier cutting-off problem	KEN CADWELL	1/23/98 12:53 PM	1KB
Re: Cavlaier cutting-off problem	goodwrench	1/23/98 9:09 PM	2KB
Re: Charging Problems	Mj.	1/23/98 3:27 PM	2KB
Chev V8 diesel	Scam	1/25/98 1:20 AM	1KB
Re: Chev Vortex Pings	Jim Walker	1/23/98 7:34 AM	3KB
Re: chevrolet suburban engine noise	M & R	1/23/98 11:11 PM	1KB
Chevy Cavalier Limited Slip Differentials	@www.isuzuperfor...	1/24/98 6:09 PM	1KB
Re: Chevy Malibu Sunroof	Brian T. Kennett	1/21/98 4:57 PM	1KB
Chevy Monte Carlo	Katherine L Nelson	1/23/98 11:59 AM	1KB
Re: Considering Cadillac Catera	microserve	1/23/98 3:33 PM	2KB
Re: Considering Olds Integra	Ali Nabeel	1/20/98 7:08 PM	2KB
corsica no start	Violet G. Bergeron	1/23/98 6:51 PM	1KB
Customized Vehicles	Jason	1/24/98 3:57 PM	1KB
Re: desperate for advise on 1990 lumina eu	Shirley Gray Nino	1/23/98 2:46 PM	2KB

From: Ermina Britt **To:** alt.autos.gm
Subject: Cavalier cutting-off problem

I have a 1983 Chevy Cavalier with the 4cyl engine. I've replaced the O2
sensor, have a rebuilt carb, replace the fuel filter, cleaned the gas tank
and lines. The car doesn't like running in the cold, but after it warms up
for about 5 minutes runs fair. Everytime you try to push down on the
accelerator to speed up, the car bogs down.

Any ideas on what I might need to replace next or how to fix this problem?

Please respond to ninamike@worldnet.att.net.

of Internet users, including those who access the forums through commercial online services such as CompuServe and America Online. Thus, the audience is broad. Demographics of Internet users also suggest the audience is prosperous and well-educated, with household incomes exceeding $60,000 per year.

Listserv mailing lists use Internet e-mail to facilitate the same kinds of discussion that occur in Usenet newsgroups. Listservs are managed by software that resides on a server. The software manages subscriptions to a mailing list along with subscriber access to the list's various functions. At its most basic, a mailing list works by automatically distributing e-mail that a subscriber sends to the server to all other subscribers.

Let's say we participate on a mailing list dedicated to public relations. (There really is one, called PRFORUM, managed out of the journalism department at the University of Indiana in Indianapolis.) You want to get information on methods of scanning the Internet for references to your company. You send an e-mail to the list with the subject "Scanning the Internet," which all other subscribers would receive. If I have some thoughts to contribute, I would reply to your message, and the server would distribute that reply to all subscribers, with the subject head "Re: Scanning the Internet." If somebody responded to my message, it would appear in all our in-boxes as "Re: Re: Scanning the Internet." Thus, it becomes a simple task to follow a threaded e-mail-based discussion.

Mailing lists are often more focused than Usenet newsgroups and represent a potentially more action-oriented audience. Mailing list subscribers are serious enough about the subject that they don't mind receiving the volumes of e-mail the list generates. Anybody who participates also needs to subscribe. Whereas Usenet newsgroups tend to attract hit-and-run participation (including juvenile pranks and deliberate baiting), mailing lists are more likely to stay on topic.

Newsgroups and Their Impact

Discussions on newsgroups can be devastating, enlightening, troublesome, annoying, or beneficial. When something hot appears in a newsgroup, it can be discussed in short order, and the participants can elect to take some kind of action based on the results of the discussion. These actions can be taken individually, or the group can band together in an activist mode.

Let's look at the consequences of negative or false information posted on the Internet. Perhaps the most famous case involves the Intel Pentium chip, the math flaws of which were first discussed online among mathematicians using computers with the chip. Intel probably could have defused the situation by participating in the discussion and listening to the concerns of those few customers who actually needed to have that particular math function work correctly. Instead, the debate spilled over the newsgroup environment and into the public media, where it became a significant crisis for the company.

What happened to Lexis-Nexis—the online database of articles from newspapers and magazines, along with public records and other information—provides another view of the consequences of ignoring messages posted to newsgroups.

Case Study: Lexis-Nexis

P-TRAK was a catch-up product for Lexis-Nexis, since several of its competitors already offered access to databases that contained information on individuals. The legal community and private investigators use these databases to track down litigants, heirs, and others being sought in relation to legal cases. The information includes names, addresses, and phone numbers. Initially,

Lexis-Nexis also included Social Security numbers, but that feature was withdrawn (although a user can type in a Social Security number to learn to whom it belongs). Competing databases do offer Social Security numbers.

Concerns over privacy, however, led to the following Usenet newsgroup posting *months* after Lexis-Nexis withdrew Social Security numbers from the P-TRAK dataset:

> LEXIS-NEXIS P-Trax Database WARNING: Your name, social security number, current address, previous addresses, mother's maiden name, birth date and other personal information are now available to anyone with a credit card through a new Lexis database called P-Trax. As I am sure you are aware, this information could be used to commit credit card fraud or otherwise allow someone else to use your identity. For Lexis response to this post go to: http://www.lexis-nexis.com/lncc/about/ptrak.html.
>
> LEXIS-NEXIS has been swamped with requests to remove personal data from this database (thanks to the wonders of electronic communication, no doubt). It is no longer possible to remove your name from the database simply by calling the LEXIS-NEXIS phone number. To remove your name from the P-trax database, you must make a request in writing. You can either mail or fax this in: fax: (513) 865-1930, or surface mail to: LEXIS-NEXIS P.O. Box 933 Dayton, Ohio 45401-0933. If you would like to register any additional comment against this product, the product manager is Andrew Bleh (rhymes with "Play"). He can be reached at the LEXIS-NEXIS toll-free number: 800-543-6862. Ask for extension 3385. According to Lexis, the manager responsible is Bill Fister at extension 1364.

The post was copied and reposted in hundreds of newsgroups, from privacy-related discussions to such unlikely venues as a forum for Pakistani culture. The message also was copied into e-mail messages that well-meaning individuals sent to their lists of friends, business colleagues, and acquaintances. Lexis-Nexis public relations officials began to recognize the post as the source of complaints from the misspelling of the service: P-Trak is the official name of the service; P-Trax is how it was spelled in the Usenet post.

In 1998, two years after the story erupted, Lexis-Nexis was still taking heat over the perceived impropriety of providing sensitive information to subscribers. The company was still receiving calls from reporters who, upon reading the post for the first time, believed they were breaking a hot news story. Had Lexis-Nexis caught the erroneous message early, however, the inaccuracies could have been corrected and the spread of the message through the Internet probably would never have happened.

Clearly, though, you can do far more than stem a crisis by monitoring discussions about your organization. You can, for example, detect trends, such as dissatisfaction with a particular product or service.

In Chapter 4, a case study about SPSS showed how a company was able to target a customer complaint and address it quickly, resolving the issue and enhancing the organization's reputation as a responsive, customer-focused business. In June 1997, the *New York Times* reported the following incident:

> *Catherine Stanton is an ordinary consumer, but when she logs on to the Internet, her product complaints have power that rivals Ralph Nader's. She discovered that power last October when a $10 late fee charged her by a Blockbuster video store was referred to a collection agency. Ms. Stanton tried to clear up the problem over the telephone, but despite several calls, she said, she continued to receive bill collectors' "nastygrams." Frustrated, she took her complaint to the Internet, where she posted her story on a bulletin board. "Five minutes of my time to complain to thousands of people is a good turnaround," she said. "I vented and felt better."*
>
> *But she felt even better in December, when Blockbuster's vice-president for operations, Tim Hicks, got in touch with her. He offered a written apology, canceled the late fees, called off the collection agency, and sent a $20 gift certificate. The reason, Mr. Hicks explained recently, was simple. Blockbuster's research, he said, suggests that a customer who had a bad experience tells ten to twenty other people. "Imagine how many people see it on the Internet," Mr. Hicks said. "The Internet becomes a very powerful consumer tool."*

In fact, Blockbuster's policy is to respond to every discussion group article that references the organization.

Tip: Educate Employees on Using the Internet
Among the audience subcategories you find online are your own employees. When a company is attacked, many employees jump to its defense—often with information that is inconsistent with official company messages and sometimes by giving away proprietary information. You cannot keep

> your employees off the Internet, nor should you *want* to. You can, however, educate them about the proper way to discuss the organization online. When the organization faces a big issue that will be a natural topic of online discussion, make sure your employees have all the facts they need to present a united front rather than a disjointed mess.

Pages Posted to the World Wide Web

If discussion groups provide individuals with a means of engaging others sympathetic to their issues, the World Wide Web establishes a forum for publishing any kind of position about any organization or issue. The Web is rife with sites that attack organizations, praise products, condemn practices, and idolize celebrities. Because the cost of publishing on the Web is so low and the process so simple, anybody with an ax to grind can find an audience of like-minded souls, along with those cruising for whatever information they can find. Some of the sites that have gained notoriety for their attacks on organizations include NutraSweet, Ford, Microsoft, Allstate, and McDonalds.

These sites gain not only the attention of others on the Internet who share an interest in the topic but even those who are not online. Consider the site dedicated to getting the president of Disneyland reassigned within the Walt Disney Company. The site represents what the author calls an online campaign based on his disenchantment with some of the directions Disneyland has been taking. The home page of the site notes that it has been covered by the *Los Angeles Times* and *Harper's*.

Once a page containing damaging information appears on the Web, the allegations can spread through Usenet newsgroups, e-mail, and other vehicles. By monitoring these pages, you can deal with the inaccuracies before they spread. You also can develop a plan to address divergent viewpoints the Web site may take.

Legal action is one way to handle attack sites, but that strategy can backfire on the Internet. In discussion groups, individuals can comment *ad nauseum* about your company's strong-arm tactics to remove a page rather than deal with the issues it raised. Legal threats—even successful ones—can lead to worse problems than the page itself created. It is better to use the conventions of the Internet itself to address misinformation.

Case Study: Mrs. Fields Cookies

Following O. J. Simpson's acquittal on murder charges, *Hard Copy* reported that several companies donated congratulatory products to a party Simpson held at his home. Among the companies making such contributions, the tabloid television show claimed, was Mrs. Fields Cookies. Despite the fact that the allegation was not true (*Hard Copy* and others that repeated the information wound up issuing retractions), the claim found its way to a site devoted to initiating boycotts against companies and others that were somehow contributing to Simpson's welfare. That led to newsgroup discussions.

Mrs. Fields representatives were monitoring the discussion group, however, and were able to learn of the claims before the posts had spread across the Internet. By participating in the newsgroups and presenting accurate information, the organization was able to shut down the rumor before it became common on the Internet (as in the Lexis-Nexis example given above).

The Hybrid of Web-Based Discussions

The rapid development of the World Wide Web and software to facilitate a wide range of functions on it has led to the emergence of Web-based discussion groups. There are several reasons why these discussion groups are cropping up everywhere and attracting audiences and participants.

First, they are easy to create. You can purchase off-the-shelf software that allows you to manage the establishment of groups. You can even create them yourself using some of the over-the-counter software packages, such as Microsoft FrontPage.

Second, they offer other material beyond talk. A Web site that includes a discussion group is more than just the sum of the discussions. Other resources are available from the site. The information on the site can generate discussion, and the discussion can lead the site owners to offer additional information. In fact, not everybody who joins a Web-based discussion came to the site with the intention of engaging other users. Often, a new participant came in search of information and discovered the existence of the discussion group. (See the discussion of Web-based virtual communities in Chapter 4.)

Third, Web-based discussion groups are highly targeted. They appeal directly and uniquely to the audience of people who visit that particular site. And finally, Web-based discussion groups are easy to use. They use the same interface as any other Web page: Just point and click.

How to Monitor Company-Related Internet Activity

Individuals—armed as they are with the publishing and information-sharing tools of the Internet—are putting the Net to effective use. Combining online discussion with Web publishing, it becomes simple for anybody to wage a campaign in favor of or opposition to their particular cause.

Two options are available for monitoring Internet activity related to your company:

1. Outsource the work.
2. Do it internally.

Outsourcing

Several companies have sprung up to monitor the Internet on your behalf. The prices they charge vary as much as the range of services do. Some report on Internet activity, others provide analysis and recommendations, still others apply measurement principles in order to help you appraise the effectiveness of your efforts.

When you select a company, make sure its services are consistent with your information needs. The services available are provided by:

- E-watch (on the Web at *www.ewatch.com*), which monitors as many as 250,000 messages daily on 40,000 public discussions in cyberspace. For an extra fee, it can alert you whenever a change is made to any Web sites you designate.
- M3, a service of Middleberg + Associates (on the Web at *www.middleberg.com*), which combines three services: monitoring, analysis, and response.
- The Delahaye Group (at *www.delahaye.com*), which offers an image analysis based on the content of online discussions.

Doing It Yourself

There are a number of reasons to consider doing your own monitoring (or at least, supplementing the work done by the company with which you have contracted). First, nobody understands the issues that face your organization the way insiders do. Companies contracted to look for key information could miss something subtle that only an insider would be able to identify. You also benefit from the immediacy of doing your own monitoring. If something is brewing online, you won't have to wait to get a report in order to act on it.

Methods of Monitoring

The methods of monitoring fall into four basic categories:

1. Reading newsgroups
2. Using search engines and other Web services
3. Utilizing software
4. Subscribing to mailing lists

Reading Newsgroups

Any newsgroups that are dedicated to your company, the products your company makes, or the issues your company faces should be added to your regular reading list. Once you get the hang of reading newsgroups (and using newsgroup reader software), you are able to scan a day's worth of messages in just a few minutes. You learn the kinds of subject headers that warrant your attention and can dispense with the remaining headers quickly.

Make sure you limit the newsgroups you read only to those that are directly related to your business. Those that occasionally address the business should not be added to your regular reading list. For example, just because your company's stock is mentioned now and then in one of the investment newsgroups doesn't mean you want to start scanning all the various messages posted to that newsgroup.

Participating

You may sometimes have to go beyond reading newsgroups. You may need to participate. If a message to a discussion group sends up a red flag, how do you respond? Before jumping in and engaging the audience, follow these steps:

1. Lurk first, for several days at least. This means retrieving and reading articles posted by others in the newsgroup without posting yourself. Unless you post a message, nobody knows you are there. By lurking for a while, you can learn the lay of the land.

2. Determine who is posting to the newsgroup. Is it an audience that's worth your time? Are they taken seriously? Are messages from the newsgroup cross-posted elsewhere on the Internet? Who are the players in the newsgroup—that is, who has influence?

3. Learn the culture of the newsgroup. How do people reply to messages? What's the ruling netiquette?

4. Find out if the group has an FAQ (Frequently Asked Questions) document. If so, read it to learn more about the group.

5. Assess the current situation. How is the group likely to respond if you jump in? Are you better off dealing with the individual who posted the article in question, or is there value in speaking to the entire community? (Remember, as recounted above, Blockbuster responded directly to the individual who posted an objectionable message rather than to an entire group.)

6. If you decide to contribute, make sure you participate as a new member of the community rather than preach as a representative of the company.

7. Don't succumb to "flame bait." Some participants in a newsgroup drop messages deliberately constructed to make you lose your temper. You're best off ignoring these and engaging in discussion only with those who post substantive messages.

Using Discussion Forums and Listservs for Focus Groups

Focus groups are part of every communicator's research arsenal. There are drawbacks to focus groups, however. One is the difficulty of getting participants to come to a central meeting location. Another is what experienced facilitators refer to as "herd mentality," in which quieter participants in the group tend to agree with dominant personalities rather than stake out their own positions.

Neither of these are issues when focus groups are conducted online. Monica Zinchiak and Bob Novick are both public relations research experts who conduct some of their focus groups using e-mail.

Zinchiak: The Entire Process Online

With twelve years of experience in market research, the San Diego-based Monica Zinchiak's Z Research Services serves a national client base that includes high-tech companies, consumer goods operations, advertising agencies, and public relations agencies.

Most of her online focus group participants are prerecruited, although Zinchiak says she has done some online recruiting from lists of people who have expressed an interest in participating. While the recruitment process—including invitations and confirmations—is handled by e-mail, diligence in the process is particularly important in an online environment. Certain parts of the process are designed to surface issues that are of no importance in a live, face-to-face environment.

For instance, you need to make sure that the unseen participant at the other end of a keyboard is, in fact, part of the demographic group you were seeking. And qualifying participants requires more than an e-mail message, as far as Zinchiak is concerned. She calls the participants on the phone. That's how she learned that one participant recruited for a group designed for people over age 50 was in fact the target participant's son. "He was Steve Junior," she says. "The list just said 'Steve,' so the son didn't know he wasn't supposed to participate, but if I hadn't called, I would have had a seventeen-year-old kid answering questions instead of the fifty-four-year-old Steve Senior—and I would never have known."

Before the focus group begins, participants receive printed information about the focus group that covers such things as how to express emotions when typing by using "emoticons" (typed characters that, turned sideways, look like facial expressions). Just before the focus group begins, participants visit a Web site where they log on and get some last-minute instructions. Then they move into a Web-based chat room in which Zinchiak and the participants type to each other in real time. The Web environment in which Zinchiak conducts her focus groups is based on privacy. "If Bob has something interesting to say, I can pursue that line of thought with him in a separate window that I'm controlling. The rest of the group never sees it," Zinchiak says.

Still, many of the issues that arise in focus group facilitation are the same online as they are in the real world. Zinchiak needs to keep the conversation focused, deal with rogue participants who get out of line, and handle other nuances. Plus, the online environment presents new challenges. "First of all, you have to use more colorful language, more exciting phrases. You don't want people drifting off because the kids are talking to them, the television is on, or something is distracting them. You have to keep their attention." As a result, online focus groups tend to run shorter than live ones. "Sixty minutes is about as long as most people can stay focused."

Participants tend to be less inhibited online—there is a detachment that comes from the anonymity of the keyboard, which diminishes the herd mentality issue and tends to make everybody more equal. On the other hand, some people can type faster, have a higher-speed modem, or are more adept at getting their responses in quicker. You generally have fewer people in an online focus group than in a face-to-face meeting because too many voices can confuse the discussion.

Still, there are tremendous advantages to online focus groups, Zinchiak says. They are fast; the text is recorded as it is being typed, which makes it easier to jump into analysis and fire off results to the client. And with e-mail as the medium through which recruitment is handled, the entire process can be completed in less time than traditional groups.

There are, however, instances in which Zinchiak says traditional focus groups will continue to be preferred. "For instance, you really can't explore highly emotional issues or subject matters online," she says. And of course, there are clients unfamiliar with the technology who just won't permit a focus group to happen online.

But new technology will expand the scope of online focus groups, Zinchiak says. "With the software we use, we can put visual material on-screen for participants to see and react to," she says, "and video and face-to-face focus groups are coming."

Novick: What's the Rush?

Bob Novick uses listserv software to control the subscriber list so that only focus group participants receive list mail. Focus group participants are recruited from Usenet newsgroups and other listserv mailing lists where the target audience tends to congregate. "We pay them the way we normally do in a focus group and pretty much conduct the groups the way you conduct a normal one, except it's not live," Novick says. "It takes longer, but the quality of response is much better. People have more time, so when they write their responses, they are more thoughtful, longer, and they get less carried away by the emotion of the moment." Novick or his partner serves as the facilitator of the group, just as they do in a live setting.

There are some drawbacks to these e-mail-based focus groups that operate asynchronously (that is, not in real time). "First of all, they take longer," Novick says. "It's more difficult to show visual and other kinds of exhibits if you want the group to evaluate an advertisement or taste a product. And not every audience is available on the Internet—although we haven't yet had a project where we weren't able to find the people we needed."

While online focus groups—or, for that matter, live ones—do not provide quantitative results, Novick insists they are wonderful forums for qualitative research. As for more statistical research, he says, "You do need to be aware that it's very difficult, if not impossible, to do statistically accurate surveys on the Internet because of the voluntary nature of the medium. It's very difficult, if not impossible, to reach everyone, which makes it difficult to sample. People need to agree to participate, and most don't. That makes for low response rates."

But the dynamics of focus groups can't be beat, Novick insists. "We've had several cases where the participants in the focus group asked to keep the listserv going even after the focus group was concluded," he says. "In one case, a focus group about a particular medical condition, the participants kept the discussion going for several weeks, then formed their own support group by establishing a Usenet newsgroup."

Using Search Engines and Other Web Services

Of course, you won't find every message that deals with your organization in the few topic-specific newsgroups you identify. To find messages that are contributed to discussion groups that do not routinely deal with your organization, you should make it a habit to use search engines and other Web services to help ferret out important themes you might not otherwise find.

There are different types of search tools, and each has different characteristics. In order to take advantage of the information on the Web without turning the search into a lifelong activity, communicators need to familiarize themselves with the tools and how they work.

There are two fundamental types of search tools available online: (1) search engines, and (2) directories.

Search Engines

Search engines routinely send programs called spiders to scour the Web, collecting information about what's out there and putting that information into a database. When you type in a search term, the result is a list of items in the database that match your query.

Search engines include AltaVista (on the Web at *www.altavista. digital.com*) and HotBot (at *www.hotbot.com*). Both of these search engines (and several others) allow you to select whether you want to search the World Wide Web or Usenet newsgroups. Other engines are limited to information published on the Web. DejaNews (at *www. dejanews.com*) is designed specifically for searches of Usenet newsgroups. These and most other engines include a link to a "Help" page, where you can get details on how to strategize your search.

Strategy is the key when using a search engine. Resist the temptation to just fire off a couple of words and see what comes up. Instead, take a step back and think about the information you're trying to retrieve. Let's say your company is introducing a new managed care benefits plan, and you want to find out what the negative consequences of a managed care approach might be so you can plan a communications effort that proactively addresses the issue. Simply typing *managed care* will produce more results than you can cope with—everything online about managed care, along with every link that contains the words *managed* and *care*. Instead, think about the information you *really* want. This might cover such combinations as:

Managed care and *employee*
Managed care and *communication*
Managed care and *reaction*
Benefits and *managed care*

When you are finished, you can combine the queries to come up with a search request that might look like this:

```
(managed care or benefits or managed health care or health
care or PPO or EPO) and (employee or employee communication
or change or reaction or consequences or resistance)
```

Other approaches to using search engines depend on how they were constructed (which is why you should always spend some time on the "Help" page learning the nuances of that particular engine). Some of the different search methods adopted by the various engines include:

• Boolean searches, which allow you to group terms using connectors such as *and, or,* and *not.*

• Phrase searching, which allows you to string words together in a phrase (such as "animal rights activism").

• Proximity searching, in which you specify how many words may separate your search terms (such as "animal" within five words of "rights").

• Truncation, which allows you to add a wild card, generally an asterisk, at the end of a search term in order to retrieve all the documents that contain any variation on the term. (Entering communic* will return *communicate, communication, communicator,* and *communicating.*)

• Field searching, which lets you specify where the query term resides—in the URL (address), the title, the headlines, or the body copy.

The more you can use these tools in conjunction with a clear search strategy, the more quickly you will find the results you need.

Directories

Directories, unlike search engines, are produced by hand, with people filtering and classifying resources and, in some cases, annotating and rating them. You pick the subject heading that most closely matches the subject of your search, then browse the results or drill down through deeper levels of category headings. Popular Internet directories include Yahoo! (on the Web at *www.yahoo.com*), and Info-Seek (*www.infoseek.com*). Just as with the search engines, you can use the "Help" page to learn how to get good results. And, as with the search engines, some directories (such as InfoSeek) also allow you to search Usenet newsgroups.

Directories take the form of catalogs and let you type in a search query. However, since real people have reviewed and classified the sites, the value of the index increases with the amount of information those people have provided. Look for ratings (and a rating system, including the criteria that help you determine what the ratings mean), annotation (in which the individuals compiling the index tell you something about what the site contains), and a sense that the index is discriminating in which sites it includes (whether it offers only sites it has determined have real value, or whether it lists everything that it comes across).

Mixing It Up

As you become more proficient at your searches, you will probably find a favorite search tool that, more often than others, produces results that meet your needs. Don't ignore the others, though. Some tools are better for some searches than others. Get a sense of which tool gets you better answers for different *types* of searches. For instance, if you are looking for a particular product or information outlet, a directory may allow you quickly to drill to that information. If, however, you are trying to find what authorities have posted about a particular issue—with information appearing on sites that could easily be listed in dozens or hundreds of different categories—you may be better off using a search engine.

Utilizing Software

You can obtain software that automates the process of scouring newsgroups and the Web.

Newsgroup Searching Software

The software that searches Usenet newsgroups allows you to input a high level of detail in order to narrow your search so you get precisely the kind of information you want without having to sift through a lot of messages that literally match your query but ultimately are of little or no value. One such software package, NewsMonger (information is at *www.techsmith.com*), works in conjunction with the AltaVista search engine. You specify key words to search for, then you can refine those searches with filters. For example, you can filter out messages with certain key words in their "Subject" or "From" fields. You can schedule how often these programs run.

Web Searching Software

A whole crop of intelligent agents has sprung up that allow you to create detailed queries, then send the program onto the Net to find pages that match. Once you find them, you can be alerted whenever something new has been added to the page. Two excellent programs that fit this description are NetAttache (on the Web at *www.tympani. com*) and WebSnake (at *www.anawave.com/websnake*).

The latest versions of Microsoft Internet Explorer and Netscape Navigator include monitoring capabilities. Once you have identified a Web page or site that interests you, you can instruct the browser to alert you whenever a change occurs. Internet Explorer even lets you instruct the browser to download a page that changes so that it's waiting for you on your computer hard drive when you get to work in the morning.

Subscribing to Mailing Lists

If your company or issue is discussed in a listserv, it would be a good idea to subscribe to that list in order to monitor the discussion. Unlike subscribing to a newsgroup, a listserv subscription is recorded by the list owner, which means it's possible for people to know that you—a company representative—are receiving messages contributed to the list. Therefore, lurking is not an option. Still, most subscribers won't know you're there unless you distribute your own message.

Many of the software programs that are used to manage mailing lists allow you to receive a "digest" version of the list—all the day's messages consolidated in a single message—or an "index" version—just the subject headers; you retrieve the messages you want to read separately.

Unfortunately, there are over 84,000 mailing lists and no equivalent to DejaNews or InfoSeek to help you search them. However, there *is* a service that can help you identify the lists that may be pertinent. The Liszt page (on the Web at *www.liszt.com*) allows you to use search terms to find lists that match your interests; you also can drill through a subject category listing. Starting with "Business," for example, leads to nineteen subcategories, including "Public Relations" and "Marketing." Selecting "Public Relations" takes you to a page of information about PRFORUM, the mailing list handled out of the University of Indiana.

Once you subscribe to a mailing list, you generally receive an e-mail that contains all the information about commands used to manage your subscription. Save that file! It helps you temporarily log off (if you're going on vacation, for example), retrieve older messages, and end your subscription should the list not meet your needs.

Using the Internet to Monitor the Press

Not only does the Internet give you resources to monitor your company's online image; it also lets you monitor the traditional media. You can supplement the information you receive from your clipping service or transition your existing online database accounts (with companies like Lexis-Nexis or Dow Jones News Retrieval) to a Web-based account.

Web-Based Subscription Services

Several subscription services are available on the World Wide Web that deliver news reports from a host of traditional print publications via e-mail, a personalized Web page, or both. *San Jose Mercury News*'s NewsHound (on the Web at *www.hound.com*) is an example of a subscription news reporting service. Your several "profiles," which you complete in order to specify the kind of information you want to retrieve. The profile enables you to find articles that contain certain words, to discard articles that contain other specific words, and to select the newspaper or wire service to which you want to limit your search. Your profile is stored on a computer that also receives articles from the Knight-Ridder chain of newspapers, Associated Press, Reuters, the business news wire services, and the Kyodo News Service. The articles are fed through an engine that matches them to queries and instantly stores them for you. You can choose to receive them by e-mail, get a daily digest of the articles that have been retrieved for you, or simply logon to the Web site to read them. Using NewsHound, you can enter your company's name, making it a required word or phrase, then add relevant words with which to match the company name, such as "environment," "boycott," or "strike." The articles you retrieve could alert you to emerging communications challenges. Other terms, such as the

names of your products, can help you track your products' images in
the press.

NewsPage from News Edge (on the Web at *www.news
page.com*) is another subscription service. NewsPage scans some
20,000 articles from about 600 sources, then categorizes and cross-
references them. The site is updated daily. For your subscription fee,
you have access to the full text of most stories but also can create
My Personal NewsPage, a personalized Web page that features those
categories of information that are most important to you. You also can
request daily e-mail delivery of a summary of the articles retrieved
for your Personal NewsPage. Figure 5-2 shows the author's Personal
NewsPage, which provides links directly to articles related to intranets,
the Internet, the U.S. Public Relations Industry, and other selected topic
areas.

Figure 5-2. A Personal NewsPage.

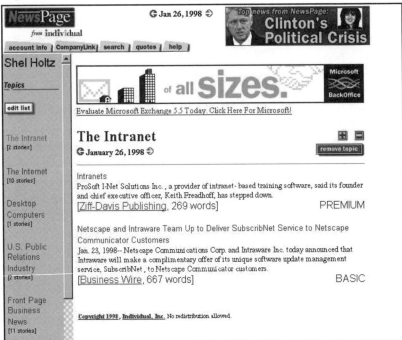

Major Databases

Lexis-Nexis and Dow Jones represent the two biggest databases of articles from newspapers and magazines in the world. Tracking your company name and other key words through these more robust (and proportionally more expensive) services can result in more detail and greater depth. Both services have begun providing access to their databases through a World Wide Web interface.

As of early 1998, Dow Jones Interactive allowed you to search its entire publications database for free, then charged for each article you retrieved. Lexis-Nexis offered telnet access to its databases for existing customers and opened a Web-based service for Lexis, its legal database; Web access to many of its other services began shortly thereafter.

When to Monitor Online Resources

How often should you check your online resources to identify references to your organization and issues in which you have an interest? That depends on the organization and the issues. In general, try to follow these guidelines:

- *Reading targeted newsgroups.* Check the newsgroups that are directly related to your business once a day.
- *General image monitoring.* Review the articles that match your queries at least once a week.
- *Crisis monitoring.* Maintain separate queries that retrieve articles about key issues (such as boycotts, environmental topics, and other issues that require immediate attention), and review them once a day.

Conclusion

Being vigilant about what is said about you on the Internet is most likely your single most important Internet-based activity. Unfortunately, it also is one of the most time-consuming and—most of the time—dullest. Don't let it slide, though; make sure you either undertake the monitoring yourself or contract it out. While the cost may seem high, it is be a pittance compared with having to deal with a crisis you could have prevented had you been monitoring the Internet. (Just ask Intel!) Once you know what is being said about you and where, it becomes easier to implement strategies to communicate with your various strategic audiences using the Internet. In Part Two, we explore the means by which you can bring the Internet to bear in your communication with your various key publics.

Part Two

Audiences and Measurement

6

Media Relations

Different types of organizations must address a wide variety of constituent audiences, but they share the press in common. The press is not only one of the most important groups with which an organization must communicate, it also is one of the easiest groups to apply to the Internet. Most organizations already have this figured out to some extent. You can hardly find an institutional Web site that does not feature a link to material produced by the media relations department.

In general, this material is not available only to the press but to anybody else who happens by the site, a situation that can be problematic for reporters looking for proprietary information they can incorporate into an article. What good is a story about something everybody already knows because it was trumpeted all over your Web site? The real benefit of doing media relations on the Internet comes from targeting the media as a dedicated audience and crafting a strategy that specifically addresses their needs.

Contrary to the apparent belief of many observers, the role of an organizational media relations department is not to make the company look good in the press, nor is it to keep the company out of the news. Most reporters who cover business are savvy enough to know when their chains are being yanked and are experienced enough to know how to circumvent a flack-oriented public relations department. Ideally, the job of the media relations department is to help reporters do their jobs. That objective is entirely consistent with the broader goal of public relations, which is to manage the relationship between the organization and its various audiences.

Reporters have a job to do. It involves covering news and events and reporting on their beats, categories of news and information that some reporters have assigned to them. A beat might be the chemical industry, all companies in Orange County, high tech, or mergers and acquisitions. Every story has a deadline; news stories have the most unforgiving deadlines.

Journalists on the Net

Is the effort to target the media on the Net worthwhile? After all, how many reporters actually use the Internet, and to what extent? Fortunately, the answers to these questions are not a matter of speculation. Middleberg + Associates, a New York public relations agency, has since 1997 (in conjunction with Dr. Stephen Ross of Columbia University's Graduate School of Journalism) conducted a study called "Media in Cyberspace," which seeks to quantify the print media's growing reliance on the Internet to do its job. As a result, we can with reasonable certainty determine the prevalence of reporters on the Internet and the ways in which they use it to do their jobs. With that information in hand, it becomes easy to establish online communications processes and programs that meet their specific needs.

The most important thing to know about newspaper reporters is that they are online. In 1998, more than half of daily newspaper reporters went online every day (up from 34 percent in 1997); 54 percent reported that they used the Internet "continuously." Another 29 percent used the Internet at least weekly (an increase of 34 percent in 1997). They used the Internet primarily for research. Two-thirds of the print media used the Internet to research articles and as a source of reference material. (Financial information, photos, the ability to search a site, and press releases ranked high on reporters' lists of valuable material to find on a company's Web site.) Reporters also used Internet-based e-mail as a means of corresponding with sources *after* initial contact was made and the identity and credibility of the source established.

The second most important thing to know is that the Internet, while dramatically affecting the way reporters go about doing their job, has not altered the principles of good reporting. Despite their use of the Net for a variety of tasks, reporters and editors do *not* undertake stories based on pitches they have received by e-mail. Few reporters randomly surf the Web in search of stories; only about 10 percent of reporters say they use listservs, e-mail, the Web, and Usenet newsgroups *combined* as a principal source of story ideas. That's about the same number of reporters who count on wire services to give them leads on stories to cover.

> **Tip: Don't Send E-Mail to Public Media Addresses**
> Several sites on the World Wide Web offer extensive lists of e-mail addresses for media outlets (such as newspapers, magazines, and TV news operations) and the reporters who work for them. Resist the temptation to send press releases or story pitches to these addresses. Reporters and editors note that they are increasingly annoyed at the growing use of their e-mail addresses for routine or junk mail. News organizations have pulled back on the use of public e-mail addresses, having decided that it is not cost-effective for journalists to answer countless public messages and scroll through hundreds of unsolicited press releases. It may seem cost-effective to send releases or pitches by e-mail to public lists of reporters, but the practice could backfire. Not only will you *not* get the coverage you wanted—you could earn the enmity of the reporters on your list.

Still, reporters do take advantage of free services that businesses offer them—at least, the number of reporters who are willing to use those services is growing steadily. More than half either use such services now or say they would be likely to give them a try. While they are more inclined to use sponsored online sources, they give greater credence to material provided by nonprofit and public-interest groups than that posted by businesses. Nevertheless, they do visit the business-sponsored sites, albeit with varying degrees of wariness. (The solution to this dilemma is to tell the truth and to cover all reasonable aspects of any issue under discussion. Remember, in a many-to-many environment, reporters have immediate access to all the information others are publishing about the same subject. As Stephen Ross, one of the authors of the "Media in Cyberspace" study, notes, "Sins of omission will be punished.")

Based on what we know about the public relations role with the press, the needs of reporters, and the way the media use the Internet, we can identify some effective applications of the Internet:

- Developing media relations Web sites
- Providing customized information delivery
- Engaging in positive e-mail relationships

Tip: Use the Internet an Enhancement, Not a Replacement
As powerful and valuable as Internet-based media relations tools can be, they are not a substitute for personal contact. Reporters are clear that they plan to stick to personal and public relations contacts as the source of their leads. Fewer than 5 percent of reporters use the World Wide Web to generate leads. The Internet is a tool to enhance your relationship with reporters (and, by extension, to obtain better coverage) by providing a valuable service to those reporters who cover you. It will not replace the traditional practice of effective media relations. It is also important to remember that there still are reporters who do not use e-mail or the Internet.

Developing Media Relations Web Sites

A World Wide Web site dedicated to the press can be one of an organization's most potent public relations tools. The source of that power is in the Internet's basic "pull" model. Reporters can get the information they need, at any time of the day or night, often in a format that's ready to use. I can remember from my days as a newspaper reporter the frustration of an approaching deadline and needing to speak with sources who were away from their desks. In the years during which I was responsible for company media relations, reporters often waited on hold, their deadlines approaching, while I spoke with another reporter who had called first. Today, if you provide answers to reporters' questions on the Web, they often don't need to call at all.

Some media relations experts are concerned about reporters retrieving company information without their knowledge. Often, it is the reporter's call for this or that bit of information that tips the company off to the fact that the reporter is working on a story about the company. But reporters will not limit their research to the Web. They will still seek interviews, responses, and quotes directly from authoritative live sources. The Web is just the resource for background material. Accordingly, media relations sites should be *loaded* with background material and categorized in a way that makes it easy for reporters to find what they're looking for.

Basic Media Relations Site Elements

Media relations sites should be carefully targeted to the reporters they are meant to serve. These are not general company news sites. Given the nature of reporters and their jobs, we can identify some online resources that are useful enough to motivate reporters to visit your site often and rely on it for accurate and candid information.

Breaking News

The home page for your media site should not be limited to a static presentation of links. Prominently display your most current news. During a crisis, reporters will know your site is a resource for information. In the normal course of day-to-day business, you can make sure your most important messages are front and center.

Contact List

Nothing irks a reporter more than getting routed from one person to another. ("I'm sorry, I don't handle that issue. You need to talk to one of my colleagues who has responsibility for that division. I'll transfer you.") A list on your site of the appropriate media contacts can end that misery. Your public relations staff directory should include:

- Name, phone number, and e-mail address
- Areas of responsibility

You can create links to the listings on the contact page from other parts of the site. For example, a position paper on a labor issue can include a link to information about the media relations representative handling all labor-related inquiries.

Position Statements

Every company is involved in something that is likely to raise somebody's ire. Animal rights activists pay attention to the pharmaceutical industry, children's advocates watch the toy business, and environmentalists keep tabs on the oil industry. Various business practices can meet with disapproval from the government, consumer affairs activists, competitors, and people in your own industry. You should already have a position statement for each issue with which your company grapples. Put them on the Web.

Activity Calendar

Let reporters know about your upcoming events, and give all the information they might need. Include:

- The time and date of the event
- The location
- The nature of the company's involvement
- The media contact (hyperlinked to detailed contact information)

These calendars can help editors make coverage decisions and assist reporters assigned to the event.

Press Release Archives

Post your press releases to the site, but make sure reporters can easily find the releases they want. Organize them chronologically (starting with the most recent) *and* by any other categories that make sense (e.g., product line, country, issue).

Tip: Use a Database for Press Releases

If you put your press releases into a database, you can create a simple query form for reporters to use to find a given release. Establish separate fields for the date of the release, the headline, the author, the text of the release, and any other pertinent information (a plant location, a brand name, a key executive). Now the reporter can use the form to conduct a search of your press releases, making it easy, say, to find a release that was issued six months earlier about the promotion of a particular executive. The programming required to create such a service is fairly quick and simple.

When assembling an online press release, remember that whether it is listed on a World Wide Web page or is destined for delivery by e-mail, it is not the same as a paper press release. The medium is different, and the form of the press release should accommodate and capitalize on those differences.

Three main elements differentiate online press releases from their print cousins:

1. *Limited opportunity to gain attention.* A printed press release is available for a quick read-through. If it is accompanied by a photo, it takes a mere second for an editor to pull out the photo and give it a glance to see if it's interesting; the photo alone could motivate the editor to read the release. The online version, though, offers only the amount of text that appears on the screen. Anything below the screen requires a conscious effort on the part of the editor to scroll down. If the part of the release that appears on the screen is not interesting or compelling, or if it does not contain the heart of the release, it could motivate the editor to move on to something else. E-mail press releases are even more challenging, since an editor can dispose of the release with a single tap of the *delete* key, and the only tool you have at your disposal to capture the editor's attention is the text you type into the "Subject" line.

2. *Ability to build internal links.* One way to address the issue above is to build a mini-table of contents for your readers at the top of the release. This also serves to help those who have used search engines to find your release. Reading just the headline may not prompt a visitor to recognize the value of the release; it may even seem that the search engine has found a less-than-pertinent link (they have been known to do that from time to time!). However, a table of contents can list, in order, the elements that appear in the release. An editor can click on any element that interests him and jump directly to that element, enhancing the possibility that the release will pique his interest.

3. *Access to other material.* The press release that appears online is not limited to material you can stuff in an envelope. You can make the entire realm of cybermaterial available to a reporter or editor with the click of a mouse. You can offer links to related material, full text of background documents, video, audio, animation, and executable programs.

Look at the following mock-up of an online press release to see
how one might appear on a Web screen (underlined elements represent
hyperlinks):

```
Press Release                          Release Date: 02/16/99
Contact Information: Shel Holtz, shel@holtz.com, (925)
673-9896
```

New Book Offers Online Press Release Template

This press release features the following information:
• <u>Using a table of contents-like listing at the top of
the release</u>
  • <u>Incorporating multimedia elements into the release</u>
  • <u>Linking to related material</u>

NEW YORK, New York (February 16, 1999)—*Public
Relations on the Net*, the new book from AMACOM Books,
includes information on how to develop a press release for
online use. "It takes less energy to hit the delete key than
it does to crumple up a piece of paper and throw it away,"
according to Shel Holtz, author of the book. "But there are
ways to capture an editor's attention online."

One of those ways is to include a contents-like listing
at the top of the page, allowing editors to move quickly to
information in which they have an interest. Another method
is to hyperlink to related materials, such as an <u>archive of
sample press releases</u> that meet Holtz's criteria.

Finally, press releases that appear online can contain
multimedia, such as an audio clip from a speech that is
being reported, a video of an event you would like covered,
even an animation of a new process to make it easier to
understand.

Boilerplate information should be kept for the end of
the release. The boilerplate is the block of text that tells
editors about the company that issued the release.

E-mail press releases can work in virtually the same way, since
most current e-mail packages support hyperlinks to Web pages and
launch a new e-mail message template when a hyperlinked e-mail address is invoked. However, be sure to use a compelling subject line, as
noted above. Do not hope that an overworked editor on deadline will
open up your e-mail message based on a subject line that reads something like: "New Public Relations Book Offers Tips on How to Get
Your Press Releases Read." First, tell the editor that the e-mail is, in
fact, a press release. Then be sure to use a compelling subject line
that will at least make her want to open the release to see if anything
worthwhile is hidden there. An effective subject line might look like

this: "PRESS RELEASE: Companies learn how to keep YOU from ignoring them!" You can bet most editors will at least be curious about just what you think companies can do to get their attention!

Speeches

The text of speeches delivered by your key executives should be archived online. You have the option of including a sound file of the actual speech. Reporters are not dazzled by multimedia, though, and rate simple Web sites among the best. But a streaming audio capability allows you to segment speech highlights. Listening to the twenty-second clip in which the president outlines plans for a stock repurchase may be just what a reporter needs to decide it would be worthwhile to go ahead and read the entire speech.

Government Filings

Most of the documents your company files with the federal government are public anyway, so you may as well put them on your site and save the reporter the time she would have to spend digging them up somewhere else.

Company and Executive Background

The company information section should include all the little tidbits that constitute the majority of phone requests from the press. When was the company founded? When was it incorporated? In what state? When was Product X introduced? How many employees work at the plant in Kuala Lumpur? How many are expatriates and how many nationals?

The executive section should include biographies and photos. If you use a standard Web photo format (GIF or JPEG) for your executive pictures, offer a better quality file for download so editors can snatch them and print them without having to request a glossy print from you.

Product/Service Information

You can simply link to product/service information on your general company Web site, but reporters have different information needs than the general public. Include downloadable product photos, package art, label information, manufacturing details, customer profiles, and other material that might be likely to find its way into an article. If a press kit was distributed related to a particular product or service, make it available here too.

Links to Alternative Information Sources

If the Internet is indeed a modern multimedia version of the old party line, reporters have access to everything being published about an issue that is important to your organization. By using the various search engines available on the Net, reporters can root out any information available, whether or not it's favorable to your company. Since they are going to find the information anyway, you may as well save them some time and provide pointers to it.

Granted, pre-Internet media relations efforts never included guiding reporters to your critics and naysayers. Today, though, you give yourself a distinct advantage when you create these links. A reporter who finds such information on his own may not think about checking its accuracy with you. But if he finds it because you provided a link to it, the link can include a disclaimer about the source and an offer to discuss what he reads there. By displaying the link, you imply that the organization is aware of the content of the material and untroubled by it.

Include links to Web sites, mailing lists, and discussion groups where your company, operations, products, or services are being discussed.

Special Press Kits

When special events or activities occur, you can create a special section dedicated to it. Bell Atlantic, for instance, created a special online press kit that provided information and links related to the company's merger with NYNEX.

Real-world press kits can be a pain. You have to print several versions of press releases, add fact sheets and data sheets, reproduce photos, print captions on the backs of the photos, and mail the whole thing out at high postage rates. And then you have no way of knowing how well this one-size-fits-all kit meets the needs of each individual editor.

Online press kits are much easier and more effective. These virtual resources for journalists can include original material as well as links to related resources scattered throughout your Web site. The only thing that binds these elements together is that the links to them are gathered onto a common page as a means of assisting journalists research a given issue.

Let's say you want to assemble a press kit about the introduction of a new product. You can link to all related press releases, giving reporters hints at the spin each release offers (e.g., one release was crafted for the trade press, one for the financial media, one for consumer publications). Photos, logos, and package shots can be archived under an "Image" link. The environmental issues addressed can be found in the company's environmental policy section. Government approvals received appear in the regulatory section.

Other, more heady issues—such as a merger, a crisis, or a lobbying effort—can include other original resources, such as a list of the benefits of the action (or the damage it can do, depending on the company's point of view and the nature of the influence it is trying to exert).

Extra Goodies

Depending on your industry, the business climate, and the media that cover your institution, you can add other services to your media relations Web site. Symantec, the computer software company, offers case studies—short articles about people who successfully use new Symantec products. Reporters who have wanted to interview somebody using a Symantec product have been known to copy segments of these case studies directly into their stories. Some other extra features of media relations sites include:

- Video, such as the commencement ceremony at the University of Southern California. You can view the entire ceremony or select segments, such as the procession of graduates or the commencement address.
- Story ideas, just in case a reporter with a beat is coming up dry.
- The chief executive officer's Web page, such as the one Bill Gates maintains on the Microsoft site. Gates uses it as a personal forum for his key messages as well as an archive for his speeches and columns.
- News clippings—compilations of coverage your company has

received from other media. Reporters can use this archive to get a sense of how other reporters are spinning a story.
- Online press briefings, which allow reporters to cover a briefing without leaving their desks.
- List of newsroom participants, for those sites that require registration.

Tip: Decide if You Want Visitors to Register or Not
How do you keep people who are not members of the working press from getting into your media-dedicated site? One way is to require users to register, then enter a password each time they want access to the site. This approach has its pros and cons. In its favor, reporters who register can rest assured that the information on the site is proprietary to them; the public won't find it on their own. Registering credentialed members of the press keeps traffic down on your site and ensures that the server is available for, say, editors who need to download a large graphic file in order to include a picture in the next issue of their magazine. On the negative side, reporters (already a skeptical lot) might worry that their visits to the site are being monitored or that registering will lead to unsolicited e-mail from the company. The best way to determine whether registration would work for your site is to survey the reporters who cover you the most and get their feedback.

Organizing Your Media Relations Web Site

The structure of your media relations Web site should accommodate the likely ways reporters will look for information. The hyperlinked nature of the Web allows you to create more than one path to the same information. Consider providing such paths based on elements including:

- Basic information
- Products
- Markets or lines of business
- Issues

Figure 6-1 shows the different paths that can lead reporters to the same information released by the company. Each reporter selects the appropriate path based on the story he's covering. In the figure, a pharmaceutical company that manufactures drugs for the elderly has announced a new policy to ensure reduced prices for its senior consumers. One reporter visiting the site might be researching a story on pharmaceutical pricing. Another is on the senior citizen beat. A third covers health care in general, and a fourth reports on the company. Each reporter begins at an intuitive point, but the resources listed under each heading direct those following that path to the press release of common interest to all of them.

Figure 6-1. The different paths that can lead reporters to the same information released by the company.

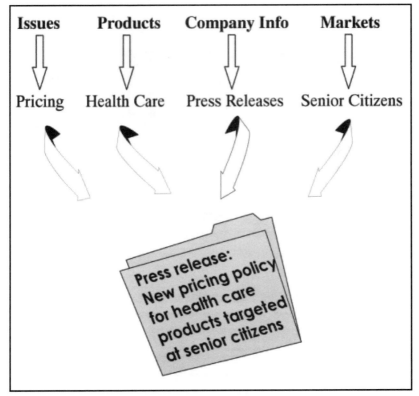

Case Study: Chrysler

Chrysler knew why it was important to take advantage of the Web, according to Rita McKay, director of corporate media relations at Chrysler's Auburn Hills, Michigan, headquarters. "We had conversations with some reporters who were using the Web," she says, "and discovered it would be a valuable resource for a growing number of the department's audience members. The goal, once the decision to build the site was made, was to create a one-stop information resource for reporters.

McKay and her staff talked with more reporters as the project evolved. "We had several reporters use the site as it was developed in order to get their feedback. We wanted to know how easy it was to use, if it had the kind of material they needed." Reporters participating in the pilot came from both the public and the trade media, as well as wire services, from the U.S. and international locations. "Most of the comments we got were asking why we didn't have this or that type of information—it was all content-oriented. None of it was about the way the site was laid out." Figure 6-2 shows Chrysler's media relations home page. Note that media information is reconfigured depending on whether it is aimed at print or broadcast media.

Figure 6-2. Chrysler's media relations home page.

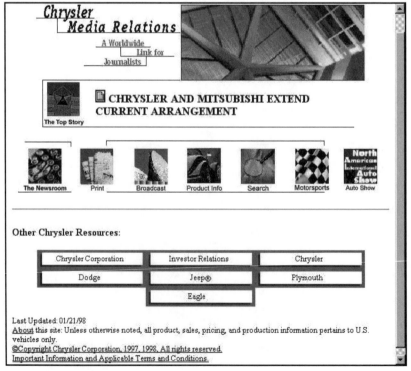

Most of the site is open to the public, although reporters need to register in order to gain access to the Newsroom. Reporters' credentials are checked before they can enter this area, which contains a warehouse of photography. "The pictures can be downloaded," McKay says, noting that the images are of high quality so they can be used in publications. "But we couldn't afford to have everyone who wants a photo download it," she says, explaining one of the reasons for limiting the Newsroom to credentialed reporters. "We also have copyrighted material there, such as articles from other publications about our products. If reporters remember seeing something about the subject they're covering in another publication, they can go to that area and find it." On any given day, there can be as many as eighteen or twenty stories posted to the "News Clips" page, from sources such as the *New York Times*, Associated Press, or Japan Economic Newswire.

Figure 6-3 shows the Chrysler Newsroom. The information in this section is available only to working members of the press, who gain access by using a login and password. The Newsroom also has press kits and an activity calendar. During the 1996 Democratic National Convention, for example, when the United Auto Workers and Chrysler jointly hosted community groups, delegates, and political honorees at a 50,000-square-foot exhibit at Chicago's Navy Pier,

Figure 6-3. The Chrysler Newsroom on the media relations Web site.

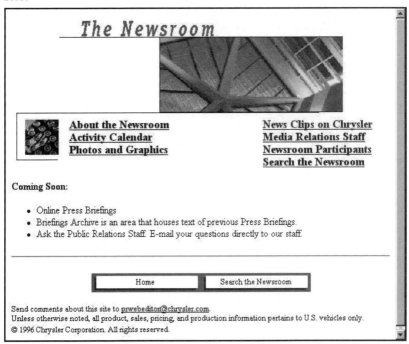

details were available on the Web site. A search engine makes it easy for reporters to find specific information quickly by specifying the nature of the content: Biographies, press releases, press kits, corporate history, and a number of other categories can be searched independently.

By 1998, over 200 reporters had registered, from such media outlets as CNN Business News, *Car and Driver*, the *Washington Post*, *Popular Mechanics*, *The Today Show*, National Public Radio, CNBC, the *Chicago Sun-Times*, NBC Nightly News, *Consumer Reports*, Bloomberg Business News, *USA Today*, CBS Radio, Reuters, *Esquire*, *The Wall Street Journal*, *Motor Trend*, *Business Week*, and the *Boston Globe*.

Registrations began pouring in shortly after reporters were notified individually of the site's availability. "We have a core group of automotive journalists and business journalists we work with," McKay says. "That's our audience, so we contacted them and asked them what kind of computer equipment they had. We asked if they'd be interested in getting a password to get into the Newsroom, then followed up with subsequent communications to ask if they'd tried using the site, if they had run into any problems. When reporters get into the site and find everything that's there, they're pleasantly surprised."

McKay uses the registration process to track the usage of the site. "We can tell as soon as we put something new on the site whether there's a spike in hits. We can tell what parts of the site they're looking at, what time of day is good for reporters to be checking our information, and what information they're interested in."

Other than the Newsroom, reporters and the public have access to information in sections titled Print and Broadcast (including speeches, press releases, biographical material, financial information, and the like) and Product Info. The media relations home page also offers a link to the top story of the day which, according to McKay, can change as many as four times in a twenty-four-hour period.

Chrysler's media relations staff has taken to using the Web site routinely as its own source of information as well. "Nobody uses paper any more to get information they need for whatever they're working on," McKay says. "The Web site is very integrated into what we do day-to-day in the media relations department."

Still, while the entire staff uses the site and contributes to its content, there are only three full-time employees maintaining it—an editor and technicians who handle the computer side of things.

The future of Chrysler's media relations site includes a variety of enhancements and additions. McKay plans to replace sections that are no longer relevant with new material. She also plans to take advantage of the Web's worldwide nature to serve the international media. "We have international journalists who call on us, and the Web allows us to serve their needs twenty-four hours a day, seven days a week. That's a top priority." At a recent meeting of the company's international public relations staff, one of the most popular suggestions for the site was the addition of foreign languages, an option McKay is exploring.

Announcing the Site

Once you have a site available for the media, you need to let them know it's there. You can achieve this in several ways:

- Issue a press advisory or release alerting the media to the presence of the site.
- Include the URL* on all press releases and other written material.
- Have the URL printed on your business card.
- Include the URL in your e-mail signature.
- Provide a link from the top-level corporate home page.
- Make sure your site is registered in appropriate directories and that business services such as Hoovers and Dun & Bradstreet know the URL so they can include it on their Web sites.

Example: Media Web Site Announcement Press Release

Smith Bank Opens Web Site for News Media
BOSTON, Massachusetts, May 1, 19XX—Smith Bank announced today that it will offer an area with special content on its corporate Web site exclusively for the news media. Smith Bank's media area is designed to provide the media with real-time information about the business.

"At Smith Bank, we understand that the importance of the World Wide Web as an information resource is growing daily," according to John Jones, vice-president of public relations. "As a result, our media area will provide real-time information to reporters, as well as serving as an easily accessible source for bios, downloadable photos, and broadcast-quality audio clips quoting our experts on the news of the day. Time is a premium in the news business, so we've made it easy for the media to access the information they're most interested in about Smith Bank."

From the media Web page, reporters can get information about:
- The latest Smith Bank news events, including downloadable sound bites for use by broadcast media on breaking stories
- Advisories about upcoming news events at the Bank and sources to contact for topical stories
- A list of contacts in Smith Bank's media relations units around the world, with phone numbers and email addresses
- Current and relevant past Smith Bank news releases, with useful background

In addition, media visitors to the media page will be able to follow links to key recent senior manager speeches; bios and photos of Smith Bank senior executives; a photo file with a variety of downloadable print-quality images; a summary and timeline of major events in Smith Bank's history; and a page with links to a variety of banking information sources, including regulators, trade associations, trade publications, and legislative and other government bodies concerned with banking issues. A special search engine allows searches to be targeted to an archive of all the news releases Smith

*The URL, or uniform resource locator, is the address you type into a browser to retrieve a page from a server.

Bank has posted on its Web site or to speeches, as well as to the entire Smith Bank site.

The media page also includes links to a variety of resources publicly available on the Smith Bank Web site that may be of special interest to the media. These include the news release archive, which includes all the releases Smith Bank has posted on its Web site since 19XX, sorted by topic; financial information about the corporation, including links to earnings releases, stock price history, analyst presentations, and SEC filings; economic outlooks, data, and reports issued by Smith Bank; a reference list of the acquisitions Smith Bank has done since 19XX; and information on Smith Bank operations. The Media site is exclusively for the news media and is accessible by password only. A quick application form can be found at http://www.smithbank.com/media.

Smith Bank is the largest regional bank in its region, with assets of more than $1.5 billion. Smith Bank provides commercial, retail, and real estate services.

# # #

NOTE TO EDITORS AND WRITERS: To obtain a password to access the Media Web site, go to the Media at http://www.smithbank.com/media and follow the link to the quick application form.

Providing Customized Information Delivery

While reporters are clear about their contempt for unsolicited e-mail, they can be delighted to receive information they do want. And as noted earlier, journalists are likely to take advantage of free services that sources provide. You can combine these two facts and offer journalists a news-and-information subscription service.

Customized information delivery services are becoming commonplace on the Web. Several technologies can be employed to make such a service work. One example of a customized delivery service, discussed in Chapter 5, is My Personal NewsPage, a service of News Edge's general NewsPage. NewsPage archives articles from several hundred publications and categorizes them. An article about enrolling for employee benefits on an intranet, for example, might be placed in both the Benefits and Intranet categories. You can find the article by starting at a top-level hierarchy, such as Business Management, then drilling down through successive levels (Human Resources, then Benefits). But if you subscribe to My Personal NewsPage, you can specify the categories of special interest to you and sign up for Benefits as one of your desired categories. When you visit the site, your name appears on the page along with the categories you selected—no drilling required.

Edelman Public Relations, one of the world's largest public relations agencies, was an early PR adopter of this approach. Edelman represents clients from a myriad of businesses and institutions, producing thousands of press releases. No single reporter would be interested in *all* of those releases, and one of the biggest challenges faced by Edelman's account representatives (or, for that matter, *any* agency's account representatives) is targeting journalists with releases they would want to see. On an early iteration of Edelman's Web site, journalists could sign up to receive releases based on the industry they covered. For instance, a reporter could subscribe to the category of High Tech and receive e-mail copies of all releases related to Edelman's high-tech clients. Figure 6-4 shows the current news-delivery subscription page from Edelman Public Relations.

Figure 6-4. The news-delivery subscription page from Edelman Public Relations.

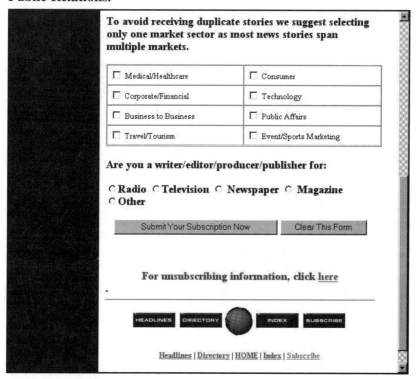

The potential for such customized delivery increases when you are representing a single organization. Bell Atlantic offers an excellent approach, for example, allowing reporters to select information from across a spectrum of categories. A reporter could want to receive press releases based on a geographic region (such as Boston or international) or subject (like financial or executive staffing). Each release is stored in a database with fields that identify the various categories to which it relates. The database recognizes the profiles of each subscribing reporter. Thus, a release identified as "Financial" and "Boston" would automatically be sent as an e-mail to those reporters whose profiles list those criteria. This way, reporters receive information pertinent to the stories or beats they are covering. Figure 6-5 shows Bell Atlantic's information subscription page.

A variety of other approaches can be applied to help media representatives get just the information they need. Auto-responders, for example, allow reporters to send an e-mail message that generates an automatic response. A reporter interested in the entire text of a particu-

Figure 6-5. Bell Atlantic's information subscription page.

General Information about Bell Atlantic
Below is a list of general information documents that will be distributed by Bell Atlantic. To select multiple items, press and hold either the SHIFT or CONTROL key while clicking on an item.

News Releases
Regions
| None |
| ├─All Regions |
| │ ├─Boston |
| │ ├─Connecticut |
| │ ├─Delaware |
| │ ├─International |

Subjects
| None |
| ├─All Subjects |
| │ ├─Announcements |
| │ ├─BellAtlantic-NYNEX Merger |
| │ ├─Executive Staffing |
| │ ├─Financial |

Filings
| None |
| All Filings |
| ├─All Regulatory Body |
| │ ├─FCC |
| │ ├─Public Service Commission |
| ├─All Subjects |

lar speech can send e-mail to a designated address (or click a link from the Web page to that address) and receive the entire text of the speech in response.

Reporters also can subscribe to a mailing list in which you list the headlines of the week's press releases and other information. The reporter can scan the list and follow a link to the Web site for the complete information on any items about which they'd like to know more. (*See Chapter 3 for details on how to craft an e-mail newsletter.*)

Engaging in Positive E-Mail Relationships

You *can* engage in a fruitful and positive e-mail relationship with a reporter, but *only* after you have established yourself as a reputable and credible source. Then, the reporter works with you in any fashion that meets her objectives (timeliness of information generally is at the top of this list). If e-mail fits the bill, e-mail is the tool the reporter happily uses.

Case Study: Larry Mathias

The best way to find out if a reporter would be willing to receive e-mail from you is to ask. That's the approach taken by Larry Mathias, currently public relations manager for Acacia Technologies in Lisle, Illinois. "I started out by including a simple questionnaire with the paper press releases I sent out," Mathias says. The questionnaire featured one question, asking the reporters' preferences for press release receipt. The options included paper via U.S. mail, e-mail, and fax, along with having their name removed from the list altogether.

"I got some response from the written survey, but much better response when I started asking during conversations with individual reporters," Mathias says, noting that media relations is, at its core, relationship building. "Person-to-person has been a far more successful approach. Even over the phone it's more personal than responding to a piece of paper.

"Initially, the subject of e-mail just came up as part of conversations about other subjects," he says, "and if a reporter felt comfortable, he might say, 'Here's my e-mail address.' Now I incorporate it into the conversations."

It comes up in other ways too. "During a business card exchange, I might see an e-mail address on the reporter's card. I'll remark on it and end up with an OK to communicate with him via e-mail."

What Mathias has found is that there is no single answer. "Technology has been both a blessing and a curse," he muses. "When e-mail was new, a lot of reporters loved it because it was something only a handful of people had. They could get a few useful items every week. Now everyone has e-mail, and people are publishing reporters' e-mail addresses in online directories. Reporters are getting inundated. Some of them are changing their e-mail addresses just to avoid the flood of unwanted releases they're getting."

Which is, Mathias is quick to note, the antithesis of building strong relationships. Mathias takes the time to build the relationships, which leads many reporters who have added a second, private e-mail address to pass it along to him because they know he'll send them only information of value.

Tip: Be Concise in Your E-Mail

Even for those reporters who *are* willing to accept company information via e-mail, the same rules that govern old-fashioned paper distribution apply. You wouldn't send a pitch letter that exceeded two pages, so don't send long e-mail pitches either. People have a tendency to get sloppy in their online writing, and that can be dangerous. It's easier to click on the *delete* button than it is to wad up a two-page letter and throw it in the trash.

Step-by-Step: Online Media Relations

Before undertaking an online media relations effort, you should follow these steps in order to ensure that you are delivering the kind of material that will be beneficial to the reporters covering you:

1. Segment the media covering you. Are you covered regularly by trade media? Are you a *Fortune* 1000 company? Are you an industry or profession that receives regular coverage (e.g., high tech, health care, tobacco)? Are you covered as a leader in your business?

2. Identify the kinds of information required by reporters working for each major segment you identify.

3. Query the reporters with whom you already have regular contact. Find out if they want to receive any information by e-mail or would be inclined to avail themselves of a Web site in order to obtain company information.

4. Determine the nature of the information these reporters would like to receive through each online medium. Use the answers to prioritize your list of information categories.

5. From your priority list, determine which information reporters would want to *pull*, and which you may want to be able to *push*. Those that qualify as *pull* items should on your media relations Web site, while those that are *push* should be available through a customizeable subscription service.

Measurement

Then you must measure the effectiveness of your online media relations. Use the following questions to guide your assessment:

- How many reporters have given you their e-mail addresses for receipt of press releases, press advisories, and other materials?
- How many reporters have subscribed to any e-mail distribution services you offer?
- How many reporters who have registered to use your media relations Web site actually visit the site? Where do they go? What materials have they downloaded, and how many of those materials have shown up in their publications?
- How much material from your Web site appears in stories written by reporters who cover you?
- How many reporters check with you or your site after reading other information about your organization elsewhere on the Internet?
- How many reporters participate in online activities such as press conferences?

Conclusion

Your job as a media relations professional is to make a reporter's job easier. In doing so, you best represent your company and make it more likely that reporters will listen to your point of view, your story pitches, and your requests. Use the Internet to facilitate this approach to media relations by making information available, not by invading reporters' e-mail boxes with unwanted e-mail. Reporters are using the Internet more and more, and be aware of *what* they use it for. Then build communications efforts that accommodate those trends.

7

Investor Relations

Investors and the financial community—and all their related subaudiences (e.g., mom-and-pop investors, institutional investors, large individual shareholders)—constitute one of a company's most significant audiences. Not only must you convince the kinds of investors you want to attract to view your stock favorably, you must also keep them informed about the progress of the company they own so they will not sell their stock or seek to take action against the company. Shareholder suits are among the most debilitating actions a company must deal with, and there are law firms that make their living seeking reasons to file suits on behalf of shareholders. In addition to lawsuits, shareholders can engage the company in proxy battles.

The financial community is, in general, heavily wired. Bloomberg helped pave the way to the widespread use of electronically delivered financial information. Everybody from investment analysts to stockbrokers to corporate investor relations managers keeps computers on their desks that flash stock prices, earnings reports, and other important financial news. Business Wire, PR Newswire, and First Call have grown their businesses considerably by providing electronic communications systems that satisfy Securities and Exchange Commission rules that insist that financial communities get first notice of any company news that could have an impact on share price.

Yet the average corporate Web site treats investor relations as an afterthought. Most investor relations sites are dusty corners of the overall corporate homestead, featuring little more than earnings reports, financial-oriented press releases, and annual reports. The annual reports are little more than "shovelware," Webified reproductions of the printed report that was distributed by mail to shareholders.

There is so much more that can be done on the Internet to promote the company's brand as a sound investment. But even if you are going to limit your offerings to an annual report, at least make it useful to your audiences so that it does serve to brand your company as a worthwhile investment.

Annual Reports on the Web

The argument for making an annual report available on the World Wide Web begins with your definition of an annual report and your understanding of the Web. Most definitions of an annual report describe a book bound by covers and produced in a traditional linear fashion. Far too may organizations seem to believe they have taken the big step into cyberspace by storing a portable-document version of the annual report on their Web site. This way (the thinking seems to go), any interested investors, brokers, or analysts can download the file and read the annual report just as if they had the hard copy in their hands!

There are many problems with this approach. The key disadvantages include:

- The amount of time required to download a graphic representation of the printed report (generally several megs large)
- The presumption that people have Adobe Acrobat installed on their system, or that they will take the time to download and install it just so they can read your annual report
- The fact that the printed report wasn't designed to be read on a computer screen
- The fact that a linear presentation of information defeats all of the advantages of making information available online

From the invention of the printing press on, publishing has hinged upon an economic model: You need to justify the economics of publishing, and those economics drive what you can publish. Annual reports are published based on an available budget that necessarily limits the number of pages and, consequently, the amount of content. A finite number of copies are printed and distributed to people whose names appear on an established mailing list; a small number are held in reserve for others who may request a copy.

The World Wide Web explodes these historic publishing models. Consider these two characteristics of the Web:

1. No matter how many people may visit your Web site, you need to produce only one copy of the document.
2. There is no cost associated with Web-based publication, beyond the hard-disk space the information occupies—which is minimal.

The information on your Web site is available to everybody, including potential investors who are not on your mailing list. Many of these people may never have discovered your organization without the Web. What if one of them is a just-hired investment analyst working for an investment fund? And what if, based on information she finds in your online annual report, she decides to invest a considerable portion of the fund's assets in your organization's stock?

Some public relations professionals believe that it makes more sense to use the Web as a vehicle for publishing highlights from the annual report. Highlights are important, but only if they provide pathways to increasingly detailed levels of information. Recognition of how people use the Web makes this rationale clear. Since the Web is a "pull" medium, the receiver seeks and extracts just the information she is looking for.

The information contained in an annual report—along with greater levels of detail that couldn't fit in the printed report—accommodates this model *ideally*. The trick is to reduce each chunk of information to its lowest common denominator and then provide pathways that visitors can use to find the information they want. Start by providing the highlights, but with each highlight include a link to greater detail. The nature of the Web suggests that we should allow the visitor to decide what information is important. Making that decision on the reader's behalf is old-media thinking.

It is absolutely true that there may be only four people who ever visit your Web site hoping to learn the three-year history of your organization's earnings from continuing operations. But the fact that the Web enables you to store that information where it's easy to find makes the Web the perfect place to retain it! Those who have no interest in the information never need to see it, but it's accessible to those who *are* interested.

If you are going to put your annual report on the Web:

1. Do it in HTML rather than PDF.*
2. Start with overview information (with lots of visual represen-
   tations of data designed for the computer screen) and provide
   gradually more detailed levels of information.
3. Create the paths to data based on the paths your audiences
   might take. Ignore the old linear format of the annual report.
4. Leave behind all but the most important artwork from your
   printed report. People come to the Web for information—
   particularly when they are seeking financial information.
5. Keep your annual report up-to-date. The Web is an immediate
   medium that screams for currency.

Beyond the Annual Report

A well assembled, Web-based annual report can be of real value to an
investment analyst, investor, or broker. But why stop there? Look at
the range of information your investor relations department addresses,
the scope of questions it receives every day. Many in the investment
community will regard your making this information available on the
Internet as a service. It also will lighten the load of lightly staffed
investor relations departments. Most IR departments focus 90 percent
of their efforts on 5 percent of their organizations' shareholders—those
institutional investors (and an occasional individual) that own the lion's
share of the company's stock. By making information available online,
members of the investment and financial communities can retrieve
facts and data on their own without encumbering you with the work.
For each call you *don't* get asking about this or that SEC filing, you
have that much more time available to focus on the one-to-one conversations with key investors that your job genuinely requires.

Let's look at some other ways to use the Internet for investor
relations.

---

*HTML, or Hypertext Markup Language, is standard code that can be produced by
any browser. PDF, or portable document format, is produced by Adobe Acrobat software and can be viewed only by someone who has an Acrobat reader.

Investor Conferences

The use of technology to meet virtually with investment analysts is hardly new. Audio teleconferencing has been used for years to conduct meetings with analysts upon the release of quarterly earnings figures. The Internet now provides you with a new tool to add to the mix, allowing investors at their desks (and on the phone with you, your CFO, or your CEO) to follow an on-screen slide show—actually a series of sequential HTML pages. "You can see by the chart that earnings rose," you can say, then instruct those who are following along to click the arrow at the bottom of the screen to proceed to the next slide. "As for income from continuing operations. . . ."

Participants can click the buttons on their own, or you can take advantage of new software, such as Teepee, to control the on-screen tour you give to the audience. All investors participating in the conference would need to install Teepee on their computers, but you could supply the software while touting the advantages of the analysts immersing themselves in a multimedia experience without ever leaving their offices.

You also can forsake the telephone altogether and introduce an online conference using computer-based videoconferencing (such as CU-See-Me). Participants with their own video capabilities would be able to engage in conversation with you face-to-face, while those without such capabilities would at least be able to watch the conference even if you could not, at the same time, watch them.

Online Roadshows

Companies invest considerable sums in roadshows, sophisticated presentations made to groups of analysts and investors in a large meeting environment. The invitation list to these shows is limited, but you can make sure elements of your presentation are available to your larger audience as soon as the show is over by posting them to your Web site. Even if your presentation was produced in a presentation software package, such as PowerPoint, you can convert the presentation to HTML or make the PowerPoint Web viewer plugin available for free from your Web site. Microsoft was among the first companies to upload their investor presentations to their Web site immediately following the initial presentation to key members of the financial audience.

Communication of the News Behind the News

The law requires that you use traditional means to communicate information that could have a bearing on the value of your organization, such as a merger, an acquisition, or a divestiture. Also use the Internet to provide the details various members of your audience may seek, from complete legal documents to lists of assets of a company you are acquiring. As long as the information is not confidential, there is no reason to keep it secret. An obscure piece of data may be *just* the information an analyst is seeking before making a "buy" recommendation.

If your company is affected by regulatory agencies, you can offer information about any government developments that could influence your stock price.

Providing the Numbers

The financial community can't have too many numbers. Offer performance history, stock charts, comparison charts (to the Standard & Poor's 500, for example), trend information, and detailed numbers from your various public filings. Be sure to segment topics so each visitor to the site can quickly find exactly what she is looking for without having to wade through irrelevant numbers.

Case Study: MCI's Total Investor Web Site

Unlike most investor relations sites, MCI's is not only complete, it has its own domain (on the Web at *investor.mci.com*). The unique domain symbolizes the importance the telecommunications company places on the investor audience, and the effort that has gone into the site bolsters that sense of importance. The MCI investor relations site is as rich and detailed as many corporate sites— and more than some! (In late 1997, MCI announced that it was accepting a takeover bid from WorldCom to form MCI WorldCom. While the merger may lead to an even richer investor relations Web site, nothing is certain and the site as it existed at the time of this writing may be lost.)

Upon entering the site, you are first struck by the degree of multimedia work that has gone into its development. Recognizing that the most important members of the financial audience are likely to be accessing the site at high speeds (from within companies via T1 or T3 lines instead of from homes dialing in with 28.8 bps modems), the company has built a site with movement and pizzazz. The movement, however, is neither overdone nor overwhelming. A ticker, for example, offers insights into valuable new resources on the site. Watching the words scroll by, you learn that you can dynamically chart the company's performance or get information on its merger with WorldCom. Figure 7-1 shows the home page of MCI's investor relations site.

Figure 7-1. The home page of MCI's investor relations site.

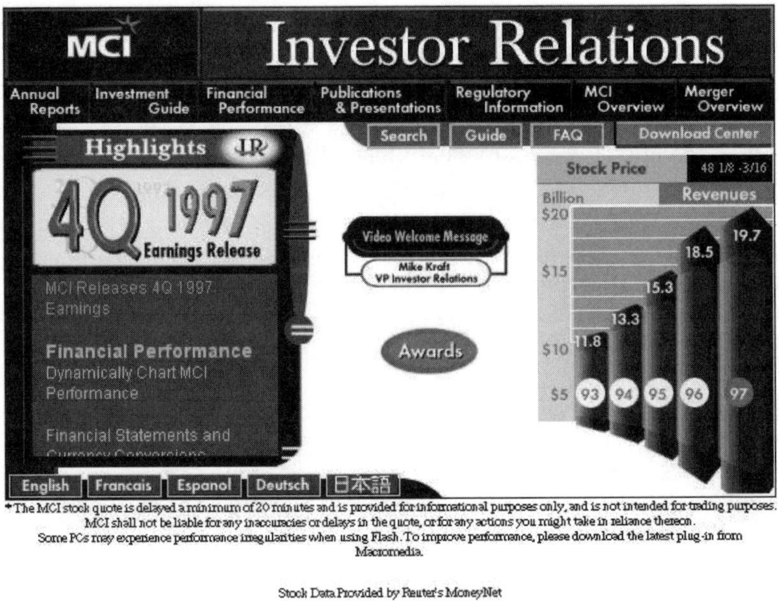

The home page also serves up a graphic displaying the company's key numbers for the last five years: total revenues and profits. The current stock price (delayed twenty minutes, consistent with New York Stock Exchange rules) also appears on the home page, along with a video welcome from the company's vice-president of investor relations. In addition to links to the several key sections of the site, icons also invite visitors to view the site in other languages, from Spanish to Japanese.

Annual reports are available going back eleven years. All of the annual reports have been redesigned for the Web, with quick access to just about any element of the report. All of the annual reports share exactly the same format, so that you use the same navigation to view the 1990 annual report as the 1996 report. In addition, a Microsoft Word version of each report is available for downloading. Brokers who need to print out a section of a report for a client can grab a small Word file they can use on their own computers and printers; they can even cut and paste elements of the Word document directly into their own word-processing file, such as a letter to a client.

One of the most intriguing elements of the MCI site is the investment guide, which is divided into two sections, one for individual investors and one for fund managers. Both sections are available in a high-speed version (taking advantage of leading-edge multimedia technology) and configured for a low-speed connection for those logging on through a dial-up modem. On these pages, visitors can research MCI's financial history, get to know the relation between the company's lines of business and its financial results, and manage MCI investments. The merits of the company as an investment (reinforcing the brand) are listed here. On the individual investor side, you can access a glossary of investment terms, review shareholder services (such as transferring stock or changing your name as a registered shareholder), and get financial facts (like the company's position on the *Fortune* 500, its market capitalization, and its long-term debt).

The financial performance section of the site includes stock price performance data and financial statements, along with interactive features. Using the "investment evaluator," investors can enter the number of shares they own and when they were purchased in order to determine the increased value of their investments. A Java applet* contains annual and quarterly data. Visitors use a drop-box to select a time period; they also can switch between quarterly and annual time frames. Managers and individuals seeking investments can review performance using the criteria that are important to them in order to assess the quality of MCI stock.

A publications and presentations section offers the company's most recent earnings release and quarterly statement. The presentations archive is particularly impressive, featuring PowerPoint presentations by a number of MCI executives, such as a business markets overview by the company's chief operating officer. The presentations require visitors to use a free plugin from Microsoft, but if you don't already have it on your system, you can download and install it directly from the presentations page.

Regulatory information is available, including proxies and government filings. An overview page provides insight into the company, its business, and its management. A special merger overview section offers details into MCI's acquisition by WorldCom. MCI investors can, for instance, use a special calculator to determine how many shares of WorldCom stock they will receive when the acquisition is complete. Fact sheets, FAQs, and press releases related to the deal are available here, as is a detailed description of the merger process. You can even watch a video of the merger announcement.

A download center lists all of the documents available for retrieval from the site, including financial information in spreadsheet format (so it is of immediate use to anybody seeking to use the data), earnings releases (in Word format), and presentations (in self-extracting executable files). The investor relations site also features its own search utility, a general series of FAQs, and a site guide.

Clearly, as much work went into the MCI investor relations site as many companies put into their entire Web presences.

An Investor Relations Internet Checklist

Use the following checklist to assess the investor relations presence your company should have on the Internet.

*This is a small application program, running on a Web page, that is associated with the Java programming language.

1. Is your company public or privately held? If it is privately held, financial information may be limited and the audience too small to make a significant investor relations presence worthwhile.

2. If you are privately held, are you considering an IPO (initial public offering)? If so, it is critical for you to begin branding the quality of your company as an investment as quickly as possible, using an investor relations site as one method for doing so.

3. What are your company's most commonly requested investor-related documents?

4. What are your investor relations goals? Are you trying to attract more individual investors? Institutional investors? Are you trying to retain institutional investors that are seeking to diversify their portfolios?

5. How will your key investment audiences seek information? How can you cross-reference information to make it as easy as possible to find?

6. Is your current financial health good or not so good? How do you want to position your company's investment brand in light of current performance? (For instance, if the company has been performing poorly, the focus could be on long-term growth plans.)

7. What issues are you currently facing that could have an impact, positive or negative, on your company's financial value?

Measurement

How do you know if your online investor relations efforts are paying off? Try using these measures:

• Draw a correlation between the number of times your annual reports and other materials are downloaded and the reduced number of telephone or written requests you get for such materials.

• Track the number of visits to your investor relations Web site, particularly after key announcements and events. If you have developed materials to support or oppose an action such as a merger, assess the number of visits to the topic-specific page, and correlate that information to shifts in public opinion.

• Ask your key investors to rate the value of the Web site. You can even include a mini-survey directly on the site.

Conclusion

Investors constitute a distinct and important audience—one that rates its own strategy for online communications. Use all the tools of the Internet to develop communications that support your objectives for this audience *and* to streamline the operations of your investor relations department.

8

Government Relations

In many organizations, the government relations department is not part of the company's public relations effort. It should be, at least in a dotted-line relationship. The government—legislative and regulatory branches of federal, state, and local jurisdictions—constitutes an audience no less important than customers, consumers, investors, media, and activists. The same principles are involved in communicating with government (notably negotiation). And it is particularly important that messages sent to various government audiences are consistent with those that have been woven into any communications strategies targeted at all other strategic publics.

Perhaps the disconnect between government relations and public relations is the perception held by many executives that PR is closer to propaganda than it is to negotiation. If that's the case, it is incumbent upon communications professionals to create the link. The first step is the strategic management of relations between the organization and its other, nongovernment audiences. The exploitation of the Internet for government communications can be a major element in uniting the two functions to the ultimate advantage of the organization.*

Government is fast catching on to the Internet. Several regulatory agencies are requiring companies to communicate with them via e-mail when sending submissions, filings, and reports. Government servers actively promote activities undertaken by legislatures and agencies. Every state in the United States has a home page. (You can access yours by going to *www.state.xx.us*, replacing the *xx* with the two-letter

---

*In some companies, public relations is a component of a larger department known as public affairs. In these organizations, public relations and government relations often are peer units reporting to the same public affairs executive. Other departments incorporated under this heading include employee communications, community relations, and investor relations.

postal code for the state; California, then, would be at *www.state.ca.us.*) The White House has a home page, as do all of the cabinet departments and the agencies that are part of each cabinet post. If you like, you can visit the Internal Revenue Service online (all of their forms are available for download) or the Central Intelligence Agency.

Some government sites are better than others. Most states have yet to provide valuable resources configured in a manner that is useful to people visiting the sites. The U.S. Postal Service, on the other hand, has created a lively and informative site that ranks with the best business-oriented sites.

But the bottom line is that government is online. Shouldn't we be communicating the messages targeted at government using the same tools government representatives use?

Setting Objectives

Internet-based communication with government can be established in support of any objective in which the government holds the company's future or fate in its hands. Use the following checklist as a starting point to assess the usefulness the Internet can play in communicating key organizational messages to government:

Government Communications Checklist

1. Is your industry regulated? Do you produce materials, such as pharmaceuticals or construction materials, that are subject to government regulations?
2. Do you rely on government funding?
3. Do you work in a controversial industry, one that is subject to attack from activist groups?
4. Do you lobby the government for considerations beneficial to your organization, its customers, or its stakeholders?
5. Do you wish to engage in a merger or acquisition that requires government approval?

The rest of this chapter examines these five categories.

Regulated Businesses

Two channels can aid in your effort to communicate issues related to regulation of your business or products:

1. Communication to general audiences about your adherence to regulatory requirements
2. Communication directed toward regulatory bodies to reinforce your commitment to compliance and to provide up-to-the-minute information about progress related to efforts to gain regulatory approvals

As much as possible, you should coordinate and leverage the two sets of audiences. For example, you can dedicate a section of your Web site to the processes your company employs in its compliance efforts. Use a range of communications methods with both audiences.

E-Mail

Use traditional communications vehicles to invite government regulatory personnel to sign up for regular e-mail updates on regulation-related activities. Send brief updates whenever you purchase new equipment, enter new alliances, tighten procedures, or take any other action that strengthens your ability to comply with regulations. For each product going through the approval process, provide a separate update to the agency representatives involved in the approval process, either administratively or as decision makers.

Discussion Groups

You can develop a password-protected discussion forum using Web technology for ongoing discussions between the company and regulatory representatives. A similar discussion forum, accessible only by authorized individuals, can be used by those involved in the actual testing process. The forum can facilitate communication between company scientists managing the testing and independent researchers contracted to conduct clinical trials.

File Transfer

Archive all test-related documents. Use your Web site to list and briefly describe the documents and make them available for download. The multimedia capabilities of the Internet enable you to include not just written documents but video as well. One pharmaceutical company included a video of a child, part of a clinical trial, who was able to walk for the first time after a few treatments with the drug undergoing tests. It was powerful video that could be made available to regulators, giving them a real glimpse of testing in addition to a clinical report. While videos are certainly not required as part of the approval process, they can provide compelling additional evidence of a product's efficacy.

The World Wide Web

Include a section on your public Web site dedicated to regulatory activities. Document the extraordinary steps your company takes to ensure compliance. This site can raise the level of consumer confidence and help build support for the approval of certain products. List the types of products currently in the process, and provide details about the steps through which the products are going (e.g., the organizations contracted to conduct the actual studies). For each of your existing products, note the steps that were taken to obtain approval and offer (or link to) the regulatory agency's actual documentation of the approval. This can be particularly valuable should the product come under attack for any reason. Having government documentation already available lends credibility to the use of the product for its approved indications. You also can provide access to all the laws and regulations that govern the approval of your products or services.

Government Funding

Institutions that rely on government funding generally compete with other similar institutions for piece of a very limited pie. The Internet can serve as a means by which you can make your case for funding. Let legislators and legislative staff members know about the means by which you provide such information by prominently displaying the URL of your related Web site on all printed documentation. On the Web site, you can report on:

- *The need.* Tell why the publics you serve are more deserving of funding than those of competing organizations.
- *Your programs.* Show how the funds you have received to date have been put to use, articulating the fact that your institution makes outstanding use of the funds it receives.

- *Your plans.* Detail the uses to which you would put future funds and the publics which those funds would serve.

The fact that this information is readily available to members of your other strategic audiences and the general public can raise additional support for the disbursement of public funds to your organization.

Case Study: Housing Authority of the City of Los Angeles

"The target audience for our Web site is the people who are passing laws—Congress," asserts George McQuade, director of communications for the Housing Authority of the City of Los Angeles (HACLA). The press release announcing the site also lists the general public, but it is deliberate in noting that politicians ranging from those at Los Angeles City Hall to the U.S. Congress and the White House are the key audience.

"Politically, with the climate of Congress wanting to do away with public housing, one of the things we talk about in the Web site is promoting self-sufficiency and creating a sense of family," according to Ozie Gonaque, chair of the HACLA Board of Commissioners. "We're not just in the housing business, we're about forming partnerships with our residents and helping them climb the ladder to success. We want our residents to grow out of public housing and into self-sufficiency." This is according to the press release McQuade distributed upon the launch of the Web site (at *www.hacla.org*). "We're 95 percent funded by the Department of Housing and Urban Development," McQuade explains. "The Web site is a way for us to tell our story to HUD."

Telling the HACLA story is not a new idea. When McQuade first joined the agency, he was asked to develop a video that got the agency's message out to important constituents. "We spent $35,000 on the video and had no way to ensure that it went to the right person. When you call up a home page on the World Wide Web, on the other hand, you're *choosing* to look at it. You're selecting yourself as the audience. So we're giving people that ability, the option to look at it when they want to."

What kind of information might be of value to government agencies scanning the site? "One of our main sections features success stories about how people got off public assistance thanks to Housing Authority efforts," he says. "This site gives us a chance to tell that story to anybody who will listen, about how HACLA can establish programs to divert children from gangs and other examples that clear up the misconception about public housing. Ninety-five percent of the residents in HACLA public housing are law-abiding citizens."

The problem, McQuade insists, is that the media create a different perception that becomes a reality for government officials. "I had a good-news story about public housing I wanted to tell," he recalls. "But one news director of a large Los Angeles all-news radio station flat-out told me, 'We don't have listeners in public housing,' and he wasn't going to run the story. The next day, I had to go to our largest housing project because there had been a shooting there. One of the reporters from this station was there and asked me for information.

I shot back, 'Why are you interested? You don't have listeners in public housing.' "

Of course, McQuade wound up giving the reporter the information, but he tells the story to make a point. Those who *are* interested in the positive results of public housing won't hear about it through the public media, but a Web site can make that information available.

To make it easier to find, McQuade planned to establish links to the HACLA site from the HUD page, the City of Los Angeles page (which is visited about 600,000 times a day), and the pages of other housing authorities all over the country.

Five days before opening the site to the public, McQuade distributed a press release announcing the impending Web launch over Reuters. "That was on a Monday or Tuesday before the Friday of the launch," he recalls. "I went home and started up my computer and did a search using the key words 'government,' 'real estate,' 'Internet,' and 'interactive.' I found the release right away using a search engine." As a result, McQuade registered a lot of media interest and visits to the site the day it went live.

Just because the HACLA site is designed to encourage government funding doesn't mean it can't serve multiple purposes. As a result, the agency includes a variety of other services on the site. One of the services McQuade has placed on the public relations section of the site is a guide to HACLA's filming potential.

"I spend a lot of my time working with filming companies; they use HACLA sites for movies, television shows, and the like," McQuade says. "We'll be putting up pictures from movies that have been filmed at our sites, a list of sites that are available for filming, photos of each of HACLA's twenty-one housing developments, and our policy." The policy, about twelve pages long, includes all the rules a film production company must meet, including federal regulations and guidelines. "They can download the policy and make sure they've taken care of all the details before bureaucratic snafus arise."

Other departments are including forms and applications on the Web site, along with job listings, lists of new construction projects, and other features—all of which further serve to put the agency's services to its public on display to government funding decision makers.

Offsetting Activist Attacks

Your organization can experience a full-blown crisis if one of your government-regulated products comes under attack by an activist group opposed to some aspect of the product—how it is marketed, the impact it has on customers, how it is made, its effect on the environment. The documents that show the product meets (or exceeds) government standards can be powerful evidence that the company has taken steps to guard against just the kind of problem about which the activists have made an issue. Links to related materials can support the company's commitment to the environment, patient safety, and other issues activists might be likely to attack. These links can provide access to:

- Related policies
- Testing procedures
- Special measures the company takes to ensure adherence to policies
- Documentation of the steps taken to obtain government regulatory approval
- Any FAQs you maintain that address environmental safety, product safety, etc.
- Customer testimonials, particularly from those who activist groups claim are at risk from your products

If the government agency that approved your product maintains records on its Web site or elsewhere on the Internet, you can provide links to the site or information about how to retrieve the documents. You can even offer information about how to get documents via U.S. mail.

These measures will be far more effective if they are in place *now*, before an activist group targets your product, than they would be if you build such links and add such documents only as a reaction to an assault. And of course, all of the foregoing are valid *only* if the information is accurate—if your environmental record stands up to scrutiny, your product safety measures are valid and thorough, your values are sincerely and fully reflected in your business practices.

Building Support for Lobbying Efforts

Regulated companies often seek changes in regulatory processes. Pharmaceutical companies, for example, would like approval processes for new drugs speeded up. Other industries and the businesses within them have similar issues. And some unregulated industries suddenly find themselves facing regulation. Since politicians respond to public pressure, companies and industries can use the Internet to drum up public support for their positions in order to exert influence on the politicians that oversee regulatory agencies, as well as the agencies themselves.

Based on solid research and empirical evidence that a change in regulatory practices—or the decision not to impose such practices— would be in the best interest of the public, you should take your case to the people.

Legislative issues could benefit from the same approach. When I was working in the late 1970s in the petroleum industry, most of the industry was united in its opposition to the end of the oil depletion allowance. Taking the case public was difficult, since few people understood (or cared about) the issues, and those who did were difficult to target. There were no mailing lists of individuals who might be willing to call or write a legislator to extol the virtues of a special entitlement. If the case could have been taken to the Internet, though, those interested would have been able to find the company's position by following the cognitive links that represented a pathway constructed of their interests.

Individual companies posting their own position pages can be effective, but the power of the medium is diluted when each company buries such a page within the structure of its larger Web site— constructed, perhaps, to address other objectives. Far more forceful would be a single site dedicated to the issue that represents the policies and positions of a coalition of companies within the industry. Each individual company could offer a small but prominent link from the appropriate place on its site to the coalition site. Each company could then provide a path to the advocacy site, leading more people to it. Once at the site, visitors would see a united front, many entities sharing a common set of ideas and embracing a common position.

Making the Case for Mergers and Acquisitions

If there is any company activity that segregates people into camps of winners and losers, it is the practice of mergers and acquisitions. In many instances, the government (in the United States, the Federal Trade Commission and, in some cases, the Justice Department) must approve mergers, and courts often are called upon to uphold them.

When a company announces a merger or acquisition, those who believe they will be on the losing side invariably take action to block it. Building support for the merger can help influence the ultimate decisions. A merger-related Web site—such as that built as a component of MCI's investor relations site during its acquisition by WorldCom, described in Chapter 7—can list the various reasons for the merger and the benefits that will be accrued by various publics.

Conversely, opposition to a merger can also be taken to the Net. Refer to the case study on Slocan Forest Products in Chapter 3 to see how a chairman employed Internet-based tactics to defeat a hostile takeover attempt, soliciting the support of shareholders and others.

Measurement

Measuring the impact of your online communications with government entities can be a little more difficult than with other audiences, such as the media. However, you can still draw some conclusions using these methods:

- How many agencies and legislative staffs have opted to communicate with you by e-mail? How many have elected to receive updates you deliver by e-mail?
- Of the visits to your government-oriented site, how many come from the *gov* domains, signifying the visitor is from the government?
- Can you draw a correlation between the increased activity on your site and changes in public perception or support?

Conclusion

You can streamline your communications with government agencies and legislative staffs through the Internet, but you can also influence government decision making by building support for your initiatives among the publics that vote.

9
Community Relations

Businesses, it is said, function only by the consent of the communities in which they choose to locate. As a result, a company needs to address the people who live, work, and raise their families in the geographic areas surrounding its various facilities. This includes not only the company's headquarters but also remote offices, plants, factories, refineries, sales offices, and any other locations where company employees do business.

Unlike most of the other publics with which institutions must communicate, the community is hard to pin down. You can slice the community audience in any number of ways:

• *The community at large.* This is everybody who lives near the company's operations. The impact of the company's operations on the community is largely economic. The company pays taxes to the community, the salaries it pays local employees are recycled into the local economy, and the company and its employees buy goods and services from local vendors. Hard times for the company can translate into hard times for the community. (Just ask the people who live in Flint, Michigan.) A layoff can devastate a community.

• *Those who live in the immediate proximity.* These are people who would feel the impact of a factory construction, increased factory emissions, or the addition of a new division that would increase vehicle traffic in the immediate area.

• *Civic participation groups.* Local politicians expect organizations to be good corporate neighbors, participating in civic activities and contributing to the community's welfare. Doing so also builds goodwill in the community, which can be used to bolster a company's credibility in times of need or crisis.

• *Educational groups.* The academic community seeks to involve companies in teaching children. Involvement ranges from contributing classroom supplies to the active participation of employees in classroom activities. An oil company geologist, for example, might spend time in a classroom while children are studying geology.

• *Community organizations.* The Lions Club, the Elks Lodge, the Boy Scouts, the Girl Scouts, the Rotary—they all want your company's involvement. At the least, they want financial support and employees to speak at their meetings. Ideally, they would like the use of your facilities for group events and direct sponsorship.

• *Charitable organizations.* The local Red Cross and United Way, along with charitable organizations that exist only in your community, look to your company to help pay their expenses and support their causes.

• *Special audiences.* If your facility is in an agricultural region, farmers constitute a special audience. Similarly, a facility in a mountain resort area makes merchants and resort operators an audience that rates special consideration.

In a perfect world, it would make sense to subdivide the community into many smaller strategic publics. The world is not perfect, however, and most companies commit only a token amount of resources to community involvement. Some companies cast the entire responsibility for community relations to a nonprofit foundation whose sole task is to distribute money to organizations that seek support. In other companies, community relations is the orphaned stepchild of a public relations department more concerned with bigger issues; only a limited sliver of the total PR budget is earmarked for local community. As a result, these diverse audiences are lumped together under the "community" label.

The Internet can help businesses target specific elements of the community relations audience—if not to actually engage them in direct, two-way symmetrical communications, then at least to target messages to each segment. This chapter explores some tactics for achieving this goal.

The Community at Large

The most important objective of a community relations effort is to garner the support of the community at large—shown in the following case study.

Case Study: Suncor Energy

Suncor Energy is a Canadian oil and natural gas producer with worldwide operations, several of which require community support. "Much of our Web site is dedicated to building that community support," says Ron Shewchuk, manager of external communications for the Calgary, Alberta-based company.

Community-based efforts are at the heart of each of the three major elements of the Suncor site, one for each of the company's primary businesses: Oil Sands, a business that extracts oil from the oil sands deposits of northern Canada; its overall Exploration and Production business; and its Sunoco refining operation. Each of the company's businesses are readily accessible from clearly identified icons on the Suncor home page at *www.suncor.com,* and the two most significant operations feature prominent links to community-related information.

The Oil Sands operation, situated near Fort McMurray, Alberta, has been targeted for a significant expansion—$2.2 billion worth, designed to increase production to 210,000 barrels per day by 2002. That would double the current extraction level and require a significant infrastructure investment to upgrade the existing facilities. The expansion plans are not part of a $600 million effort already under way, which is designed to bring production to 105,000 barrels per day by 1999.

"Earning the support of the local community is critical," says Shewchuk, explaining that the company launched its Project Millennium public consultation effort specifically as a means of communicating the company's plans to local residents. Project Millennium also occupies a prominent place on the company's Web site. Included with the information the site offers is a "Public Consultation" section, where the company makes its desire for public input clear. As Rick George, Suncor's president and chief executive officer, says on the site, "A comprehensive consultation process throughout the project will ensure the needs of the public are addressed. We believe the project will be most successful if stakeholders are given the opportunity to be meaningfully involved."

Highlights of the project are outlined, including the geographic areas slated for expansion, the employment outlook ("Temporary jobs will be created during the planning, design and engineering states, and new permanent positions will be created once Project Millennium is operational"), environmental issues, and information on the public consultation process.

The media conference in which the project was announced is available as a text transcript as well as a RealAudio file. Also online are the company's official public disclosure document and an environmental impact assessment. This information is readily accessible to any member of the community with a question about the possible effect of the expansion on just about any aspect of their lives.

The Oil Sands site also includes a Web-based copy of the company's annual *Report to the Community,* which chronicles the company's involvement in the community in which it does business. "Suncor has been actively involved in the Fort McMurray community for over 30 years," notes the introduction to the report. The contents provide a comprehensive review of the company's Fort McMurray activities, written to satisfy the specific informational needs of the members of the local community. Figure 9-1 shows Suncor's *Report to the Community,* reviewing the company's involvement and impact on the communities where it operates.

The balance of the Oil Sands site, while potentially of interest to a variety of audiences, is most likely to be visited by locals, Shewchuk notes. For example, a simple but effective animation illustrates the process by which Suncor extracts oil from oil sand. Anybody living nearby concerned about the impact of Suncor's operations on the environment would find quick answers in the animation and associated information.

Suncor maintains a separate Oil Shale operation in Queensland, Australia, where a demonstration plant near the community of Gladstone will produce 4,500 barrels of oil per day once it is operational. Again, Shewchuk notes, community acceptance and support are vital. "We produce a newsletter that we send to the local community," he says, the contents of which are reproduced on the Web site. "We've made an effort to integrate all of our media," he explains. "If we print it and distribute it, we also make it available for retrieval from the Web."

Figure 9-2 shows the printed newsletter received by residents of Gladstone, Australia, which also has a home on the company's Web site.

A visit to the Sunoco section of the Suncor site provides a direct link to "Community," where the refinery's involvement in local activities is highlighted. Among the activities promoted here are:

- *Charity lunches.* Each month, an employee selects a charity. Other employees attend a lunch, the proceeds from which are distributed to the selected charity.
- *Partners Active in Resource Sharing (PAIRS).* The refinery provides job placements for students of the St. Clair Secondary School in Sarnia, Ontario.
- *Corporate challenge.* Employees hold an annual athletic competition that raises funds for local charities.

Other Community Relations Ideas

Any company activities that will build support for the business among the community at large can be leveraged on the Internet. The simplest use of the Web (as employed by Suncor) is to publish your company's community relations report on the Web. Another example of this practice can be found at the site maintained by Ashland, Inc., which covers the company's investments in civic affairs, education, arts and culture, the environment, and health and human services. (You'll find the excellent report on Ashland's site at *www.ashland.com/community/annual*

Figure 9-1. A Web-based copy of Suncor's *Report to the Community*.

Suncor has been actively involved in the Fort McMurray community for over 30 years. The people in this photo represent just a few of the not-for-profit groups Suncor supports through its community investment program.

From left to right: Megan Jahn, Brittany Lauersen, Brent Mills, Carolyn Slade, Kevin Gazzard, Sean Parsons, Eric Inder, Sharon DeBleyser, Margo Strong, Dr. Pari Razvi, Karen Gooden, Ed Kamps, Brigitte Parent, Anne Marie Szucs, Catherine Grant.

Report to the Community – A New Look

In 1995, Suncor Energy was actively seeking regulatory approval for the proposed Steepbank Mine and an expansion of its operating plants when it launched "Report to the Community." The newsletter was created **to inform the residents of the Regional Municipality of Wood Buffalo** and initiate dialogue to help identify concerns about Suncor's growth plans.

This fall, the report is bigger than ever before. Suncor is celebrating its 30th anniversary as the oil sands pioneer and has just announced its intention to more than double oil production by 2002. This report is intended to celebrate the successes of the past 30 years and look ahead to the challenges of the next 30.

The vision of Dr. Karl Clark became reality in 1967 with the opening of the world's first commercial oil sands plant. From his Edmonton lab, Dr. Clark had perfected the hot water extraction process more than a decade earlier.

1967 — 2027

Contents

The Early Years

New Times, New Technologies

The early years of the Great Canadian Oil Sands plant were fraught with technical challenges, and seven years after opening, the plant had not yet achieved its initial design capacity of 45,000 barrels per day.

Strategic initiatives introduced in 1992 included a fundamental change in mining technology. The aging bucketwheels were phased out and replaced with more efficient and cost-effective trucks and shovels.

About the Company

Suncor Energy Inc. is a Canadian integrated energy company operating an oil sands plant near Fort McMurray, Alberta, an exploration and production business in western Canada, a refining and marketing operation in Ontario and Quebec, and an oil shale development project in Queensland, Australia. Suncor common shares are listed on the Toronto, Montreal, Alberta, Vancouver and New York stock exchanges.

For a hard copy of this publication or for more information contact:

Suncor Energy Inc.
Oil Sands
Communications Department
P.O. Box 4001
Fort McMurray, AB
T9H 3E3

tel (403) 743-6479
fax (403) 791-8300
E-mail

In 1997, Suncor unveiled Project Millennium, a detailed plan to more than double production from the oil sands plant by 2002 at a cost of $2.2 billion.

Suncor maintains a high commitment to environmental protection in the Fort McMurray area, using state-of-the-art equipment to monitor air quality.

Suncor Home   Oil Sands Home

The National Oil Sands Task Force predicts that by 2010 production from the oil sands will exceed one million barrels per day.

September 1997

Figure 9-2. The newsletter received by residents of Gladstone, Australia, on the Suncor Oil Shale Project.

update
on the Stuart Oil Shale Project

Issue No. 1, October 1997

CO-OWNERS:
Suncor Energy
Southern Pacific Petroleum NL
Central Pacific Minerals NL

In This Issue:

- THE STUART OIL SHALE PROJECT
  - Turning Oil Shale into "Black Gold"
  - Twenty Years of Work Pays Off
  - A Staged Development
- PROJECT TEAM SPANS THE GLOBE
  - SPP/CPM
  - Suncor Energy Inc.
  - Bechtel
- UPCOMING ACTIVITIES – October to January
- FREQUENTLY ASKED QUESTIONS
  - For Further Information
  - About "update"

Welcome to the first issue of the Stuart Oil Shale Project newsletter, a publication designed to keep the community informed on the progress of the demonstration plant located near Gladstone, in Queensland. This cooperative venture between Southern Pacific Petroleum (SPP), Central Pacific Minerals (CPM) and Suncor Energy is designed to test the commercial viability of producing oil from Australian oil shale.

Turning Oil Shale into "Black Gold"

Stage One of the Stuart Oil Shale Project is a ground-breaking pilot that Stage One of the Stuart Oil Shale Project is a ground-breaking pilot that will determine the feasibility of converting Australia's ancient sedimentary shale rock into '*black gold.*'

The Stuart deposit alone is estimated to contain the equivalent of three billion barrels of shale oil. 'If the project is successful,' says Suncor Energy's managing director, Peter Hopkins, '*It's the first step in the development of a whole new industry in Australia. With this project, we're looking at a technological breakthrough that makes this oil shale economical. There's no real limit to how much you could produce. There's so much oil.* '

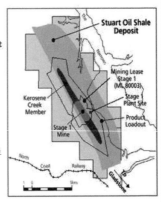

Contents

_report/index.html.) But building an online version of a print publication only scratches the surface of the online potential for community relations. Following is a laundry list of ideas you might apply to your site:

• *Subscriptions to community mailing lists.* On your community relations page, invite local residents to subscribe to an e-mail mailing list to receive notices of activities related to the community. Use the mailing list to announce construction that might affect traffic, job fairs, sponsorship of a booth or event at community fairs, major grants, and other goings-on you want residents to know about. The goodwill you build comes in handy in the event of a crisis, since you can use the established mailing list to distribute your point of view to the community, particularly when the crisis hits close to home, such as a toxic gas release or a plant explosion.

• *Invitations to open houses.* The open houses can be virtual or otherwise. If you host an actual open house at your company, you can promote it on the Web, as well as through an e-mail to local residents who subscribe to a community-based mailing list. Whether you host an actual open house or not, you can provide a virtual open house twenty-four hours a day by building a Web-based tour of your local facilities.

• *Information about grants.* If your company provides grants to the local community, offer information about the criteria for distribution. You can even offer advice to those who plan to apply for a grant, as does Quantum, the Silicon Valley manufacturer of computer hard drives.

• *Promotion of joint projects.* Toys for Tots is a classic example of a community relations activity sponsored by third parties that are no-brainers for companies to join. The Web can be used to publicize the company's involvement as well as to appeal for contributions at company locations. Even employees—regular visitors to their own company's Web sites—can be the target of such messages.

• *Contributions to arts and culture.* Many companies contribute to local art and cultural resources (often because that is a personal interest of the CEO). If that's the case with your business, you can do more than note the dollars contributed. You can produce virtual galleries on behalf of the museums to which you donated money or provide space on your site to promote local theater productions.

Community relations is one of those aspects of public relations that invites creativity and flexibility based on the needs of the local community, its character, its culture, and the means by which your institution has elected to be involved. Use your imagination!

Those in the Immediate Proximity

Sections of company Web sites could be dedicated to those who live in neighborhoods that surround company facilities. Many companies already produce printed newsletters that are distributed to neighboring residents, particularly companies with controversial facilities such as refineries or plants that handle toxic products. A Web site allows the company to expand the volume of news it makes available and maintain related archives of information that would be too voluminous for publication in each issue (such as detailed safety information). The site could help calm any fears some of your neighbors may have about your facility.

Neighbors also could sign up to receive e-mail bulletins on issues that interest them, subscribing through the Web site. One bulletin could list local employment opportunities, another could keep neighbors informed about upcoming construction or maintenance, and a third could be about any activities that might temporarily increase traffic. The more you communicate with the local residents, the more likely they are to appreciate your interest in them and their welfare.

When you undertake a major expansion or construction project, providing detailed information can help secure public support for your efforts. A pharmaceutical company for which I worked could have benefited from the Web (had it existed at the time) when it sought to build a plant that produced a near-miraculous drug from the deadly botulism toxin. The local residents vehemently opposed the effort, and the company was limited in the means at its disposal to reassure them of the process's safety. For instance, local meetings—attended, naturally, by those most opposed to the construction—often degenerated into shouting matches. A Web site, promoted through local newspaper ads, could have made a strong case for the plant and offered information on upcoming employment opportunities as well. A site designed to curry neighborhood favor for such a project can include environmental information, details about the benefits to the community, and even a forum through which residents can express their concerns and get answers directly from a company representative.

Civic Participation Groups

Let your community know that you do more than occupy space: You play an active role in the community's affairs by encouraging your employees to participate. When I worked in the communications department at the natural resources company ARCO, we reported regularly on employees who ran for public office and who served on city councils, boards of education, even state assemblies. The company's public affairs department supported employees in their efforts by giving them time and encouragement to run and to serve. A company can celebrate the employees who dedicate their time to such activities by featuring them on Web pages. You could consider a site under your community relations label that is dedicated to employees who are elected officials in the community.

Ashland, mentioned above, lists all of the public policy organizations with which its employees are involved, from local chambers of commerce and Junior Achievement to the Public Agenda Foundation and the Pacific Research Institute for Public Policy. Each month, the site also focuses on one employee who is particularly involved in civic and community functions. The report on the employee costs the company virtually nothing, but the article reflects the degree to which the company values and supports its employees' involvement in the political life of the community.

Other opportunities for using your site to highlight civic involvement include:

• Position pages that outline the company's stance on local political issues and the steps the company is taking to support or oppose local government action.

• Listings of the contributions from your political action committee (if your company has one) to political candidates. (In many PACs, the members—the employees who join—determine who receives contributions, and a listing can contradict popular public opinion that contributions are heavily weighted toward those candidates who would vote in the company's interests.)

• A regular report on local issues of interest to the company. Cover such items as education decisions, showing your support for improvements to the schools your employees' children attend and that will furnish your future workforce.

Educational Groups

Public schools, always in dire need of funding, seek support from the local businesses that ultimately recruit employees from the local education system. Those who advocate reductions in government spending assert that it is the responsibility of business to provide this kind of support since they are ultimately the beneficiaries of an educated population. Many companies do, in fact, find innovative ways to contribute to local education efforts. The Internet represents a new vehicle for communicating, for facilitating company activities, and even for providing new educational opportunities.

Tip: Make Your Educational Site Educational
For an excellent example of an education-oriented corporate site, visit Apple Computer's education page at *www. apple.com/education/.* The site features resources for teachers, newsletters geared toward K–12 and higher education, seminars, and a Distinguished Schools program.

Following are some approaches to using the Internet—and primarily the World Wide Web—to enhance your institution's reputation as a patron of education in your community.

Promote Your Efforts

Whatever your activities to support education, be sure to promote them on your company's Web site. Computer storage manufacturer Quantum, for example, spotlights its participation in NetDay, the California-based volunteer effort to circumvent government stagnation and wire public schools for Internet access. Figure 9-3 shows how Quantum celebrates its participation in NetDay on a page that is part of its community relations Web site. Another page promotes the company's involvement in Take Our Children to Work Day.

List Available Employees

Employees who have volunteered to spend time in local schools generally do so in order to share an area of expertise. Many employees enthusiastically give their time in classrooms in order to generate excitement among students for their chosen line of work. At ARCO, employees participated in a program sponsored by the Los Angeles Unified School District in which they spent a half day each week in the classroom, teaching an overview course on their profession (engineering, chemistry, geology, etc.). Teachers would be equally delighted to know that your employees are available for a onetime visit to the class-

Figure 9-3. The page of Quantum's community relations Web site highlighting its participation in NetDay.

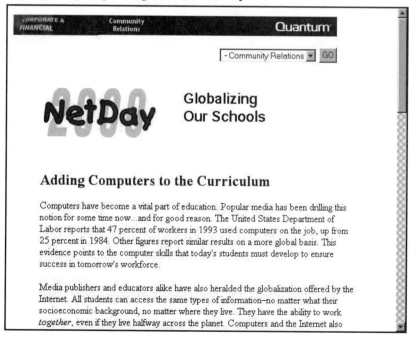

room. Most schools lack information about the employees available for such a program. Develop a section of your Web site that catalogs the employees who can spend time in the classroom, and promote the listing via other media to your local schools.

Sponsor Contests

Use your Web site to promote competitions to help surface the talents of students in the community. Apple Computer, for example, sponsors the International Environmental Essay Contest, in which undergraduates describe environmental issues.

Offer Used Equipment

Outdated computer and office equipment can be donated to classrooms. Create a page on your Web site that allows teachers or school administrators to list their needs. You can then match the equipment that becomes available to the needs of the local schools and publicize the dollar value of the equipment you have donated.

Educate Students About Your Business

One function of Web sites that several companies have adopted is providing information about the business or the underlying profession. Students can access these sites directly, or they can be crafted as teacher's aids. Alcan, the Montreal-based aluminum company, gives information on its site that shows how aluminum is made. Photos and diagrams are included. Figure 9-4 shows one of the Alcan pages, explaining the aluminum manufacturing process and elaborating on the casting and fabricating part of the business.

Provide Distance Learning

The next step beyond offering a site to educate students about your business is to actually sponsor a class. Your expert employees can serve as virtual professors for classes that focus on specialty topics. These can be mini-classes appropriate for grade school or full-blown classes for which community colleges offer course credit. Distance learning programs take advantage of a variety of Internet applications, including the Web, e-mail, and discussion groups. Students can sign up for the class using an interactive Web form. Reading assignments can be deliv-

Figure 9-4. One of Alcan's pages on how aluminum is made.

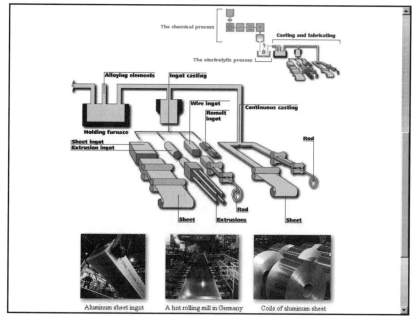

ered on a Web page, via e-mail, or in books that students purchase or your company supplies. Lectures can be delivered on the Web, via e-mail, or as articles posted to a discussion group. Discussion groups also are used for asynchronous discussions about the reading and lectures. Testing can be delivered on the Web or in person.

Community Organizations

Organizations gather in every community, catering to interests ranging from social interaction (such as the Elks) and business contacts (like the Rotary) to personal development (Like Toastmasters, which help individuals advance their public speaking skills in a social setting). The simplest forms of communication can be enhanced online. If your organization hosts Toastmasters meetings, for instance, you can display meeting times on your Web site and use your online facilities to provide an e-mail bulletin to members. If you already maintain listserv software, you can even provide Toastmasters participants with a mailing list they can use to engage in discussions on various speaking-related topics between meetings.

As for other community organization activities, consider some of the following ideas to enhance your image with the often-influential members of these groups.

Electrify Your Speakers Bureau

One of the best ways to increase your visibility in the community *and* to respond to the needs of organizations is to provide guest speakers. Your company employs individuals with a wide range of specialties and interests who can represent it at monthly organization meetings. Many companies include speakers bureaus as part of their community relations efforts. Publicizing the availability of specific speakers, though, can be problematic. But on the Web, you can easily produce a roster of speakers with information about their topics and even build a simple interactive form that allows an organization to request a speaker. A smidgen more sophistication would enable you to produce a calendar displaying the availability of your various speakers. Figure 9-5 shows the page posted by Rice & Stallknecht, P.C., a Virginia-based law firm that gets greater community exposure by offering speakers to the local community on topics related to its areas of expertise.

Build a Community Forum

Budgets are tight for volunteer organizations and many cannot afford a Web presence, but you can offer them a page or two of space on your server to promote their local activities. At the bottom of the page, include a small banner ad that reads something like, "This volunteer organization Web site provided as a community service of Acme, Inc."

Charitable Organizations

Your community includes organizations dedicated to helping others in need—and there are many different types of needs, leading to an array of charitable organizations that all compete for your limited contributions. You can help with both money and time.

Figure 9-5. The page posted by Rice & Stallknecht promoting the firm's available speakers.

Speakers from
Rice & Stallknecht, P.C.

For years, attorneys from Rice and Stallknecht, P.C. have given speeches on legal subjects of widespread interest. Our talks are at no charge to qualified community organizations and business. We view providing such talks as a method of public service, similar to distributing legal information through this web site.

Here are examples of subjects that our attorneys have addressed recently:

Social Security Business Estate Planning	Leslie Ruth Stallknecht
Like Kind Exchanges under section 1031 of the Internal Revenue Code	Karl M. Rice
Wage and Hour Violations - The Fair Labor Standards Act Americans with Disabilities Act Sexual Harassment in today's workplace Hiring and firing issues	Sydney Rab

The topics listed above are not exhaustive. Our attorneys sometimes use audiovisual aids in giving presentations. From this page, you can link to our sample slide show on Social Security disability. Contact us for more information if you are interested in having an attorney from Rice & Stallknecht, P.C. address your organization.

Giving Money

The fact that you make contributions is worth noting on your Web site. If you already produce an online community relations report, be sure to include a review of your corporate giving. Discuss the amounts contributed to each organization and the process by which the money is collected (e.g., a percentage of after-tax profits, an employee-giving campaign). For those who would solicit your organization, you also can offer a summary of the process by which the company decides which charities are the beneficiaries of its giving program.

While in the middle of an employee campaign (such as United Way or Red Cross), be sure to offer updated information on the campaign's progress. The visibility of the campaign on your Web site serves as a reflection of your company's commitment to charitable giving.

Include links to the Web sites of organizations to which the company regularly donates money, or craft overviews of each recipient of company monies that focus on the reason those organizations are worthy of your attention.

Giving Time

While companies are limited in the amount of money they can contribute to charity, there is bountiful time. The focus of many charitable institutions is not on contributions but on voluntarism, since the amount of time people donate to charity-related efforts has diminished in recent decades.

An online community relations report should chronicle the company's organizing efforts over the past year. Even if an effort was not an official company project but instead was organized by an employee, you can spotlight the employee and note that the company provided the time and office supplies to bring the project to its completion.

Projects that are in the planning stages should be highlighted as well, and progress reports should be posted to update the public about efforts in progress. Photo spreads showing your employees engaged in volunteer efforts have special value, since people especially like to look at pictures of other people from their own community. If your senior management is represented in the pictures, so much the better. The kinds of projects that are particularly applicable to photography are characterized by Habitat for Humanity, the volunteer effort to refurbish substandard housing to make homes livable for poorer members of the community. Pictures of employees hammering, sawing, and painting display genuine community-based pride and dedication.

Special Audiences

Communicating with every member of a special audience can be prohibitively expensive. It can even be impossible, given that many special audiences are not easily defined: There are no mailing lists for many of the special-needs groups with which you may wish to communicate. But there is little expense involved in developing a simple Web page (or series of pages) that provides information that meets the unique needs of these special audiences. The Web can even be used to help you identify the individual members of these singular communities so that you can communicate with them using other media as well.

Alcan Smelter & Chemicals

Alcan Smelter & Chemicals, a division of Alcan Aluminum, Ltd., identified just such a special community in the agricultural business in Canada's interior, according to Kathleen Bourchier, Alcan's manager of corporate communications for British Columbia. The company maintains the Nechako Reservoir in the central interior region of British Columbia. The reservoir's Skins Lake Water Spillway releases water into the Nechako River. "Depending on how much we're being asked to release or for fisheries protection or flood control, the amount of water going into the river tends to fluctuate," Bourchier explains. "The farmers who live downstream need to be kept informed. Our commitment to community relations includes providing as much information on water flows as we possibly can."

Even before the company launched its Web site, it made water flow information available through a variety of media. A call-in phone line offered a recording with water level information, and farmers could subscribe to a fax service. "But the amount of information you can put on a recording is limited, and not everybody has a fax machine," Bourchier asserts. The agricultural community, on the other hand, is one of the most wired, using the Internet to obtain detailed weather reports, crop reports, and a variety of other data. (See Chapter 4 for an overview of Agriculture Online, a successful commercial Web site for farmers.)

Using the Web (at *www.sno.net/alcan/*), Alcan is able to provide current reservoir levels and water flow rates, as well as a graphic chart that shows the year's historical release information—data that can be useful to farmers planning their activities. Clearly, the water flow information is of use to only a very small, special-interest audience. However, it is invaluable for those individuals and generates goodwill within the community. Figure 9-6 shows one of Alcan Smelter & Chemicals's Web pages for special-interest farming community.

The Internet can provide any number of special-interest audiences with information that meets their particular needs, enabling your company to engage in a targeted communication effort with individual members of an audience otherwise difficult—or impossible—to reach.

Measurement

Assess the effectiveness of your online community relations efforts using the following techniques:

Figure 9-6. Alcan Smelter & Chemicals's Web page for its special-interest farming community.

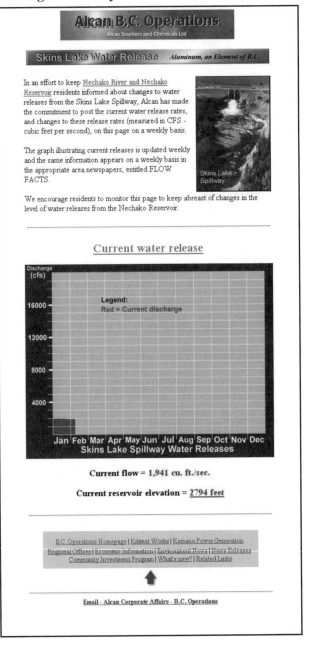

• Build a survey on your site that asks members of the visiting public to rate the online effort and submit ideas for future enhancements.

• Measure the number of visitors to community-specific sites (such as those dedicated to educational programs), and record the number of requests for information, sign-ups, or other actions that denote an individual took advantage of a program or service.

• Determine the savings involved in providing information online that otherwise would have been expensive to produce and distribute. Carrying this notion a step further, you can quantify the audiences your Internet presence allows you to reach who would be impossible to identify without the medium.

Conclusion

Identifying the various subaudiences within the community is an expense most companies cannot afford. The Internet allows those audiences to be targeted and lets them pull the information they need. In this way, they can take advantage of programs that would have been unwieldy before the Internet provided the company with a means by which to communicate and facilitate those programs.

10
Activism on the Internet

The nature of the Internet makes it the perfect place for people and organizations with an agenda to drum up support from other like-minded individuals as well as from people with only a passing interest in the subject. Existing groups promoting social causes, disgruntled customers, and everybody in between can apply the potential afforded by the Internet.

Before the Internet, organizing an effort required that activists follow a fairly well-prescribed sequence of activities, beginning with an individual or small group handing out leaflets on street corners. A few recipients of these makeshift communications were likely to be sympathetic to the cause and to respond to the flier. As the group grew, members began meeting in auditoriums and attracted more attention. The larger membership was able to pool its resources in order to buy more effective promotion. Eventually, the group would band together with similar organizations in other geographic locations in order to leverage its influence. The process could take months, even years.

On the Internet, the same process can occur in a matter of hours or days. Three factors unique to the Internet account for the speed with which activist groups can coalesce:

1. *The many-to-many model.* Everybody is a publisher on the Internet. While traditional activist groups needed to use rudimentary publishing tools just to have fliers to distribute, the Internet provides anybody with the means to publish high-quality material that is available to a global audience. There are no editors to assess the usefulness or appropriateness of the material. Neither good taste nor accuracy is required. All anybody needs to communicate with a large audience is

a $10-a-month Internet account, a computer, and a connection to the Net.

2. *The receiver-driven model.* The mass-media process is based upon the likelihood that distributing information to huge numbers of people will result in the message hitting home to a small percentage of the audience. In direct-mail models, response rates in the range of 2 percent to 3 percent are considered effective. On the Internet, there is no need to distribute information to those who are not interested. Web pages with the key words "gun control" will attract those who have an interest in the subject (pro and con); nobody else is likely to go there. Several methods exist by which activists can alert prospective colleagues to the existence of such sites, including careful placement of the sites in various online indexes and announcements in topic-specific discussion groups.

3. *The Internet's global reach.* There is no need to identify the geographic areas in which interested individuals are likely to live, nor is it necessary to start locally and only later expand to larger geographic reaches. Instead, the Internet can compel attention from anybody, regardless of where an individual might live.*

As a result, every activist group imaginable, on every side of an issue, has staked out territory on the Internet, from mainstream causes (e.g., reproductive rights, environmentalism, and capital punishment) to the fringe (white supremacy, Holocaust revisionism, and government UFO cover-ups).

Often, society's institutions are targets of activist groups. Some organizations are obvious targets, like Planned Parenthood (attacked by abortion foes) or Playboy Enterprises (which incurs the wrath of feminist organizations). But just as often, companies that are simply doing business can run afoul of a group with a cause. By way of example, in just a brief trip through the Internet one rainy Sunday afternoon, I uncovered the following:

• A site dedicated to an effort to stop Exxon from mining for coal in Wisconsin, including information on where to write, phone, fax, or e-mail opposition.

---

*Science fiction writer Neal Stephenson suggests that the Internet provides people with the online equivalent of a wormhole. Whereas a wormhole theoretically brings two

- A site announcing a labor-backed boycott of Monsanto as a result of the company's production and marketing of bovine growth hormone.

- The Association of Flaming Ford Owners, a site focusing on the alleged potential of Ford vehicles to burst into flame.

- A site focusing on getting the president of Disneyland a different job. The site—which received editorial coverage from the *Los Angeles Times* and *Harper's*—claims to be a "positive online campaign with one simple goal: getting current Disneyland Resorts President Paul Pressler promoted to a new job *somewhere else* within the Walt Disney Company. The site catalogs the reason the site developer believes the executive is "killing" Disneyland and offers visitors to the site the opportunity to post their own observations.

- Several sites dedicated to a boycott of Nike because of the company's reported use of cheap overseas labor in sweatshoplike environments.

In each case, the Web-based site was also the subject of some discussion on Usenet discussion groups. The synergy of the two Internet media serves to reinforce key messages and target new members.

Activism Directed at Existing Causes

People promoting causes that have been around for some time—before the Internet, in fact—have found the Net to be a worthwhile place to establish a presence. From their online venues, they can attack the institutions they perceive as obstacles to the change they seek. From the environmentalist sector, for example, the Sierra Club—one of the oldest and most mainstream of activist groups—maintains a Web site. One section, "Activism," includes "Action Alerts" that are updated weekly. The alerts include the names of companies engaged in activities that contradict the club's agenda and phone numbers of legislators to call in opposition to the companies' activities. The Sierra Club also is the focus of a Usenet newsgroup (*alt.org.sierra-club*). Greenpeace

---

distance parts of space together, the Internet connects two distant parts of the world. When you are online, you are simultaneously in your own location *and* at the location of the individual or institution you are in contact with.

also maintains a Web site, as do dozens of smaller environmental organizations.

The National Organization for Women (NOW) and Planned Parenthood have sites, as does the National Right to Life Council. The National Rifle Association is online, as is the Center to Prevent Handgun Violence.

In general, these organizations restrict their activities to Web sites, although individual members have been known to post messages in discussion forums. Some organizations maintain their own discussion groups within the confines of their Web sites, which generally attract only those who already are sympathetic to the cause.

What You Can Do

If your company engages in any activities that might attract the attention of an existing, mainstream activist organization, you are likely at some point to become a target. Here are some things you can do:

• Monitor the sites of the organizations about which you know. Not only will you discover when your organization has been mentioned but you will get a better handle on the issues and agendas of the organizations that can conceivably turn public opinion against you. Armed with the knowledge of what disturbs the organizations, you can mount an effort to offset the negative publicity. You may even wind up altering your approach to the issue based on what you learn from your opposition.

• Provide information on your Web site that reinforces your position. Be sure not to approach the information defensively. Assume that individuals who visit your site with an interest in the topic stumbled upon the activist group's message and are curious to see your point of view. You're never going to change the minds of those who are active in the cause anyway, so you may as well focus on those who are still willing to be influenced by a candid, credible, accurate presentation of information.

• Be a regular lurker in pertinent discussion groups. Make individual determinations about whether to reply to potentially damaging posts, and if you *do* reply, determine whether to respond to the individual or the entire group.

Instant Activists and Individuals With Agendas

While the traditional activist groups have adopted the Internet as a new and important medium, the Net is also serving an entirely new community of individuals and groups who have never before had the resources to communicate to a worldwide audience. These individuals and groups represent a new frontier for companies seeking to maintain their positive reputations, since anybody—for any reason—can lash out and raise opinions against you.

It doesn't take much for someone with a cause to organize a campaign to attack your products, activities, industry, or market. You do not have to work in the tobacco industry to attract the attention of a homespun group of protestors. The following two case studies illustrate the point. In the first, a loose coalition of individuals who genuinely believe a product to be a health hazard are using the Internet to seek its abolition. In the second, individuals who share a common zeal for a popular product banded together in order to try to stop the company that makes the product from blocking distribution of a publication for enthusiasts.

Case Study: NutraSweet

The Internet is a genuine venue for an activist group's opposition effort to the artificial sweetener NutraSweet, produced by NutraSweet Kelco. The activist group does not fit the mold of traditional groups: It has no name, no membership roster, no meetings. Instead, online activists play follow-the-leader, taking their cues from others. Their issue: a belief that NutraSweet (and its core chemical substance, aspartame) represents a health hazard, causing brain cancer and other illnesses.

These activists post attack Web pages; one flagrantly employed Nutra-Sweet's own logo, changing the words so it read "FDA Approved Brain Cancer." They lurk in discussion groups, ready to make their point whenever anybody innocently asks if NutraSweet is a healthful alternative to sugar. In fact, over a thirty-day period, some 870 messages were posted to Usenet newsgroups featuring the word "NutraSweet." Most of these posts appeared in a newsgroup titled *misc.health.diabetes,* although some messages were cross-posted to other related newsgroups, such as *sci.med.pharmacy, alt.support.diet, misc.health. alternative,* and *sci.med.nutrition.* The nature of the groups represented indicates that they are populated by people with a specific agenda. Most of the participants are diabetics or people seeking information on behalf of friends or family. And (embracing the model of the market sample of one, discussed in Chapter 2) the activists were there waiting for them.

A common article reads much like this one from Betty Martini, whose activist-oriented posts make regular appearances on *misc.health.diabetes* (with cross-postings to *rec.food.drink, sci.med.pharmacy,* and *misc.kid.pregnant*). The article is a reply to a question posted to the same newsgroup. (Errors are reprinted as they occurred in the originals.)

```
Subject:       Re: what's up with NutraSweet™
From:          Betty Martini <betty@noel.pd.org>
Date:          1996/07/20
Organization:  Emory University, Dept of Math and CS
Newsgroups:    misc.health.diabetes
    Dear Jonas:    Richard Wilson, widower of Joyce Wilson
who went blind and died from NutraSweet™ says it kills fire
ants instantly, and he used Equal. He was about to market
aspartame as an ant killer because not only does it kill
ants just like it killed the monkeys and rats in the stud-
ies, and his wife and other victims, but he thought he would
make a point.
    Recently, someone wrote and asked for information on
aspartame because she said she was doing a study of whether
dogs and cats liked sugar or aspartame best. I thought it
was a joke and wrote back and said: "You wouldn't really do
that to pets, would you? This is a joke, isn't it?
    However, I am sending you all the information you re-
quested and more on aspartame including independent stud-
ies." Then a few weeks later I get a letter from her saying
it really wasn't a joke and they did do the experiment. They
made two piles and neither the dogs or cats would touch the
aspartame and then she said: "Would you believe even the
ants wouldn't touch it!" Well, ants are pretty smart,
aren't they? They won't knowingly consume poison! Humans
should be so smart!
    Regards,
    Betty
```

Martini posted 556 articles during 1996, some 80 percent of which generated follow-up articles from other Usenet users. Of her 498 articles, 189 were posted to *misc.health.diabetes,* more than twice the number posted to any other group. Martini's single-mindedness is an example of how Usenet can be used by an individual to generate an activist movement in a manner that simply was not possible prior to the development of Internet-based many-to-many communication.

Given the many-to-many nature of the Internet, those who disagree with the activists have an equal opportunity to convey their message. There are a number of posts that dispute the facts presented by those who disparage Nutra-Sweet, such as this article:

```
    Betty's crusade against NutraSweet™ leaves me some
questions about myself. First of all I use NutraSweet™
without any apparent side affects and since my last
HB1ac was 5.1 my control is good. Without sounding
sarcastic, after reviewing the various anti-
NutraSweet™ post from Betty, I don't know if something
```

```
is missing in my life that I don't have a passion for
anything like she has against N.S. or is it that I have
a life?
      D.R.
```

The problem is that the activists have an agenda and promote it proactively, while those who take issue with the activist point of view are merely reacting, responding to the messages that incite them to say something. Many people who disagree with activists simply shrug and do not take the time to reply, wondering what the point is. For every article that takes issue with the activists, there are several that support the activist point of view, such as this article that replies to specific charges posted earlier on the newsgroup:

```
I am new to this newsgroup. Maybe there are people
hawking all kinds of snake oil for getting our money.
But NutraSweet™ matter is different. Betty and others
who are crusading against the NutraSweet™ is not
looking for anyone's money. They are not expecting
anything from anyone. As one who has seen what
NutraSweet™ could do to a diabetics vision, and one
whose vision was saved by *accidental* reading of
Betty's NutraSweet™ warning, all I can say is that this
is a very serious matter. If someone wants to go ahead
and ignore even the remotest possibility of
NutraSweet's™ deadly effects, can do so and no one to
blame later if they become blind. It will be too
late. . . .
```

In general, the majority of posts are clearly based in the opposition camp. As true believers, they will not be dissuaded by rational discussions undertaken by the company. Monsanto's best defense: Use its Web page (at *www.nutra sweet.com*) to promote the healthful nature of the product. The section of the site that offers the health-related information is not reactive. Instead, it is a simple presentation of facts, ranging from physician testimonials to official FDA records from the process the product underwent in order to get government approval. Though the activists will not be convinced, the consumer who stumbles upon the activist point of view will likely want to visit the NutraSweet page in order to see what the company has to say. Its authoritative information stands a good chance of negating the information that led consumers to check out the home page in the first place.

Case Study: Mattel

Mattel, Inc., is another company that has felt the impact of the Internet on its activities. Because of the Net's power, collectors of Barbie dolls were able to coordinate opposition to the company's trademark violation suit against a publisher.

The Pink Anger movement, as it came to be known, had been brewing for some time, the result of quality issues and other problems. But it erupted when Mattel filed suit against Miller's, the publisher of collector-focused magazines that have become the bible of Barbie collectors. According to Mattel's lawsuit, Miller's violated Mattel's copyrights and trademarks in its collectors' price guides and other publications.

There are an estimated 250,000 hard-core Barbie collectors worldwide, and the Internet—discussion groups, e-mail, and the Web—has made them strong, given them the ability to coalesce. What happened after Mattel filed the suit was reported by the *Los Angeles Times*: "Online Barbie chat groups buzzed about first amendment rights and what collectors viewed as Mattel's Big Brotherish behavior. The Iron Curtain may have fallen, but in America, they said, a toy company is stomping on the Bill of Rights. Could unofficial Barbie Web sites be next?"

Chicago Barbie collector Ian Henzel built a Pink Anger Web site using his America Online account. On the site, the instant Barbie activists could read the entire Mattel lawsuit, obtain information on how to contact Mattel, and get templates to use for letters and telephone calls.

Collectors with Web sites established a banner ad that they linked to the "official" Pink Anger site. As the word spread, other collectors added anti-Mattel rhetoric to their site. One site said:

> We need everyone's help to let Mattel know we are not happy about it. Our Web pages and others will be targeted next. I for one do not want that to happen. . . . This lawsuit against Millers is not okay and goes too far. Please take the time to write a letter to Mattel. It will make a difference. Below is the address to write to. I know I've dealt with lots of you guys and I feel like we are family. Let's get our circle of friends together and make a difference for something we believe in . . . Millers and our freedom of speech.

As Mattel stood its ground against Miller's, one legal expert—Eugene Volokh, professor of copyright law at UCLA—suggested the company could be making a mistake. "They could be alienating the customers who are most loyal," he was quoted in the *Los Angeles Times* article. "Of course, Mattel knows its business better than I do, so I'm hesitant to say they are screwing up." But collectors were not hesitant at all. "Mattel has taken action after action that is hostile to our group," according to one collector. "They are stealing our hobby. We want our hobby back."

Rogue Web Sites

In the broadest sense, "rogue" Web sites (a term coined by New York public relations agency head Don Middleberg) are unofficial sites that address a company, a product, or other entity that is owned by another group. Rogue sites break down essentially into two categories: those that merely appropriate intellectual property (such as sites established by fans of a television show or movie), and those that attack something.

Both categories of rogue sites have generated concern among companies that make major investments in establishing brand images, only to see them affected by a site that an individual with an agenda can build in an afternoon.

Fan Sites

The sites built by fans and enthusiasts present organizations with a troubling conundrum. These sites are the online equivalent of fan clubs and represent a new form of free publicity. A search of the Yahoo! online directory revealed more than one hundred sites that fans have constructed dedicated to *The Simpsons* television show, with names like "100% Unofficial Simpsons Site," "Brian's Tribute to the Simpsons," "Homer Land," and "The Simpsons Simp-A-Rama." There are approximately 860 *X-Files* sites, over 1,270 *Star Wars* sites, and some 1,760 *Star Trek* sites.

While these sites are reflections of enthusiasm for the shows and films, they also generally incorporate trademarked and copyrighted images and even sound and film clips. As a result, the Fox Network, Paramount Studios, and LucasFilms have been among the most aggressive at trying to shut the sites down, sending cease-and-desist letters from attorneys to the site owners, threatening them with legal action unless they remove the sites they so lovingly built. Mattel has taken similar action against builders of Barbie fan sites, claiming it needs to protect the trademark it has so carefully nurtured. There is a legitimate reason to protect these trademarks and copyrights. Under the law, a company that does *not* enforce its trademark for a long enough period of time can lose those rights altogether.

The risk involved in taking such action goes beyond alienating a core base of customer support. Not only will disenchanted fans turn against the companies seeking to shut them down—they will do so online, where their rants can be read by countless other fans, coloring their perception of the company as well. These online discussions can run the gamut from disparaging ill treatment of loyal fans to claims of outright censorship. Fans of *The Simpsons* have worked out what they believe is a way to post their sites while remaining anonymous, as this post to a Usenet newsgroup suggests:

```
If you go to http://www.myownemail.com they will give a
forwarding address so you can list an address and Fox will
```

```
never actually know what your real address is!! They have
the @the-simpsons.com ending to so your address looks
cool!! (It's free.)
```

Depending on the general popularity of the subject, forcing the removal of fan-oriented sites could be enough work to keep a full-scale law firm busy for years; for each site removed, another two or three could spring up overnight. (In just two months following the release of the blockbuster film *Titanic,* more than twenty fan-developed Web sites were introduced to the Internet, according to a Yahoo! search.)

Guidelines for Dealing With Fan Sites

If your organization owns the trademark or copyright for an entity that is likely to encourage the creation of fan sites, avoid a "scorched-earth" policy that treats all sites the same. Instead, evaluate each site. Do *nothing* if the site does not:

- Use copyrighted materials.
- Misrepresent the entity.
- Potentially damage the company's ability to earn profit from the entity.

Except for the use of copyrighted materials, the situations listed above do not necessarily represent any violations of trademark or copyright law. Except for instances of copyright violation, assess the site to determine the degree to which it could damage your company's investment. Only if it meets threshold criteria you establish should you proceed to take other action. Resist the temptation to send letters immediately threatening legal action. Ultimately, those threats can do your brand more harm than good. Try the following steps instead:

1. If a certain type of site seems to be gaining momentum, try to co-opt the effort and make it part of the company's official approach to branding the entity. Fan fiction, for example, has been a part of *Star Trek* fandom for over thirty years. Since it would be impossible to stop the practice, the owner of the trademark can turn the fan fiction to its advantage, publishing the best efforts, holding contests, and promoting the careers of promising talent. In this way, the company does not lose

its hold on its brand but rather brings the rogue efforts into the official fold.

2. Develop an official site from which fans can extract authorized images for use on fan-oriented sites. Use the official site to list acceptable uses of trademarks and copyrights and to explain why the company pursues efforts against unacceptable uses. Provide access to company authorities for questions. These fans are your best customers; they provide public relations that you cannot buy. Rather than alienate them, work with them so their efforts satisfy their desires to promote their favorite entity while also meeting your need to protect the way your brand is presented to the public.

3. Use e-mail to contact individuals who built sites in order to lead them to the official site and to explain what your organization objects to about their efforts. Make it clear that you do not wish to inhibit the free expression of ideas but that you wish to ensure that the brand remains as appealing for others as it did for the fans who built Web sites dedicated to it. Give your phone number or e-mail address (or that of the appropriate company representative) so the fans can discuss specific issues with the organization.

4. If these steps do not lead fans to revise their sites, send e-mail that expresses regret that these individuals are putting the company in the position of having to take less agreeable action.

5. Resort to legal action only if the site threatens the brand and the owner of the site is completely intractable.

Attack Sites

Attack sites present companies with a different type of dilemma. The whole point of such sites is to turn the general public against a company or its brand based on an individual's disenchantment. Such sites are much quicker to gain notoriety than fan sites. They can be built by disgruntled customers (such as the Flaming Ford site mentioned earlier) or by former employees.

Many companies approach rogue attack sites by engaging attorneys. This can be effective in removing the site, since few of the "little guys" who establish sites can afford the fees associated with fending off a legal attack funded by a corporate entity. However, companies need to be aware that often it is only the money that produces the desired results: The force of the law itself is questionable. Companies cannot win a case in court simply because somebody has made derogatory comments about them; the First Amendment guarantee of free speech protects such comments. Instead, the law requires a company to prove it has suffered damages. It can be difficult to make the case that the company has suffered damages specifically as a result of an attack Web site, considering that companies are still struggling to figure out how to measure the effectiveness of their *own* Web sites!

Further, sending lawyers after purveyors of attack Web sites can serve to add fuel to the fire. Somebody who already has enough strength of conviction to take his anger to the World Wide Web would not hesitate to respond to a legal challenge. For instance, when the Internet service provider that hosts the "Distorted Barbie" site forwarded a threatening letter from Mattel to the site owner, the owner added a new page to the site rather than remove it. The page begins:

> Two days ago I received an e-mail from my Internet Provider requesting that I remove this Web page from the Internet. They explained that a lawyer from Mattel had claimed that *The Distorted Barbie* violates Mattel's copyright on Barbie.

The page includes a graphic reproduction of the actual letter from Mattel, an excerpt from a *Los Angeles Times* article about Mattel's efforts to protect Barbie, excerpts from other materials that support the author's position, and the following statement:

> I do not mean to imply that there are any easy answers here. As an artist, I appreciate and respect copyright laws. What I am suggesting is that an image, when it becomes ubiquitous within a culture, ceases to be simply property. It enters into and becomes part of an ongoing cultural conversation. And the Web is a medium that calls attention to—and gives concrete form to—this conversation.

As people read the editorial opinion of the page's author, they may decide to support his point of view and develop their own sites. The effort to remove his page through legal strong-arm tactics will have backfired, even if the company ultimately wins its effort in court to have the site taken down. Another site that attacks Mattel's approach to protecting the Barbie property features quotes from Mattel executives who admit that Barbie has been marketed as a person and not a doll. How damaging would it be to the company's efforts to protect its trademark if a court determines that Barbie has, indeed, entered the realm of popular culture, open to any artistic or editorial interpretation that anybody can dream up? Finally, how much more damage is done to a company's reputation when it is branded, among a segment of the product-buying population, as an opponent of free speech?

There are, to be sure, better and more effective approaches to attack Web sites than sending the legal dogs after the offender.

Guidelines for Dealing With Attack Sites: The Unhappy Customer

Many attack sites are the product of an existing relationship gone sour between the site author and the target of the attack. One insurance company, for example, was the focus of an attack site built by an individual whose claim was denied. In these cases, the customer often has tried a number of other avenues before resorting to the construction of an attack site. Building the site is a last resort, a means by which the customer can vent frustration and anger. More often than not, the source of the original dispute is a misunderstanding. Therefore, a site that appears to have been built because of a customer grievance can usually be addressed by solving the original problem.

Again, taking the legal approach does not always result in satisfactory publicity for the company, even if it results in the elimination of the site. By way of example, look at the case of a customer upset that his car, under warranty, was not repaired. He received no satisfaction from the manufacturer or the dealer and vented his frustration on a Web page. As a result, the dealer nullified his warranty and threatened him with a libel suit. The customer wrote to the *alt.consumer. experiences* Usenet newsgroup seeking help. In addition to presenting the situation in a new venue, he obtained advice about how to proceed from some very knowledgeable newsgroup participants—advice that covered everything from ignoring the threat because the suit was unwinnable to filing a class action lawsuit of his own. This is certainly not going to improve the public perception of the dealer that sought only to remove the negative site in the first place!

The best approach is to send an e-mail to the site author. The following templates can serve as models for constructing your e-mail to the author of an attack site borne of a bad experience with your company.

Template: E-Mail to Attack Site Author When the Site Focuses on a Case of Perceived Mistreatment

Dear *Name*:

I was recently directed to the World Wide Web site you have built and was quite distressed to learn of your grievance with our company. The circumstances you cite contradict the core values of our organization and the approach we insist our representatives take with customers.

I hope you will give me the opportunity to rectify the situation. Please call me at *phone number* so I can get the details of your situation and take action to make sure we appropriately and adequately address your concerns and rectify any misunderstandings for which we may have been responsible.

Company Name certainly respects your right to use the World Wide Web—and any other legal means—to express your feelings. However, we feel it would benefit both of us if we can achieve our ultimate goal of meeting your needs and returning you to our community of satisfied customers. I am looking forward to hearing from you.

Template: E-Mail to Attack Site Author When the Author Is Not Satisfied With a Company Decision

Dear *Name*:

I was recently directed to the World Wide Web site you have built and was quite distressed to see that you have chosen to take your dispute with our organization public. I have researched the case your site addresses and believe we can come to an amicable understanding if we have the opportunity to speak with each other directly. Please call me at *phone number* so we can discuss the situation. If the information you present in the course of our discussion warrants it, I will see to it that your case is reviewed.

Our goal always is to serve the interests of our customers and to adhere to the guidelines and rules by which our business is governed. I believe a candid conversation between us can resolve any differences we may have.

I am sincerely looking forward to hearing from you.

Guidelines for Dealing With Attack Sites: Activist Groups

Any group opposed to your company's activities can take its complaints directly to the public by establishing a Web site. Those sites can simply protest your activities, or they can call readers to actions ranging from letter-writing and telephone campaigns to product boycotts.

In general, companies that find themselves in such straits have not undertaken two-way, symmetrical communications to begin with. The Web site is a symptom of a larger issue that needs to be addressed through the proactive, ethical practice of public relations techniques. Using legal tactics to remove a Web site will not suspend the group's activities or cool its members' desire to have your company stop the behavior the group finds offensive. It would be far more effective to move beyond the realm of the Internet and engage in a negotiation-based communications effort that results in victory for both the activist group and your company, in the end turning the group into an ally.

Sound farfetched? Edelman Public Relations pulled off just such a victory on behalf of its client, StarKist Seafood Company (owned by H. J. Heinz).

Case Study: Star-Kist

Star-Kist—the world's largest tuna canner—was among the tuna companies targeted by environmentalists because of the practices of tuna fishermen that resulted in the inadvertent death of dolphins. Environmentalist publicity had increased public awareness of the needless suffering of the dolphins, and a boycott loomed. Consumer opposition to the incidental dolphin catch soared, although research left it uncertain how the tuna-buying public would respond to price increases associated with changes in fishing practices. Star-Kist also would face potential opposition from fishing fleets to any change in policy.

The company finally agreed with Edelman Public Relations that it should be the first tuna-canning company to announce a dolphin-safe policy—that it would buy tuna only from fishermen who adhered to standards that minimized the risk to dolphins. Edelman and Star-Kist met with representatives of key environmental groups, as well as government leaders, before making the announcement. The actual press conference featured not only Star-Kist but environmental group representatives who lauded the company's announcement.

Edelman claims the resulting publicity generated nearly a billion impressions in a one-week period. Sales increased proportionate to the outpouring of customer support. The company was able to leverage its leadership on the issue through a variety of efforts, including the development of an in-school educational program. According to Edelman sources, the two-way, symmetrical approach "helped Star-Kist turn a controversial issue threatening sales and image into a highly positive demonstration of corporate responsibility and leadership that led to improved business and overwhelming customer support."

Of course, not every negotiation results in a complete reversal of a company's position on an issue. However, you usually *can* achieve positive results through direct negotiations with the activist public that is attacking your company.

Consider the case of the Rainforest Action Network (RAN), an activist group that had initiated a boycott against two U.S. companies in the Mitsubishi group. The boycott ended in early 1998 following negotiations between RAN and the groups, which resulted in an agreement to help protect the rain forest. The negotiations went on for five years, beginning three years after RAN targeted Mitsubishi with protests over the company's environmental practices. RAN used its Web site (at www.ran.org) as a forum for the protest, as well as a platform for announcing the agreement. Both sides lauded the agreement.

Any activist group that believes its concerns are being addressed in good faith will not take a grievance to the Web (or to any other public communications vehicle). Those that already exist on the Web will be subject to removal at best and revision at the least.

Guidelines for Dealing With Attack Sites: Cases of Mistakes and Misunderstandings

Some activist attack sites find their way onto the Web as a result of misinformation or misunderstandings. Shortly after the inaccurate Usenet post about designer Tommy Hilfiger (*see Chapter 5*), several sites promoting a boycott of Hilfiger products appeared on the Web. In these cases, it would be a simple matter to contact the site owners directly and inform them of the truth, resulting in the removal of the offensive sites.

Other Rogue Sites

Not every site fits neatly into one of the categories described in this section. What do you do about the owners of sites who are not interested in talking or negotiating?

1. *Ignore it.* In the case of the Disneyland site, it's not likely the site is costing the company much business. Ignoring the site sends a message that the charges have no merit and are not worth the company's time and effort.

2. *Address the issues.* Use the company's own Web site to put a positive face on the topics with which the attack site takes issue. If the attack site disparages the quality of a company's merchandise, make information about the high quality of merchandise a prominent feature of your site.

3. *Take legal action.* But do so only as a last resort.

Then there's the case of overenthusiastic employees, licensees, franchisees, or others with a relationship to your company who build sites. At one company, an employee's personal Web site had two prominent features: (1) his dedication to his job, featuring pictures of himself and his colleagues at the workplace, and (2) his fondness for sadomasochistic sexual behavior. While many might find the site offensive, it *is* protected speech. Still, it does not help the company to have its brand associated with behavior that a significant part of the consumer public would find offensive. In another instance, an independently owned gas station owner had developed a site that addressed the policies of the company whose name the station bore. There was nothing untoward about the remarks, other than the fact that they were not official and did not accurately represent the brand image the company had spent considerable time and effort crafting.

In these cases, the solution is simple: Advise the individual who built the site of the problems it could pose for the company. In the case of the employee, asking that either the company information or the sexually explicit material be removed should be enough. (If not, it becomes a matter for human resources to address as a violation of the employer-employee agreement.) In the case of the gas station owner, the company should provide him with wording that *does* conform to the branding of the company's image.

General Guidelines for Dealing With Rogue Web Sites

Regardless of the type of rogue site you encounter—a fan site, attack site, or other type—consider the following alternatives to risking the fallout that could result from sending legal threats:

1. Assess the potential damage of the site as a means of measuring your response.

2. Contact the author of the site to determine the core reasons he is attacking your organization.

3. Offer to find a way to resolve the differences.

4. Make sure your company Web site offers your point of view on any issues of substance addressed on the rogue site.

5. Provide material the site author can use that more accurately reflects your company's position or activities.

6. Use legal muscle *only* after all other avenues have been exhausted. (That way, you can always say that the organization tried to reason with the site author before resorting to more draconian means.) Make absolutely sure that the site violates a law that can be upheld in

court. Do not use the threat of a lawsuit as a means of getting somebody to back down who is not violating the law but cannot afford to fight against the resources your organization brings to bear.

Discussion Forum Attacks

An electric utility manager bought a product that never worked right. When he contacted the customer service department of the company that made the item, he was put into voice-prompt hell and ultimately disconnected three times. After the third time, he took his frustration to a consumer newsgroup on Usenet (not unlike the consumer discussed above who took his complaint about his vehicle warranty to a newsgroup). Later that day, the manager found an e-mail message in his in-box from the company's vice-president of customer relations. The message informed him that his experience was an aberration, a complete contradiction of the company's commitment to customer service. The vice-president couldn't understand what happened but was determined to get to the bottom of it. He included his work *and* home phone number and urged the disgruntled consumer to call him.

As it turned out, the problem was traced to a snafu in the company's phone system that was corrected in a matter of hours. The defective product was replaced, and the consumer received profuse apologies. He returned to the newsgroup, where he posted a retraction of his earlier message and applauded the company's sincere, dedicated, one-to-one customer relations effort. That kind of publicity is invaluable.

Of course, the vice-president in question did not just chance to visit the newsgroup, see the article, and decide on his own to reply. It was instead part of an orchestrated effort to ensure that the company is not misrepresented or damaged by what people say in online discussions. Your company can develop a plan as well that protects its image and ensures that accurate information is presented in the global discussion of Usenet newsgroups.

What You Can Do

Assuming you are using the monitoring techniques discussed in Chapter 5, you know when somebody has posted an article to a discussion group that warrants your attention. At that point, use the following sequence of activities to determine if, and how, to respond:

Step 1. Assess the Potential Damage the Post Can Cause

During a demonstration of DejaNews as a tool for finding newsgroup references to a company, an audience member asked if her company—a major airline—appeared anywhere in the articles available for searching. I entered her company's name and found several messages dealing with the airline, including one that called for a boycott. She was about to dash for the phone when a quick read of the article revealed there was no cause for alarm. The author was recently divorced, and his ex-wife had called the airline with instructions to transfer his frequent-flier miles to her account. His anger was the reason he was calling for a boycott. The few responses the article generated said basically, "You think you can start a boycott of one of the biggest business-travel airlines over this? Get a life!"

Clearly, this article did not warrant any kind of response—the airline's interests were best served by simply ignoring it. You should evaluate each message about your company on the basis of:

- Its content
- The number of responses the article generates
- The tone of the responses

Step 2. Determine to Whom You Should Respond

If an article warrants a reply, determine how to reply—either to the individual who submitted the article or to the newsgroup itself. Often individual contact can result in a swift resolution to the situation, leading to a converted customer who sings your praises instead of damning your inadequacies. If the reference to your organization has become a general topic of discussion in a newsgroup, it may be more appropriate to make your statement to the entire group.

Tip: Keep Your Contact Virtual
Never make direct contact with an individual who has posted something to a discussion group or mailing list. (For instance, don't find the individual's phone number and

---

> make contact by telephone.) Someone who posts articles to discussion groups online perceives herself as participating in a virtual environment and expects all subsequent communications to come by the same means. Making voice contact can create a sense of disconnect that can alienate the individual, making it much more difficult to engage her than if you keep the discussion where it started—in cyberspace.

Step 3. Read the FAQs and Lurk Before Posting

Find the FAQs (Frequently Asked Questions) associated with the newsgroup before you say anything you may later regret. The FAQs contain all the pertinent information about a newsgroup, including the group's charter and all of the commonly asked questions that already have been addressed in discussions that have gone before.*

Even after you have read the FAQs you should lurk for a while before submitting your own article. Lurking (reading posts in a newsgroup without participating) gives you the opportunity to make an assessment of the newsgroup. Is it a valid discussion area, or is it mostly teenagers sounding off? How seriously does anybody take anything posted here? How do people react to responses that disagree with what they have said?

Step 4. Don't Preach—Participate!

Newsgroups are virtual communities. They were well established before your company was mentioned and will continue to exist after the furor over the reference to your company has faded from memory. Members of the community expect new contributors to behave like other members of the community. If you storm into a newsgroup like some sort of authority figure, you earn the community's disrespect and possibly do more harm than good, even if you do manage to set the record straight.

Using a fictitious situation, let's say a hospital patient has been discharged after only twenty-four hours because (he says) his insurance company would not authorize a longer stay. The early discharge led to

---

*You can find a list of Usenet newsgroup FAQs on the World Wide Web at *www. cis.ohio-state.edu/hypertext/faq/usenet/*.

complications. The patient posts a Usenet article about his situation, and it has led to a continuing discussion of the company's practices, none of them charitable. Here are two different online responses the company could take.

Response 1

> I'm a representative of Acme Insurance Company, and
> your contention that we don't care about the health of the
> people we insure is absurd. Your health is our primary
> concern. If you were discharged after twenty-four hours,
> it is because the considered opinion of our on-staff
> medical experts determined that additional hospital time
> was unnecessary and would be wasteful. It is not uncommon
> for complications to follow a hospital stay regardless of
> the length of the stay. To blame your insurance company for
> your unfortunate turn of ill health is to shift the blame
> away from the real reasons your health deteriorated, which
> may be less pleasant to face.

Response 2

> I have been reading the posts that have been contributed
> to this group with some distress. I joined this group
> because I work for an HMO—the one everybody's discussing,
> in fact. Because I work here at Acme Insurance, I know that
> our first and greatest concern is for the patient, above all
> else, including profits. You can imagine how I felt when I
> read about your experience. I'd like to do something about
> it. If I can get more information about the specifics of the
> case—what hospital you were in, the dates, etc.—I can
> follow up and find out exactly what happened. If anybody
> else in the group has had similar experiences, I'd like to
> look into those as well. I can report back what I find and
> let you know what kind of action the organization is willing
> to take.

Which of these two responses is most likely to result in constructive discussion that ultimately could influence the online audience to change its perception of the company? Of course, in the second response, the company must in fact be willing to look into the allegations and take action, if appropriate (which is consistent with a public relations philosophy that embraces engagement of the audience and negotiation to achieve win-win results).

Measurement

Use the principles of monitoring to assess the impact of online activism to your organization. You can assess the savings you have produced by communicating directly with these activists or by ensuring that your company's answer to criticism is readily available and easily found. Undertaking this kind of monitoring generally allows you to forestall crises. A solid method of measuring the impact of communication is to determine the money the organization did *not* spend on a crisis that was prevented. Even as the Internet presents you with the challenge of an environment with few rules (like the Old West), it also affords you the opportunity to uncover crises before they emerge and save the company the cost of dealing with the crises after they become fodder for traditional media.

Conclusion

The Internet has opened the door to a new form of communication. As the many-to-many model predicts, individuals and organizations now have the power of the press at their fingertips—all it takes is a computer, a $10-a-month Internet account, and a little time. Companies need to understand how to address the material these individuals and groups can present in order to avoid the damage that can be done by responding as though the old one-to-many model still was dominant. Diplomacy can serve your cause far better than legal action.

11

Crisis Communication

Crisis management has always been a critical activity in organizations—one that is all too often ignored. The Internet has exacerbated the need for crisis planning. Thanks to the information age and the many-to-many communications model, crises can emerge from nowhere and turn into all-consuming emergencies with unprecedented speed.

In Chapter 5, we looked at the damage done to Lexis-Nexis as a result of an unfounded rumor that spread through the Internet. In the same chapter we also saw how Mrs. Fields Cookies was able to head off a similar crisis by responding quickly through Internet channels. On the other hand, many companies with a strong Internet presence have failed to use their Web sites and other online resources to address crises, either those born on the Net or those that had their genesis elsewhere.

When TWA Flight 800 crashed in 1996, the TWA Web site's home page was almost immediately removed and replaced with a terse statement that verified the crash but noted that TWA had no additional information. The statement promised more information as soon as it became available. That page did not change for weeks.

It is incumbent upon organizations to have plans for addressing crises, and now the Internet must be integrated into those plans. This chapter explores the various kinds of crises that can affect a company, how the Internet plays into those crises, and how institutions can manage those crises. Before we jump into the Internet angle, however, it is important to review some fundamentals of crisis communication.

Fundamentals of Crisis Communication

James E. Grunig, principal author of the academic study *Excellence in Public Relations and Communication Management,* defines a crisis this way:

> When conflict occurs, publics "make an issue" out of the problem. Organizations use the process of issues management to anticipate issues and resolve conflict before the public makes it an issue. Organizations that wait for issues to occur before managing their communication with strategic publics usually have crises on their hands and have to resort to short-term crisis communication.

During a crisis, companies and their executives are put into the position of making critical decisions under circumstances characterized by:

- Intense pressure
- High stress
- Heightened external scrutiny
- Dramatically compressed time frames
- Confusion about information

There are two basic kinds of crises: (1) the meteor crisis, and (2) the predator crisis.

1. *Meteor crisis.* Something terrible, unanticipated, random, and/ or senseless occurs. The organization is often a victim in this type of crisis, but not always. The confidence of the customer and other publics is at risk, and the organization's ability to respond well determines its guilt or innocence in the public eye and can reaffirm the organization's identity.

2. *Predator crisis.* Such a crisis occurs when someone has an ax to grind. An ex-employee airs his dirty laundry in public, a simmering dispute between the company and another constituency goes public, a company is guilty of something, or new regulations catch an organiza-

tion unaware. The organization is rarely a victim in a predator crisis, although it can happen. Regardless, the company stands to suffer loss of reputation, credibility, or other tangible and intangible assets as a result of the crisis. An effective response to a predator crisis can stop further damage, but the organization is never vindicated through communication alone.

Crisis Communication Objectives

Either kind of crisis tests a company's strengths and exposes its weaknesses. Ultimately, a company's reputation—with its shareholders, employees, customers, suppliers, the media, the communities in which it operates, and the agencies with which it deals—is at stake.

A company's objectives during a crisis should be no different than its ongoing, day-to-day objectives. However, without a plan—and faced with pressure, stress, external scrutiny, and shortened time frames—companies often lose sight of these objectives. Thus, it is important to institutionalize the objectives as paramount during a crisis:

- Present and maintain a positive and accurate perception of the company.
- Present timely, accurate, up-to-date information.
- Remain accessible to the media and other constituencies.
- Gather and monitor information disseminated through media channels related to the crisis in order to catch and correct misinformation early.
- Maintain investor, employee, customer, governmental, and community support.

Why Crises Escalate

Companies experiencing a crisis go through seven stages, characterized by:

1. Surprise
2. Actions based on insufficient or incorrect information
3. Loss of control
4. Intense scrutiny of the organization from outside publics
5. The beginnings of a siege mentality
6. Panic

7. Short-term focus (instead of keeping organizational objectives in sight)

The first hours of the crisis and the first seven days are the most critical times. These stages have led to a perception that it is impossible for a company to win a public debate once a crisis has erupted. Indeed, it is the nature of crises that a rational approach may be ineffective. Here are some of the issues companies face in a crisis that keep a rational, logical approach from being effective, and what companies can do to counteract the issues:

• *Publics attach little credibility to business advocates during a crisis.* Issues management efforts should be crafted to create substantial credibility among key publics. In addition, working to convey compassion, concern, and control over a crisis situation lends credibility where a rational debate will not.

• *The public is risk-averse.* That is, the public at large almost always takes the position in a crisis that represents the least risk. Again, conveying control—or showing the company is working to eliminate or reduce any risk—helps win over publics.

• *The media does not always provide a level playing field.* The press is often likely to have a bias toward conflict, which sells newspapers and attracts viewers. Establishing solid, mutually beneficial relationships with reporters and editors *before* any crises erupt helps maintain level communications *during* a crisis. Maintaining control over the symbols relevant to each particular crisis instead of engaging in rational debate—which perpetuates the conflict—also enhances an organization's image with the media.

• *Advocacy groups exploit brewing conflicts for their own purposes.* Identifying these groups and their issues, and engaging in two-way symmetrical communication with them to arrive at mutually beneficial resolutions *before* a crisis erupts, prevents advocacy groups from exploiting any conflicts. Should a crisis erupt despite efforts to communicate proactively, symbols again are fundamental tools. Showing compassion, concern, and control helps defuse otherwise explosive crisis situations.

• *Once a situation has escalated to a crisis stage, bias (not logic) is at issue.* Thus, logical responses to emotional issues have little impact. An institution's response should be to the perceived emotional concerns. That is, appropriate concern, compassion, and control over the situation should be employed instead of argumentative, rational debate.

  • *A company engaging in debate during a crisis—even if its point of view is logical or rational—is viewed as defensive and guilty.* Debating and arguing makes things worse, even when you're right. Companies should avoid engaging in any debate and instead address the perceptions of their publics.

Symbols in a Crisis

Symbols are a company's most powerful tool during a crisis. Usually, a crisis is characterized by symbols anyway: The chemical leak at a Union Carbide plant in Bhopal, India, had corpses littering the streets. The oil spill from the *Exxon Valdez* had dead, oil-slicked birds floating in Alaska's Prince William Sound. The space shuttle *Challenger* explosion had that one haunting image of the craft exploding at the end of its vapor trail. The Los Angeles Police Department will be long associated with videotaped images of Rodney King being beaten with batons. Even the Tylenol tampering case left us with a tainted capsule as the symbol of that particular crisis. Thus, since these images are so potent, how a company *acts* during a crisis is more important than what it *says*. In fact, a company cannot "manage" a crisis at all. It can, however, manage the perceptions it creates. Thus, a company's values count during a crisis. A crisis offers an organization the opportunity to reaffirm its values and reinforce a positive public perception.

The Role of the Internet in a Crisis

Companies that planned for crises in the days before the Internet were able to take certain things for granted, since all of the industrial-era models of communication applied. The media broadcast images— *symbols*—into the homes of other strategic publics. Newspapers carried details of the crisis. Individuals responded by writing letters to the editor, by talking about the crisis around the watercooler, and—in extreme cases—by banding together and taking tangible action. Exxon's handling of the *Valdez* oil spill prompted a boycott of Exxon gasoline and a movement to return Exxon credit cards. When Dow Chemical mishandled the publicity surrounding the severe health problems reportedly caused by its silicone breast implants, attorneys filed class action lawsuits. The ultimate fallout from most crises, though, is not felt until well after the immediate problem has passed. The long-term fallout takes the form of diminished public confidence, fear that the company's stock will not maintain its value, and the sullied reputation of a company unable to live up to the values it had presented.

None of these implications have diminished in the wake of the Internet's popularity. In fact, the Internet only accelerates them, enabling publics to talk among themselves. Worse, activist groups can seek kindred spirits in a matter of hours: People who share a common sense of outrage can find one another online and establish an activist group in a remarkably short time frame. Further, the Internet's publishing features allow anybody with an opinion, an ax to grind, an agenda, or a point of view to publicize her beliefs as eloquently and elegantly as she can using the tools of the World Wide Web, discussion forums, and e-mail.

The Internet's role in crises can be viewed many different ways. For example, there are the ways the Internet plays into meteor and predator crises. There are crises that got started on the Net and those that started elsewhere but became a subject for discussion and publication online. Most important, there are the things you should plan to do in advance to be prepared for any crisis.

The World Wide Web and Usenet newsgroups have become the most important place people turn for updated information and conversation about crises that unexpectedly and suddenly befall organizations, governments, and communities. Even before the Web achieved its current level of popularity, disasters and emergencies found their way onto custom-built Web pages. Some examples include:

- The assassination of Israeli Prime Minister Yitzhak Rabin, which prompted the immediate creation of hundreds of Web sites dedicated to his memory and the assassination itself.
- The bombing of the federal building in Oklahoma City, which prompted a local college professor to create a site that included a crude map of the building. That map became the basis of early diagrams used by network news broadcasters.
- The devastating 1995 earthquake in Kobe, Japan, which led

many Web developers to create pages that offered casualty lists, organizations to which charitable donations could be made, and photos of the destruction.

More recently, the Web has become a cultural tool for expressing feelings, opinions, and attitudes about any news item that might be important to us. Mother Theresa motivated hundreds to build memorial sites. Princess Diana's death in 1997 carried the memorial notion to a new level. The Web is a means for people to express and share their grief.

People are equally likely to hurry to the Web to get the latest information. They flock to news sites—those hosted by CNN, MSNBC, and others—because the news is updated there more frequently than on television. The audience can login any time to see what's new without waiting for the top of the news on TV. But they also turn to the sites of the institutions involved in the crisis.

Following the crash of TWA Flight 800, the people responsible for Boeing's Web site were baffled by the sudden high volume of visits to the their site. They never connected the surge in visits to public demand for information about 747 safety records and company statements about the crash. (Boeing learned its lesson well. When a 737 crashed in Colombia, the company had information on its home page within minutes of learning about the accident.)

> *If your company has a site on the Web, people will come to see what you have to say when you are facing a crisis.*

If any additional evidence is needed about the public's appetite for online crisis-related information, look no further than the news reports of increased Internet activity following the accusations of immoral conduct by President Bill Clinton involving White House intern Monica Lewinsky. Commentator Michael Kinsley noted that the Clinton sex scandal did for the Internet what the Gulf War did for CNN and John Kennedy's assassination for network television. He added that traditional news media "head to the Web at the first sign of distant smoke." According to a *Los Angeles Times* article: "News junkies, predictably, have become heavy [Internet] users, clicking on from their computers to scan Web sites set up by traditional news outlets, to trade opinions and gossip within chat groups and to visit the home pages of a new genre of journalists operating within cyberspace."

During the early stages of the Clinton crisis, MSNBC reported a peak of 830,000 individual visitors to its Web site, up from normal traffic of about 300,000 a day. The *New York Times* reported a 20 to 30 percent jump in visitors to its site, serving up about 2.5 million pages a day. CNN's Web site drew 12.8 million visits the day Clinton first denied having sexual relations with Lewinsky.

No matter what the nature of your crisis or its evolution, you need to know how to identify what people are saying and how to address it in order to achieve the crisis management objectives outlined at the beginning of the chapter.

Meteor Crises

Meteor crises, as the name implies, fall from the sky. They appear from nowhere, and there is little a company can do to plan for them. A disgruntled employee opens fire on colleagues, killing several in the workplace. A refinery explodes, spreading dangerous chemicals over a vast area.

Each of the crisis communication priorities to which companies should adhere applies in a meteor crisis. The following list offers specific ways to address a meteor crisis using online media:

• *Present and maintain a positive and accurate perception of the company.* Let audiences know what you are doing in terms of the issues that affect them. Investors want to know how you are going to protect your share value. Communities want to know what you will do to contain the impact of the crisis on them. Use your online resources to convey compassion or sympathy for victims (if any) and to explain the steps you are taking to keep such an event from happening in the future.

• *Present timely, accurate, up-to-date information.* Your Web page should not be stagnant. Use it to keep the latest details front and center.

• *Remain accessible to the media and other constituencies.* Keeping your media relations site updated can make it easier for reporters to get the information they need. It also helps you scale back the number of phone calls you can expect from the media during a crisis. Every reporter who finds information online means one less phone call, increasing your accessibility to those reporters who do need to speak to you in person.

• *Gather and monitor information disseminated through media channels related to the crisis in order to catch and correct misinformation early.* This is doubly important in cyberspace, where there are far more channels of misinformation. Watch for rogue Web pages and newsgroup-based rumors and attacks that could be harmful.

• *Maintain investor, employee, customer, governmental, and community support.* Use your online tools to solicit feedback and maintain open communications channels that do not need to occur in real time.

Let's look at the way two companies managed their online activities during meteor crises.

Case Study: Warner-Lambert

Warner-Lambert is a multinational diversified pharmaceutical and consumer products company that owns, among other things, the drugmaker Parke-Davis. The company used its home page on the World Wide Web to state its case and reinforce the value of its product after one of its drugs was pulled off the market by another drug marketer in another part of the world.

The crisis erupted over the Thanksgiving 1997 weekend, when Britain's Glaxo Wellcome PLC announced it was suspending sales of the diabetes drug troglitazone, marketed in the United States by Warner-Lambert as Rezulin. Glaxo said it was taking the step based on a review of 150 cases of liver disease that seemed to be associated with the drug. Glaxo also was withdrawing its applications for approval of the drug under the European Community mutual recognition processes.

Sandra Levine, vice-president of corporate and financial communications at Warner-Lambert, learned about Glaxo's planned announcement while she was at home preparing for the holiday. "I got a call from the head of public affairs, who was in contact with the CEO," she recalls, noting that the Warner-Lambert management team is tightly knit. Over the course of the weekend, the team worked to hash out the company's key message points, and developed a plan to communicate, translating those points to the company's colleagues (what they call their employees) and the investment community, the media, and other critical audiences.

The Internet, Levine says, was part of the planning process from the beginning, though the company doesn't have a specific plan for addressing such crises online. "With all the ways you have to do things and the frequency with which they change, you'd never be able to keep a detailed plan like that up-to-date," she maintains. In addition, a strictly defined set of crisis team players could slow down the response time. "Especially on a holiday weekend, the composition of the team is hampered by whom you can get on the phone and who can come into the office quickly." However, she says, the principles are well understood by the various team members, so the company isn't likely to miss any key crisis communication elements.

One of the people Sandy did reach was Paul Donchevsky, director of financial and corporate communications, who works intimately with the company's Web site. Donchevsky recalls, "We started to talk over the phone about a plan for the Web site." The plan, as it emerged, was to add a bright yellow link to the home page that sported the label "Latest News." Clicking on that link would take visitors to the company's statement on Glaxo's action, along with a copy of the product label. "The label is the bible of the drug," Levine says. "It shows all the elements of what's been approved by the FDA."

The site offered links to external resources, including the Food and Drug Administration "Talk Paper," which reiterated the agency's support for Rezulin, and the American Diabetes Association, which also had issued a statement.

Finally, a feedback button (which is pervasive across the entire Warner-Lambert site) was added to the page. Donchevsky knows that thousands of people availed themselves of the feedback link; that input was automatically routed to the medical affairs department, which handles such inquiries. By the time the special link was removed in mid-January 1998, the crisis page had been visited thousands of times, Donchevsky says.

The Web didn't represent the only use Warner-Lambert made of online technology during the crisis. "We used our existing e-mail communications vehicle, the daily 'Communicator's Network,' " Levine says; the e-mail goes to key contacts at Warner-Lambert's facilities worldwide. "We had our statement out early on December 1, along with a cover letter and the letter that had been delivered to the desks of our headquarters colleagues, along with instructions to reproduce the information and distribute it to colleagues." With more than 42,000 employees around the world, that's a lot of reproduction. The effort succeeded, Levine says, because those colleagues who needed the information the most (notably the field sales staff) had it almost immediately so they could respond to customer questions.

And an audio teleconference was conducted the morning of the crisis for members of the investment community. "We take the technology seriously," Levine says. "It's no longer just a lot of phone work, paperwork, and the occasional fax. You have to take the interactivity of the new networks into account too. Somebody told me it's like being on a party line all of a sudden. You have to realize that anyone out there who hears your message and has a computer can get into the action, can get onto the party line. That's what you have to be prepared to address."

In May 1998, Glaxo Wellcome announced it would seek approval to reintroduce the drug approval process throughout Europe, based on their belief that the drug's benefits outweighed its risks.

Case Study: Odwalla Juices

Odwalla Juices is a San Francisco Bay Area company that recalled its natural apple juice in 1996 when the juice was the source of an *E. coli* bacteria contamination. The bacteria, which affected mostly small children, stirred up the usual discussions on Usenet newsgroups. In a martial-arts newsgroup, one participant noted that he liked to drink Odwalla's juices after a workout and was concerned that his favorite was one of those recalled. In Seattle, where a number of the contamination cases were reported, a woman participating in a Seattle-area newsgroup noted that she had heard a news report about the juices that were recalled and she wished she had written them down: Her family had drunk Odwalla juices for breakfast that morning. In investment newsgroups, discussions focused on the rapidly plummeting price of Odwalla stock; participants wondered if the company would have to begin pasteurizing its products in order to satisfy the public's safety concerns.

To provide answers, Odwalla turned to the World Wide Web. This was not a matter of a company using its existing Web site as a forum to address a crisis. Odwalla *had* no Web site. Within one week of the crisis, however, one was established on the Edelman News Web, a site maintained by Edelman Public Relations as a place to put information about its clients.

"We first used Edelman News Web on behalf of Primatine Mist, as a consumer education vehicle following an incident involving a young person's death in Florida in mid-1995," says Matthew Harrington, general manager of Edelman's San Francisco office. Visiting the News Web home page at *www.enw.com* reveals nothing, but subdirectories are established for each client. Odwalla, for example, was at *www.enw.com/odwalla.*

Figure 11-1 shows Odwalla's makeshift site, established specifically to address its recall crisis. It includes a list of FAQs that provide answers to most questions inquiring members of the public may have had. Figure 11-2 shows Odwalla's simple statement upon the death of an *E. coli* victim. It is candid, honest, and heartfelt—emotions that may not have been conveyed through the filter of the media.

Odwalla's site was clean, simple, and uncluttered. The home page featured a brief message by the company's chairman and links to the company's news releases regarding the recall, a fact sheet, a question-and-answer section, and additional relevant health resources on the Web. The fact sheet presented a company that doesn't practice business as usual. This is a company concerned about the "nourishment of its consumers through the freshest, most nutritious beverages, ecological 'response'-ability, cultivating community and empowerment of the individual."

The press releases sported headlines like this one: "Odwalla expresses ongoing concern for sick, gratitude for public support." Rather than appear defensive, the company opened its statement by expressing "ongoing concern for all those impacted" and stressing "that the company continues to do everything in its power to identify the source of the bacteria." According to the releases, the company was working with the FDA and health departments in several states toward that end, as well as conducting its own tests. Further, "Odwalla has formed an advisory group comprised of experts in food safety, microbiology and regulatory issues, to counsel the company on this complex microbiological issue." The biographies of the group's members were included, lest anybody thought it was just a public relations ploy. Another press release confirmed the FDA *E. coli* finding.

Just about every page of the site referred to the Odwalla 800-number consumers could call for up-to-the-minute information. On no page, however, was there a place for visitors to ask questions or offer feedback through the Web—that was the role of the 800-line.

Perhaps the greatest advantage of opening the Web site was the publicity

Figure 11-1. Odwalla Juices's site established during its recall crisis.

Questions and Answers
Odwalla Product Recall
November 3, 1996

Q: *When was the Odwalla product recall announced and was it voluntary?*
A: Yes. The voluntary recall was announced by Odwalla on Wednesday, October 30, 1996, following notification by the Seattle-King County Department of Public Health in Washington State that several people diagnosed with the *E. coli* O157:H7 bacteria reported that they had consumed Odwalla apple juice.

Q: *Which Odwalla products were recalled and why?*
A: All products containing apple juice have been recalled and as a further precautionary measure, carrot juice, organic carrot juice and vegetable cocktail, all of which are processed on the same line as the apple juice products, have been recalled.

Recalled products and approximate percentages of apple juice content (could contain less apple juice than percentages indicated):

> Apple Juice 100%
> Blackberry Fruitshake 40%
> Mango Tango 30%
> Super Protein 40%
> Strawberry Banana Smoothie 10%
> Raspberry Smoothie 20%
> C-Monster 30%
> Strawberry C Monster 10%
> Mo' Beta 10%
> Femme Vitale 40%
> Superfood 50%
> Serious Ginseng 20%
> Deep in Peach 40%
> Carrot Juice 0%
> Organic Carrot Juice 0%
> Vegetable Cocktail 0%

Q: *Are any of the Odwalla citrus-based juices or the geothermal spring water associated with the E. coli O157:H7 bacteria?*
A: No. All Odwalla citrus-based juices and the geothermal spring water are not affected by the recall and are still being produced and distributed. These products include:

> Orange Juice
> Grapefruit Juice
> Honey Lemonade
> Strawberry Lemonade
> Menage a Tropique
> C Monster Light
> Lemon Juice
> Lime Juice
> Geothermal Spring Water

Q: *Have all recalled products been taken off the shelf?*
A: Yes. Odwalla has confirmed that all recalled products in its distribution system have been removed from store shelves. Consumers who purchased bottles of the recalled products are encouraged to return them to the store where purchased for a full refund.

Q: *What are the symptoms of E. coli O157:H7 bacteria?*
A: Symptoms include diarrhea, abdominal cramps and visible blood in the stool. Usually, little or no fever is present. Anyone who has developed diarrheal illness within two weeks of consuming an Odwalla product containing apple juice may wish to consult a physician. Individuals who have consumed an Odwalla product and have not developed diarrheal illness are not at risk for complication and do not need to seek medical care.

Q: *Is more Odwalla and recall-related information available?*
A: Yes. Odwalla has established a Web site at www.enw.com/odwalla. The company has also opened a hot line to answer consumer questions. The number is 1-800-639-2552.

This section will be updated regularly.

Back

Figure 11-2. Odwalla's Web statement upon the death of an *E. coli* victim.

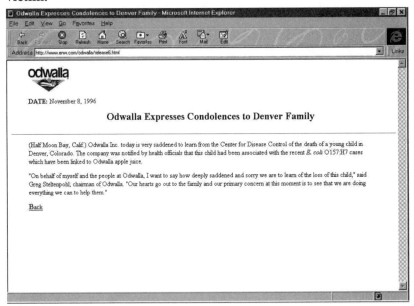

generated by the announcement of the site itself. Newspapers and television and radio stations picked up the story and ran with it, enhancing the perception among the public—notably those who don't use the Web—that the company was making every effort to get its story across. The Associated Press story on the site quoted Odwalla spokesperson Robin Joy, who indicated that an informal survey of discussion groups on the Internet was mostly positive: "I think people recognize that this is a company with strong values and vision, and a commitment to the quality of the product and the community."

The site ultimately gave way to a permanent, marketing-oriented site at *www.odwallazone.com,* but the crisis site stands out as an example of how to present symbols that reinforce a company's values using the Internet. Figures 11-3 and 11-4 show how Odwalla is communicating its health and wellness focus in a post-crisis environment.

Predator Crises

Predator crises erupt *because* an individual or institution has an ax to grind. These crises can be unexpected, as when confidential documents are leaked to the press. Some predator crises, on the other hand, give you plenty of advance warning. You know, for example, that labor negotiations are breaking down and a strike is imminent, that your product causes cancer, or that your hiring practices violate the law. In

Figure 11-3. A page from Odwalla's site as of mid-1998 drawing attention to the company's quality assurance practices.

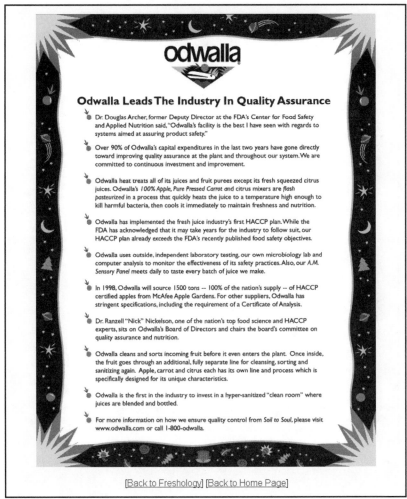

all these cases, somebody is not happy with you. While a meteor crisis is likely to elicit sympathy for your organization, a predator crisis can swiftly cause your publics to begin viewing you with skepticism and distrust.

Texaco experienced a predator crisis when tapes of conversations were made public that allegedly proved racial discrimination practices within the company. Texaco immediately updated its home page on the

Figure 11-4. A list of awards Odwalla has received helping to keep the post-crisis focus positive.

World Wide Web to include links to official statements. The text of the statements was less important than the existence of the links themselves, which established a perception that the company had an answer to the criticism, that it was being open in its communication about the incident, and that it was not afraid of the charges. Figure 11-5 shows the Texaco home page. It initially featured a link to the official press release on the incident, but later added links to statements made to employees, further enhancing the company's credibility. Figure 11-6

Figure 11-5. The Texaco home page, featuring links to a press release and statements made to employees on alleged discrimination practices.

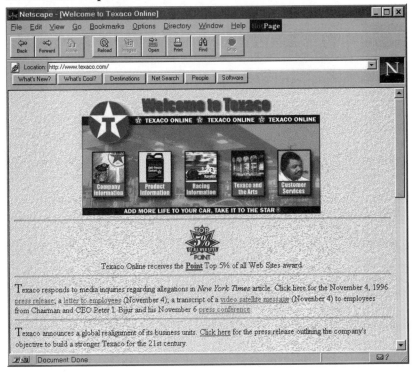

shows the Texaco Web site with a statement from the CEO about the issue. The public thus had access to the same information the media and employees were receiving.

United Parcel Service also used its home page to address a crisis when the Teamsters struck the delivery company in 1997, grinding much of the nation's business to a near halt. A prominent link provided updated information about the status of the strike and alternative delivery methods. The end of the Teamsters strike was followed almost immediately by the threat of a pilot's strike, and the update link was maintained in order to furnish information about the state of negotiations. Figure 11-7 shows the UPS home page, which maintained a link to updated information about the state of negotiations with the pilot's union.

Figure 11-6. The Texaco site with a statement from the CEO.

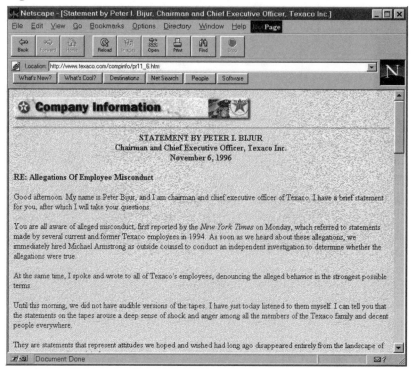

While attorneys may counsel management to say nothing during a predator crisis, the danger of remaining silent online is tremendous. Information, like space, abhors a vacuum. In the absence of authoritative information from your organization, publics use search engines to seek out secondary and tertiary sources—sources that *do* spring up.

Further, crises that emerge online can secure the attention of the media. Many companies—even those with first-class public relations departments—don't even become aware of the Internet until some on-line discussions find their way into the popular media. (The Intel Pentium crisis began as a discussion among mathematicians in a Usenet newsgroup. It wasn't until the discussion—not monitored by Intel— grew so loud that it captured the attention of the press that the company began paying attention to the problem.)

In a predator crisis, the same crisis communication priorities that count in a meteor crisis should be maintained:

Figure 11-7. The UPS home page, with a link to updated information about its negotiations with the union. (Courtesy of United Parcel Service.)

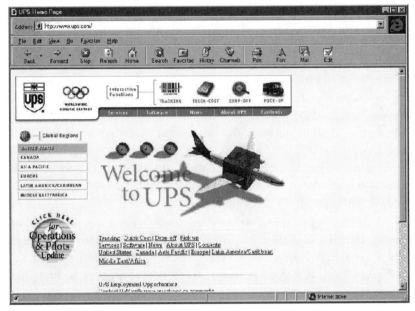

• *Present and maintain a positive and accurate perception of the company.* Be as candid as you can about the facts as you know them. Share the communications you have issued to other audiences, as Texaco shared its employee-oriented messages with its Web audience. Stress the steps you are taking to address the issue (even if your legal eagles do not allow you to admit you did anything wrong). Provide information or links to resources that can help those who may be afflicted with any conditions or circumstances for which you may be responsible. For example, if a strike has crippled your business, provide links to competitors that can satisfy your customers' business needs.

• *Present timely, accurate, up-to-date information.* When do you expect the situation to be resolved? What steps are you taking next? Offer timelines, a chronology of news releases, and other information that keep your audiences updated regarding your efforts. Make sure you keep the material fresh; include the date and time it was last revised.

• *Remain accessible to the media and other constituencies.* Make sure your media contacts know you can be reached via e-mail as well as through traditional means. Send out media advisories letting the press know that you have information available on your media relations site that can answer many of their questions, and that the site will be routinely updated for the run of the crisis. Get the official statements of your key executives online, along with the transcripts of any public interviews and press conferences.

• *Gather and monitor information disseminated through media channels related to the crisis in order to catch and correct misinformation early.* Monitoring what the opposition is saying is critical to an effective online crisis effort. It is, in fact, the *only* way you are able to develop a strategy to address the claims, rumors, misinformation, and inaccuracies that may be swirling around various newsgroups and codified on your opponents' Web pages.

• *Maintain investor, employee, customer, governmental, and community support.* Establish links to all of the relevant information elsewhere on the Web that supports your position. Let each of your key audiences know that your Web site is their best source for accurate, up-to-the-minute information.

Case Study: American Airlines and Allied Pilots Association

Contract negotiations between American Airlines and the Allied Pilots Association (APA) took place behind closed doors, and coverage of the negotiations appeared in traditional media. But the contest for votes, customer loyalty, and public support expanded into cyberspace, where both the company and the union established footholds.

"We kept communications about the negotiations on our home page relatively simple," says Tim Smith, manager of public relations for American, based at Dallas-Fort Worth Airport. "We didn't try to give large, detailed explanations of the issues or address who was right and who was wrong."

That's because the Web site (at *www.aa.com*) was developed primarily as a customer-service tool. Taking the customer-service approach into account, the company kept the home page updated with information about the negotiations that focused on concerns customers might have. "These were answers to the same questions people were asking when they called our 800-number," says Smith—questions about ticket refunds in the event of a strike or the ability to change a reservation to a later date without incurring a fee. In addition, Smith says, "We provided general reassurances to our passengers that we were working on settling this, that we were hoping to achieve a settlement that wouldn't be disruptive." The Web site was updated to reflect changes as new information developed.

There was no question, according to Smith, that the American Airlines site on the Web experienced increased activity as the APA's strike deadline approached. "In normal times, we have hundreds of thousands of pages opened each day. The closer we got to the strike deadline, the more it increased over that level by a factor of several times." Still, Smith says, that was consistent with the pattern of calls to the company's 800-reservation phone line. "The activity on the Web mirrored the phone calls to reservations," he explains. "The Web is just another avenue people can use to get information."

Recognition of the Web's new role in communicating with targeted audiences was at the top of the union's agenda when it established its Web site (at *www.alliedpilots.org*) in mid-1996. "The upcoming contract negotiations were definitely an emphasis of getting the site up early," says Captain Rich Rubin, the APA's media spokesperson and a member of the union's national communications committee. "It was designed for members but we also designed it knowing full well that it would be accessible to the media too."

While American kept its Web site updated with customers in mind, the APA updated its site as a way to disseminate information quickly to its union members. "We would get anywhere from 200 to several thousand hits each day on the site," Rubin says. "Having relevant information available to members was important, and at one point it was even critical."

That was the point at which a vote on a tentative agreement had been scheduled. The agreement was rejected, which Rubin largely attributes to the fact that information about it had been posted to the Web site. The union had also undertaken more traditional communications, sending mailings to members' homes. But those members who were able to visit the Web site took advantage of it, and Rubin is convinced of its impact. "We now live in an age where this is a medium that can be utilized to great advantage by sharing information."

The APA site clearly aimed to align union pilots with the union. The home page greeted visitors with a reminder of the circumstances that led to the negotiations, saying, for example, "Today is the 903rd day that the pilots of American Airlines are flying without a current contract." A strike-related section of the site included documentation about the contract negotiations and information about strike activities.

The site also included an information hotline, with regularly updated material and an archive of the union's press releases. Rubin says he's sure members of the media were using the site during the negotiations; several of the domains logged on the Web server indicate visitors came from media locations. Tim Smith of American Airlines also knows for a fact that the press visited American's site during the talks, although he believes most of the visits were to dig up past press releases that had been misplaced.

The APA monitored American's Web site during the negotiations but didn't get much out of it, Rubin says, because of the customer focus. He agrees that American didn't use the Web site to try to sway anybody's opinion.

Both the airline and the union also kept watch on the discussions going on in cyberspace about the negotiations. On the Internet, people talked, debated, and argued in Usenet newsgroups such as *alt.flame.airlines, rec.travel.air, alt.activism,* and *rec.aviation.misc.* In *alt.flame.airlines,* the debate kicked off when one participant posted a message that said simply, "Post your views on American Airlines." The resulting thread featured some seventy-five posts in five days.

Participants took all sides in the debate. One message read in part, "American Airlines has a record of bad employee relations. . . . AA's management has relied on harassment and intimidation as a means to an end for a long time." On the flip side: "The pilots are hypersensitive prima-donnas who are making a BIG mistake. I hope they fire them all. . . ."

The APA's Rubin says the online debate "served a great purpose. It brought to light various facets of the issue that might otherwise have gone unrecognized." According to Rubin, various "onerous provisions" of a proposed agreement were scrutinized in Usenet discussion groups. "Individuals took it upon themselves to research these provisions and provide a focused analysis," he says. "For example, American announced that they were going to purchase a fleet of new jets. Upon inspection, many discussion group participants realized that this would not result in a greater growth opportunity than simply replacing an older fleet with a newer fleet. The planes American wanted to buy required less crew—two men instead of three. The results published online indicated that the proposed fleet would benefit American by allowing them to operate more economically but would not benefit pilots as American claimed."

Much of what appeared in discussion groups helped the union determine what it would publish on its Web site. The airline, meanwhile, also monitored discussion groups, although less formally. "We determined that pilots, as a group, were very active in the online forums, and that helped us get a sense of some of the things that were being said," Smith says. "The online groups became one of many indicators we tapped into to determine how people were reacting to things the pilots were saying. It was an early warning system."

Both the union and the airline plan to continue to enhance their online presence as a means of communicating information to specific audiences—including the media—and monitoring reactions.

Guidelines for Internet Crisis Planning

The Boy Scouts have it right: Be prepared. Without a plan for addressing a crisis, your organization is bound to react with panic and a sense of siege when a crisis looms. Don Middleberg, founder of Middleberg Associates Public Relations in New York, suggests that companies without Internet crisis plans could be legally liable for the consequences of their neglect. Class action suits could, for example, claim that inattention to the Internet led to the general acceptance of a false rumor, resulting in declining sales and, by extension, falling stock prices. Following are steps to take in order to integrate the Internet into your crisis plan.

General Planning

Coordinate your Internet communication with general crisis planning. When you plan in advance, you can ensure that a siege mentality does not begin to overtake your thinking, and you can develop strategies that address what you know about how the public responds during a crisis. Answer the following questions, which reflect some key steps to factor into your thinking:

- Who determines the official company response? Nobody other than this group should develop statements or responses to queries from various publics.
- Who are your key audiences? How do you reach them quickly?
- How do you address your communications plan in the event your core planning team cannot be reached (e.g., if a natural disaster results in the temporary closure of your headquarters facility)?
- What templates do you have in place that you can use to plug in key information? What mailing lists, fax distribution lists, and e-mail lists are ready to use?

Monitoring

Chapter 5 reviewed the means by which you can monitor the Internet. This becomes even more critical in a crisis. Make sure you have the resources to scan cyberspace for references to your crisis. What you uncover could help you plan the tone or content of your communications, identify the source of a rumor, assess the degree of public reaction, and even find out what's going to happen next.

When a crisis hits, you should be able to immediately:

- Advise your outside resource (if you employ one) to launch a monitoring effort or step up an existing effort and to report to you on a prearranged schedule.
- Reallocate the time of previously identified internal resources so they can put in the hours required to regularly and thoroughly scan the Internet.
- Prepare reports for management that boil down the information gathered during the online review into digestible chunks that relate to steps the company should take.

Using Your Company Web Site

Your home page is the first place representatives of many publics look for information about your response to a crisis. Have a template for your home page prepared to drop in crisis-related information. Your approach to the home page is not limited. You can go to the extreme, replacing the existing front page (particularly if it is focused on marketing) in order to address the crisis. In this case, you can provide a link to the regular home page so those who come looking for more typical information can still find it. You can dedicate a portion of the front page to your core statement and provide links to details. Or you can simply provide a link to the page where crisis information is consolidated. The key: Don't make people go digging for the information. Make sure it is obvious that you are addressing the crisis and the information is available at your Web site.

Also have template pages ready for related information linked from the home page. These can include the typical elements of a Web page (such as navigational tools, boilerplate information, and key links such as one to your media relations site). Templates can be prepared for your key statement, a links page (providing links to such sites as government agencies whose regulatory oversight of your product plays a part in the crisis), and a Frequently Asked Questions page. You may consider having an e-mail or discussion group link as well.

Using E-Mail

Ideally, you should provide an e-mail address for the public to get in touch with you during the crisis. By providing online access, you could reduce the number of phone calls the company receives (telephone inquiries must be dealt with in real time).

If you have an e-mail link to your home page, you can invite public comments and questions. If you do so, be prepared to answer every serious e-mail you receive, even if the sender gets only an auto-response acknowledging receipt of the submission along with information about how the e-mail will be used. Auto-responses can also be sent to those who ask questions that conform to prepared answers. Frivolous e-mail (invectives and unfounded complaints) can be trashed. Serious inquiries should be forwarded to the appropriate resource for proper handling.

Being prepared for a crisis also means having e-mail addresses ready so that they can be routed to the individuals designated as contact points for such submissions. Note that e-mail submissions can provide useful information, allowing you to assess the crisis-related issues that are most important to the public.

Monitoring and Using Discussion Groups

Make sure you know which discussion groups are most likely to be forums for discussion about the crises your company is likely to encounter. Have monitoring systems in place, whether by a retainer agreement with a monitoring service, a public relations agency prepared to swing into action, or internal resources that can be called upon. (If you are doing proper monitoring in the first place, this is a moot point. If not, don't wait until the crisis hits to start figuring out how to engage in monitoring.)

If you provide a link to discussion groups from your home page, you need to decide whether company representatives participate or if it is just a place to make comments and engage in discussions with others. You can opt to respond via e-mail to messages that warrant feedback from the company.

In addition to monitoring discussion groups for references to the crisis from the public, you should be aware that loyal, dedicated employees who participate in newsgroups are likely to defend the company online—even if they innocently give erroneous information. You may be able to offset these messages in one of two ways: (1) Provide a fact sheet to employees so they can respond to discussion group messages accurately, or (2) remind them that newsgroups are no different from other media, and only designated employee representatives are authorized to make statements on behalf of the company. You can also combine these approaches: Provide accurate information to employees, but make it clear that information beyond that which is contained in the fact sheet should come only from authorized representatives.

Dealing With Attack or Rogue Web Sites

Your monitoring efforts will turn up more than just discussions that address your crisis. Web sites will crop up that focus on the situation. Some will claim to have additional information (and some actually may). Others will serve as links to resources elsewhere on the Web. Some will parody the situation, others will attack your organization, still others will take your side. Few will have been constructed based on the strategy you have developed in order to minimize damage, communicate candidly, and address public concerns.

The best preparation you can make for such sites is to anticipate their creation. Expecting they will appear helps avoid the knee-jerk reaction of sending in the lawyers. You can communicate directly with the creators of such pages in order to assess their sources and issues and what it would take to bring them to your side of the fence.

Even if activist groups are intent on skewering you in public, you can make sure your site addresses the issues they raise in a proactive manner. You can even create a set of links to the rogue and attack pages of which you are aware. Doing so reinforces the notion that you are aware of these sites and are not disturbed by them. It also gives you the opportunity to indicate what is erroneous on each page before visitors click on the link—a statement you would never be able to make if people find the sites on their own, without your assistance.

Measurement

The cost of a crisis to a company goes far beyond dollars and cents. The cost in reputation, future goodwill, and other intangibles translates ultimately into bottom-line values. You can use the Internet to mitigate these costs, and measurement is not too difficult. Consider that a study that concluded Odwalla's crisis communication had a significant impact on the consumer acceptance of its products' reintroduction to the marketplace. You can survey your publics to determine how well your Net efforts contributed to the dissipation of the crisis.

Other measures to employ include the following:

- Monitor media access to your crisis site.
- Categorize and analyze the public responses you receive at your crisis-dedicated e-mail address.
- Determine how much of your crisis material was adopted by the media.
- Monitor the tone of other material online, and try to draw a correlation between that response and the material you have made available. As you display sympathy for victims, for example, determine how much of that reaction is accepted in discussions in forums (and in reporting by media).
- Watch the symbols that others use to portray the crisis, and see how they match those you have communicated online.

Conclusion

In a crisis, the online public turns to your Internet presence to learn what you have to say, to try to understand your point of view, to hear your response, to assess your morals, and to judge you as an organization. The results can be powerful or devastating, depending on the approach you take. Plan now how to use the Internet during a crisis. Make sure your crisis plan integrates the Internet with other media and communications channels. Have the pieces in place and ready to swing into action when a crisis hits. For it's never a matter of *if* . . . it's only a matter of *when.*

12

Going Directly to the Public

For each of the audiences discussed in preceding chapters—and for audiences that cross over or combine the specific publics discussed—the Internet provides your organization with a unique opportunity to take its message directly to the public without the filters that other media can apply. This chapter offers a brief review of ideas about how to make sure your message is crafted online in such a way that you get the maximum benefit of the medium.

The Filters of Traditional Media

Before the Internet, few media were available that allowed you to get your message to your audience precisely the way you wanted it presented. Marketing and advertising, of course, were always within your control, subject to limitations imposed by law (such as truth in advertising and regulatory restrictions). In matters of public relations, however—not including those marketing communications messages aimed ultimately at selling products or services—you had to rely on third-party organizations to deliver your message on your behalf. Rarely do those organizations find that it serves their own interests to simply pass your messages along unedited to their publics.

Paramount among these third-party institutions is the news media. Your efforts to build a new factory in the heart of a small community, for example, often are explained in news releases and press conferences. While your company has gone to great pains to include all pertinent information and address all the issues that may arise, the news outlets that receive the releases and cover the press conference do not just present your information for you. Their interests are different, and they are dedicated to serving their audiences' information needs based on their charter, the feedback they get from their audiences, and any other agenda they may be carrying.

The media limit the amount and nature of the coverage you receive in a number of ways:

• Time constraints induce editors and reporters—particularly from television and radio—to shorten anything you have to say into sound bites, the two or three sentences that make the biggest impression on a viewing or listening audience. In many instances, these sound bites are taken out of context (sometimes deliberately, sometimes because of simple misunderstanding), resulting in an impression that is the complete opposite of what you had in mind. In any case, the report the public receives focuses on just a few issues, and not necessarily those that you consider important.

• Reporters already have a sense of the issues that will be important or controversial, and they focus on them. These could be minor issues from your point of view. Limiting news coverage to them keeps the public from hearing those things you consider to be most important and influential.

• If time or space is limited and your news just doesn't fit into the editorial needs of the media outlet, you receive no coverage at all. Newspapers, magazines, radio stations, and television stations are under no obligation to do your communications for you just because you produced the materials to assist them in their reporting.

Without the Internet, bypassing the media requires substantial investment, and it can be effective only if you have the means to reach your target audience. If your target audience is hard to define, making sure the public understands what you believe to be important becomes an even more onerous task.

It is not impossible, of course. Chapter 9 noted, for example, that oil and chemical companies often distribute newsletters to homeowners living in neighborhoods that surround refineries. The audience is easy to identify, and the cost is negligible. It is far more expensive to blanket the general public with information that supports your position.*

To varying degrees, companies can try to get their messages directly to their respective publics. Institutional advertising can contain 800-numbers or offers to sign up for fax service, for example. But the Internet provides you with your first real means of delivering to a specific audience the information you want them to get about any issue that involves or affects them, without filtering.

Opportunities for Direct Communication

The brief history of the Internet makes it clear that people find the information in which they are interested online, particularly when an issue heats up. As noted in Chapter 11, you can offer information to the public about your response to a crisis that the media would never cover in the kind of detail your Web site can offer. Odwalla Juices's online presentation of in-depth information—including the biographies of the scientists appointed to the task force that would review new methods for ensuring the safety of its juices—is a classic example of a company taking its message directly to the people most interested in the crisis. (And remember, the media helped by reporting on the availability of the site, even as they focused on the individuals who had become ill as a result of drinking the juices.)

But you are not limited to crisis communication when making your case or presenting your messages. In fact, any activity, event, issue, opinion, or position that generates a press release or an effort to pitch an item to the press is a likely candidate for communication on the Internet. You also can present information that you had no means of offering before, as the Army Corps of Engineers did in the following case study.

*Mobil Oil gained notoriety during the big energy crisis in the late 1970s for its campaign using newspaper advertisements to print blocks of type explaining the company's position. Not too many organizations can afford the kind of investment required to engage in ongoing communication during a crisis or public debate using traditional advertising. What's more, the value of the advertising is questionable, since many people never read the Mobil ads, and many of those who did dismissed them as one-way, top-down rhetoric that was bought and paid for.

Case Study: Army Corps of Engineers

Sandra Clawson has been the chief of public affairs for the St. Louis District of the U.S. Army Corps of Engineers since 1993. In each of those years, the St. Louis District dealt with flood events on the Mississippi River. By 1995, the volume of phone calls with which Clawson had to deal diminished considerably. She attributes the decrease to putting information on the district's World Wide Web site.

In fact, the information was to some extent *already* on the Web site. Clawson merely had to make sure the information was consistently updated and then let people know it was there for them to begin turning to the Web instead of picking up their phones.

"The Army Corps of Engineers tends to be on the forefront of technology when it comes to computers and systems, so we had a Web site before I got here, but it wasn't used very much," Clawson says. "Some of the technical people had put their stuff online, but that was about it."

During the flood of 1993, Clawson says she was struck by the number of calls coming in asking for the same information every day. "It was information on the Web site, but it wasn't being updated consistently. It would go up or not depending on whether the technicians got around to adding it."

In need of information, the media called for regular updates—5,000 times during one flood, Clawson says. And that doesn't account for calls from individuals who live along the river. "The biggest question we got was for the reading at certain mile markers," she explains. "If they live near Hannibal, they want to know what the gauge reads in Hannibal. If they live near St. Louis, they want to know the gauge reading there." The gauge measures the height the river is reaching, Clawson explains.

Without up-to-date information online, Clawson resorted to traditional techniques to handle the calls, setting up a media center. "I pulled technical people from all of our divisions to come in and answer the phone." But in the back of her mind, she continued to ponder the notion that people wouldn't need to call if the information were readily available in some other way.

An e-mail request from a local congressman to make sure updated information was available online led Clawson to push the technicians, telling them that if the information was consistently updated, she could tell people about it and cut down on the volume of phone calls. "A lot of our callers have Web access, particularly reporters and businesspeople who have businesses along the river and are concerned about high water." Other calls came in with the kinds of questions that need to be handled one-on-one.

The technicians responded, and with the 1995 flood, Clawson was able to answer every phone call by saying, "Did you know this information is available on the Internet?" She would give the Web site address and, within days, detected a drop in the number of calls—she pegs the reduction at as high as two-thirds. "We still got a lot of calls, but they were from the little old guy who lives out on the river and has no computer," she says. "But the fact that a lot of people were turning to the Web meant we had the opportunity to answer those calls."

Now, even without a flood event, those interested in water levels can login and check the "River and Reservoir Daily Report" and the "Current Conditions" part of the site (on the Web at *www.lms.usace.army.mil*). "It's important information, even when there is no flood event," Clawson says, explaining that the depth of the river is vital information for those who navigate it.

Principles of Direct Communication

Since the Internet is a new medium, no tradition has yet been established about how to ensure that direct communication with the public satisfies the needs of the organization. Use the following guidelines to improve the delivery of your Web-based public relations communications.

Don't Rely on the Web Alone

Always remember that there is more to the Internet than the World Wide Web, so use all facets of the Internet. As noted several times, the Web is a medium that works best when information is available for those who go looking for it, using the "pull" model of communication. But you may need to "push" a message. Remember the lessons of e-mail and newsgroup campaigns as a means of communicating with an audience. Consider, for example, daily one-paragraph updates on the status of labor negotiations in newsgroups populated by customers who depend on your ability to continue producing a product they use. You could distribute the same updates via e-mail to those who subscribe, either from your Web site or by sending e-mail to an address listed in the newsgroup-based updates. The updates could easily contain links to additional information that resides on your Web site, luring those individuals who genuinely desire more detail.

Offer Alternative Paths to Web-Based Information

On the Web, readers come at the information they want based on their perspective, not the way you have laid it out. Take a hypothetical situation in which a company wants to offer information on the environmental soundness of a particular product. That information might be obtainable by following any of these paths:

- Each product description contains a link to an environmental statement.
- The information is contained as part of an overall environmental component of the site.
- A public affairs site includes a listing of issues, including the environment.

You need to identify all the paths your readers may follow, and be sure those paths exist and are easy to find and navigate on your site.

Build a Dedicated Site

If the issue is important enough, dedicate a site (or a clearly delineated portion of your corporate site) to it. Crisis-oriented sites are classic examples of the wisdom of the approach, but you don't need a crisis to set aside a special-topic area. Many companies already have designated part of their Web sites for environmental issues. You could do the same for any issue you deem to be important or that you believe an audience cares about.

Set Up Common Sites for Common Issues

If, as a company, you support or oppose pending legislation or regulation, you *could* build your own page outlining your rationale and eliciting support. If every company in your industry that shares your viewpoint does the same, the message becomes diluted and confused. How many people interested in the issue take the time to read every company's statement? How many would even be able to *find* them all? Even if they do, odds are that each statement differs from the others to some degree, creating inconsistencies.

The general public already has figured a way around this problem, as exemplified by the Pink Anger campaign discussed in Chapter 10. Those individuals who supported the campaign to get Mattel to drop its suit against Miller's used a little space to have their own say, but they also featured a banner that led visitors to a common page that represented the views of the entire community. The perception created by the effort was that of a united front, of people working together for a common cause.

The Internet community at large undertook a similar campaign in opposition to the Communications Decency Act (CDA). A blue ribbon icon was made available for Web site owners to add to their Web pages. Clicking on the icon linked visitors to a central CDA opposition page. For a brief period, the page instructed all Web site owners to turn their sites black as a show of solidarity, and tens of thousands complied. While Congress approved and the president signed the CDA, the opposition effort received considerable attention as a sign of the Internet community's ability to join together in pursuit of its common interests.

(The U.S. Supreme Court ultimately struck down the CDA as unconstitutional.)

Business and industry should take a lesson from the individual inhabitants of the Internet. If trade associations will not take up the call to centralize positions shared by the majority of their members in a manner that allows each member company to capitalize on the effort, companies should band together on their own. Your company could even lead the effort, inviting your competitors to join the endeavor for the common good.

Point to Additional Resources

Since interested individuals search for information on the subject you are communicating, you may as well point them to those resources. Offer a list of additional Web sites that contain pertinent data, along with newsgroups and discussion forums where the subject is under discussion. Of course, you should highlight those that support your point of view, but don't ignore those that do not. You need to make it clear that you are cognizant of the material. By providing the links, you have the opportunity to address inaccuracies or other problems with questionable sites and discussions—an opportunity you would not have if a reader finds the information on her own and never discovers your site.

Be Candid

It should go without saying: Do not lie or twist facts. What many brand as "public relations" is really propaganda. As explained at the outset of this book, *real* public relations is the process of engaging your constituent publics in a process of two-way symmetrical communication, designed to result in both sides achieving their objectives. In that way, your organization obtains public sanction to continue its operations and engage in new enterprises.

But in cyberspace, the requirement to be candid and forthright is doubly important. The online world is nothing like the world in which traditional public relations is practiced. In cyberspace, audiences have a wealth of alternative information sources. They can talk with each other and point one another to facts that contradict your assertions.

Let Audiences Talk Back

Since the Internet is interactive, you should give your audience the opportunity to offer feedback. Letting members of your publics know that you are listening—in fact, that you *want* to hear what they have to say—enhances the credibility of your statements. Include a button on your Web page that invites people to submit their comments, or add your e-mail address to other forms of communication and invite readers to submit their thoughts. Be sure to respond to every serious message you receive, even if the response is generated by an automated program. And don't ignore the feedback you receive. Categorize the comments, analyze them, and then use them to refine your approach, your position, or the way you couch your comments.

Monitor Reactions

Using the techniques described in Chapter 5, monitor newsgroups, discussion forums, and the World Wide Web as part of your effort to assess audience response to the messages you are communicating. Incorporate analyses of the feedback into your overall evaluation and use it to tweak the message or the means by which you are delivering it.

Measurement

Content analysis of material appearing in the media gives you a benchmark against which to measure. If the media is spinning a story or focusing on one particular aspect of the story, your online communications can be targeted more toward the messages you believe are most important. You can assess public opinion to determine if your focused message is having an impact, helping the public understand your position in spite of the media spotlight shining elsewhere.

You can count the visits to your site, and determine as best you can how many came from members of your target audience. Other means of assessing the value of going straight to the public can be entirely anecdotal. For instance, media coverage of your efforts, positive responses from members of the public, and forum discussions about your site can all be used to show that your efforts are paying off.

Conclusion

If everybody is a publisher on the Internet, your company is too. The Net gives you the means to communicate directly to the public. Your candid, useful presentations to your many publics will buy you goodwill in times of trouble.

13

Measuring the Effectiveness of Your Online Efforts

Each of the chapters in Part Two of this book concluded with a review of how to measure the effectiveness of the effort. Of course, most measurement should be focused on the initial objectives you establish. Setting solid objectives must be at the core of every communications effort's initial planning stage. Why? Because a public relations effort *succeeds* only if it meets its objectives.

Objectives must be measurable. It is not enough to set a measure that says: "Increase support for our plans to build a plant in the Willow Pass neighborhood." How will you know that support has increased if you cannot measure it? A more useful objective would be: "Record a 30 percent increase in the support among residents of the Willow Pass neighborhood for our plans to build a new plant." You would determine the current level of support, then establish a public relations effort that allows you to assess the increased support. The measure you use depends on a variety of factors, including the audience, the media, and the outcome. For instance, if you held a meeting, you could begin by asking how many members of the audience supported the project. At the end of the meeting, ask again. Did 30 percent more people raise their hands? If so, you met a measurable goal and can report to management that you achieved the objective established for the meeting.

The principle of measurement applies equally to communications efforts that take place on the Internet. In fact, it may be even more critical to prove that you are achieving a return on the investment made in the Internet. Many CEOs acknowledge the need for traditional public relations but remain skeptical of the new computer-mediated communications tools. You need to be able to show that your online communications are serving the company's bottom line or helping it achieve its goals.

Considering the media focus on the profitability of World Wide Web sites, CEOs are even more interested in seeing the return on investment. The early perception of Web profitability is based on the expectation that a visitor to a site should engage in a dollar-for-dollar transaction. That is, he has to buy something. Nothing could be further from the truth. There are many ways to record a return on a Web investment without getting a sale from a customer.

Unfortunately, most efforts to assess the effectiveness of Internet communications campaigns focus on the tool rather than the results. For example, many communicators brag about the number of hits their Web sites receive, but such boasts are meaningless. Hits are a means of measuring the number of files downloaded from your server; each hit represents a request for a single file. Early Webmasters—those responsible for the technical aspects of a site—recorded hits in order to assess the load on the server. Once a server started recording a threshold number of hits, it might mean the time had come to upgrade the server's capacity. As a means of determining how many people visited a site, though, it means nothing:

• Since a hit records each file retrieved, a Web page with three graphics, a Java applet (small application program), and a sound represents six hits. Another page with only text records only one hit. Which pages were visited? How many people actually came to the site and saw what you wanted them to see? Hits won't tell you.

• Hits won't tell you if the individuals who visited your site were part of your target audience.

• Hits won't help you determine if your site influenced the behavior, attitudes, or opinions of those who visited.

To avoid the false measurement results generated by hits, software companies have developed programs that do a better job of recording visits. This is a more valid number, since it helps you determine precisely how many people visited a site. Depending on the sophistication of the software, these tracking programs can also tell you:

- Where the visitor is from (based on her e-mail domain)
- Where the visitor came from
- On what page the visitor started
- What pages were visited, in what order
- How long the visitor spent on each page
- What the visitor did on each page (e.g., complete a form, download a file, play a game)

Useful information, to be sure, but it's still not enough to satisfy the need to assess the site's effectiveness at exercising influence over targeted visitors. To stop your evaluation effort at recording information about visitors is the online equivalent of assessing a print campaign based on the demographics of the people who received it.

Genuine measurement requires that you build the assessment process into the communications effort—which subsequently requires that you begin with objectives that can be measured! Following are some sound methods of measuring the effectiveness of an online public relations effort.

Measuring the Web's Impact on an Integrated Campaign

Professional public relations efforts are integrated across a variety of media designed to achieve common results. You can establish criteria to determine the kind of impact your Internet efforts are having on the total campaign. If, for example, your efforts are aimed at the defeat of a particularly onerous piece of legislation, your Web site can include phone numbers of legislators to call, along with scripts supporters can use when they make contact. As part of the site, you can ask people to log back onto your Web page and enter the name of the legislator they contacted, then click on a button after they have made the call. When you tally the number of clicks, you find that 6,000 calls were made to that legislator's office, prompted by the Web site. That legislator winds up switching his position from supporting to opposing the legislation. You can draw the inference that, since the Web inspired 6,000 calls to the legislator's office, it played a measurable part in helping defeat the legislation.

You can even record meaningful statistics simply by heightening awareness of your cause or position on an issue. These numbers become more significant, though, if you can link the individuals who visit the page with a particular audience segment or demographic. Your Web site probably has an address like the one used throughout this book: *www.acme.com.* Everybody who visits comes to the same URL. You could, however, employ the same technique that telemarketing professionals use when they advertise on television, instructing callers to "Ask for Operator 24." Of course, there *is* no Operator 24. But when you comply with the instruction, the telemarketer on the other end of the line makes a notation that helps the organization determine what television show you were watching when you saw the ad. Operator 24 is the number associated with, say, the *Tonight Show*; Operator 31, on the other hand, is the number assigned to one of the local late-night newscasts.

You can adopt the same technique by listing unique URLs that all go to the same page. That way, you know that someone who went to *www.reply1.acme.com* saw the ad in *Popular Mechanics,* while the visitor who came to *www.reply2.acme.com* was responding to the listing in newspapers that ran your press release. Now, you can begin to determine which media are attracting the greatest numbers of visitors to the site, and you can assign demographic information to the volume of visits.

Case Study: Richmond Savings and Humongous Bank

There really is no bank named Humongous Bank, but residents of Vancouver, British Columbia, have come to recognize the name and associate it with *any* large, bureaucratic bank. That suits Richmond Savings just fine, according to Marketing Communications Manager Paul Mlodzik. He says that was the goal behind the invention of the fictitious bank.

Although the Web site for Humongous Bank is relatively new, the campaign featuring it is three years older, begun, Mlodzik says, when Richmond Savings—Canada's third-largest credit union—learned that 15 to 20 percent of bank customers at any given time were unsatisfied with their bank and willing to make a switch. "Unfortunately for us, they usually just switched to another bank," he says. "We wanted them to consider switching to the credit union as an alternative."

The way to achieve that objective was to develop the fictitious Humongous Bank, whose motto is "Your money is our money." The campaign began with radio commercials portraying beleaguered customers getting outrageously bad service. The commercials won some awards but also raised questions about Richmond's unfriendly portrayal of bank employees. "Employees are trying their best, but it's the system that's the problem," Mlodzik explains, so the campaign shifted gears to focus its attack on the overwhelming bureaucracy associated with large banking institutions.

That focus led to the launch of print ads that also generated interest and a continued increase in the awareness of Humongous Bank. The most recent print ads have taken a new approach, giving Humongous its own persona. "It's mock advertising, as if it's coming from them instead of us," Mlodzik says. "We've developed a logo for them and a jingle." One ad shows a couple of smiling banker types with the text "We built this bank one service charge at a time." Another offers, "Maximum return on our investment: That's what we expect from our customers."

The development of the direct-from-Humongous ads led to the notion that the ersatz bank should have its own Web site. "The ideas started flowing very quickly at that point," Mlodzik recalls. He interviewed several Web development companies, but as he neared a decision, the advertising agency that had developed the Humongous campaign started its own Internet division. "We worked very closely with them on the development of the site," Mlodzik says. "We were very concerned that the site be an extension of the brand, not a standalone entity that didn't relate to all our other efforts." The work was hard but also fun. "The banking industry is not noted for its willingness to take risks," Mlodzik says. "On this assignment, no idea was too wild."

Launching the site was pinned entirely on the media. Three days before the site went public, the local press received an invitation with a big *H* on it that informed them that an event was imminent that would stun them. Two days prior to launch, the fictitious CEO of Humongous sent a personal letter that noted, "I have seen the future, and it is humongous." With one day left, reporters received a press release on Humongous letterhead. The only reference to Richmond Savings was the contact phone number, although, Mlodzik asserts, most Vancouver media knew by now that Humongous was the invention of Richmond Savings.

The strategy was a success: The largest television station in town used its news program to take viewers on a three and a half minute "virtual tour" of the site, and the newspapers were generous in their coverage. With that coverage, and coverage that has continued since the launch, activity on the site has skyrocketed with hundreds of thousands of hits. "We've had about 37,000 unique visitors as of December 31, 1997, most from the Vancouver area," Moldzik says, adding that about 450 individuals have completed the "Contact Us" form on the Humongous site, indicating that they enjoyed the Web site and knew that Richmond Savings was an alternative to the banks.

The real proof, however, has been in the more hard-core measures that Mlodzik uses to assess the effectiveness of the campaign. For example, in the last year, unaided recall of Humongous Bank has leapt from 3 percent to 18 percent, and aided recall is up to 88 percent. "It's become part of the lexicon," Mlodzik says. "People don't even use bank names, they just call them all Humongous, which is great, because grouping them all together is just what we were trying to do." As for the bottom line, the credit union's membership has grown 40 percent since the campaign began, well above pre-Humongous growth.

The site itself is based on the notion of entering the Humongous Bank building. "It's a good navigation metaphor," Mlodzik says, "and we can keep it fresh easily by adding different departments, changing what's on the various floors, and even adding more floors if we need them." When visitors enter Humongous Bank, they see a row of teller windows, but as soon as you click on any window, it instantly closes. That forces visitors to go to the elevator, where they see their various options. For example, on the first floor is customer service, where your feedback options are limited to only those things the bank wants to hear. On the second floor, you can apply for a loan by completing an online application with questions like, "Have you ever cheated on your golf score? Do you occasionally lie to telemarketers? Have you ever removed the tag on a mattress? Can you be trusted? Can you prove it?" Once the application is completed, the visitor submits it and is presented instantly with the "Loan-O-Matic" machine. Pulling the handle down causes the wheels to spin, and the answer comes up with results like "Fat Chance, Pal."

On the third floor is the investments department, where a visitor's personal profile is submitted in order to draw him into investing in a Humongous portfolio. The fourth floor is the mail room, where visitors can submit their comments. Floors five through twelve are still under development, Mlodzik says, but that doesn't keep him from having fun with them. JavaScript messages appear on the screen when you click on these floors. Try the fifth floor, the vault, and you're told, "Sorry, we're busy counting our money right now." The thirteenth floor is where the CEO resides. Click on his head and you can find out what he's thinking—such musings as "They say you can never be too rich or too thin. Frankly, I've always thought being thin was overrated."

So how, exactly, does a visitor find out about Richmond Savings? The elevator buttons include an emergency exit, which leads to a screen that asks, "Had enough of big bank attitude?" and invites visitors to click through to the Richmond Savings home page. Approximately 30 percent of surfers go on to the Richmond Savings site.

Mlodzik says the Humongous site—and the rest of the campaign of which it is an integral part—will continue "as long as it's not boring and we're able to continue taking it to the next level." That means Humongous Bank could be around for some time.

Recording New Customers or Clients

An Internet presence coordinated with a larger campaign can produce new customers even if the Web site does not facilitate purchase transactions. You don't even need an interactive component on the site—any kind of tool that visitors use to acknowledge they stopped by—to produce these kinds of results.

Let's say you work for a company that manufactures digital cameras and sells them wholesale to camera retail dealers, which in turn sell them to the consumer. You produce a magazine ad that touts the benefits of your product and invites visitors to your site to see actual digital images and obtain additional detailed information. Upon visiting your site, a consumer explores the three different models you produce, then decides she wants to buy one. Your company, however, does not sell direct to the consumer. But you allow the visitor to enter her zip code into a field, generating a list of nearby retailers that have the camera in stock.

As part of your relationship with your retailers, you have asked them to ask each customer who buys one of your company's cameras to indicate where she found out the dealer had the camera in stock. The dealer tallies up the number of people who reply, "The Acme Web site," and sends a monthly report to the company (no doubt by logging into the company's extranet (network) and entering the number on a special Web page). Now you can take concrete numbers to management, showing that the Web was an integral part of the communications chain.

Measuring the Internet's Impact on Audience Behavior

Influencing behavior is the Holy Grail of public relations. Why not measure how well the Internet helps your company achieve that goal?

A friend once worked for the visitor and convention bureau of a well-known city. Her efforts focused on convention planners, the target of her Web site. The site included information convention planners would need to make decisions. For instance, a section of the site dispelled myths about the city, enhancing its desirability as a convention destination. She also included information on hotels (including capacity, room availability, and conference facilities), convention center details (including available dates), and the city's recreational facilities. (The site might well attract individual vacationers interested in the city as a vacation spot, but they were not the audience whose behavior she wished to influence.)

My friend had a lot of different hopes for the site. She hoped it would attract people to the city who might otherwise not even consider it for their conventions. She hoped it would put a better face on the city's reputation. But her measurable objective was to reduce the amount of time a convention planner would spend on the phone with a convention bureau sales representative. A convention planner visiting the site could answer many of his own questions by looking at floor plans of various facilities, checking hotel availabilities, or reviewing the ease of access to the city from hub airports. She achieved her goal beyond her wildest expectations. A caller who had not been to the Web site could take up to two hours of a bureau representative's time (not including the gaps between conversations while the representative obtained information and sent literature to the prospect via overnight delivery). The average amount of time a caller who *had* visited the site spent on the phone was less than twenty minutes. These individuals already knew what they wanted; the call was a formality to get the gears moving.

The measurement of success was based on the number of convention planners who called, armed with information obtained from having visited the site, and the number that booked conventions.

Measuring How the Internet Affects Media Coverage

When Odwalla Juices experienced its contamination crisis (see Chapter 11), media coverage shifted when the press learned the company had opened up a comprehensive crisis-oriented Web site. On its media relations Web site (when Windows 95 was launched), the software company Symantec included case studies of different types of customers who used Norton software products. Reporters were known to cut and paste those case studies directly into their stories. You can measure the impact of your online efforts by determining how much of your Internet-based materials find their way into editorial content.

Identifying New Audience Members to Target

The one-to-one nature of the Internet makes it possible for you to obtain detailed information about members of your target audience that you may not already have been reaching through conventional means. Lawrence Ragan Communications, Inc., a Chicago-based company that produces newsletters, manuals, and conferences for public relations professionals, invites visitors to its site to register to win a free registration at one of its conferences (which normally cost upward of

$500). Those who would want to attend a conference focused on public relations are clearly targets for Ragan's other products. By registering for the drawing, visitors provide Ragan with all the information it needs to add the people to its marketing database and possibly convert them into customers using the company's traditional marketing methods. The measurement: the number of new prospects added to the database.

Executive recruiting companies (better known as headhunters) are starting to use their Web sites to identify new contacts. Traditionally, each search begins with calls to a few people the recruiter already knows may be well connected in the desired profession. When visitors to a recruiter's Web site enter their personal information in hopes of being matched for a job, they wind up in the recruiter's database. Now, if a recruiter needs a chief financial officer for a manufacturing company, she can query the database for all related fields, generating a list of contacts, each one of whom may know the ideal candidate. Each new name in the database is a new avenue for identifying potential candidates; each legitimate addition to the database is a solid measurement.

Integrating Multiple Measurement Techniques

Ron Shewchuk, the manager of external communications for Suncor Energy, is responsible for the Canadian oil company's Web site. He has assembled some intriguing methods of measuring his site's effectiveness.

Case Study: Suncor Energy

Suncor recently unveiled a new graphic identity, and Shewchuck placed a series of six advertisements in appropriate print media to support the launch. After only a few of the ads had run, Shewchuck's boss called. She is responsible for both human resources and corporate communications, and her expertise is the former. Several colleagues had noted to her that the ad campaign was getting redundant. She told Shewchuck to cancel the remainder of the ads. But Shewchuck knew that the individuals to whom his boss was speaking were aware of Suncor and its new graphic identity. The ads, on the other hand, targeted new audiences, including potential investors. He believed six was a minimum number of ads and needed to convince his boss that the ad series should play out.

He turned to statistics from the company's investor-oriented Web site (at *www.suncor.com*). He found that visits to the site spiked on days the ads appeared (the URL appears at the bottom of each ad). Moreover, each ad attracted *more* visitors to the site than the previous one did. Clearly, each ad prompted those who saw it to visit the Web site, and the cumulative effect of the series motivated visits by people who might not have responded to a single ad. The statistics convinced Shewchuck's boss to stay the course with the full series of ads.

Shewchuck also closely monitors Web site activity that coincides with significant company news and announcements. Important news coincides with peaks in visits to the Web site. (He also has plotted parallel spikes in the company's stock price but stops short of attributing price gains to Web visits.) But how does Shewchuck know the right audience is visiting the site?

For that, he relies on anecdotal evidence. He has heard from enough representatives of the investment community to know that many of them have been getting their information about company activities from the Web site. The fact that the site was developed specifically to accommodate the financial community's information needs gives him a strong gut feeling that they will be the most likely to come looking for information to supplement that which they get from other sources.

A couple of points are worth noting about Shewchuck's approach:

- It's cheap.
- It relates to business goals rather than simple measurement of the Web site in a vacuum.
- It's ongoing.
- It's simple and not time-consuming.

Most important, though, is the fact that Shewchuck did not rely solely on server-based measures, but added measures from other sources (i.e., relationships to non-Web activities and anecdotal evidence).

Saving Money and Increasing Target Audience Contact

The following case study shows what one company did to serve its target audience more effectively, and save money in the process.

Case Study: AMP

AMP makes electrical and electronic connectors for every kind of machine, ranging from high-tech equipment to automobiles. Early in 1996, AMP launched an ambitious Web site designed to allow its customers to find the parts they need quickly and easily.

"We publish 400 catalogs to display our products and services to our customers," explains Jim Kessler, AMP's director of global electronic commerce. "And while AMP's catalogs are as good as anybody's, they don't do as good a job as the newer technologies allow us to do in delivering information to our customers."

Trying different technologies as an alternative means of producing its catalog led the company to produce a Web site that employs a nonhierarchical, parametrically searchable database of products. We then considered the possibility of using the then-called "information superhighway" as the delivery vehicle for our product information.

Nonhierarchical parametrically searchable? Sure, Kessler says. "It's based on the parameters that customers find most important to them." Consider a real estate search, he suggests. "Most people start a search for a house based on a few parameters—how many bedrooms, how large, what the schools are like, and so on. So most real estate information is presented that way. But what if you've just had back surgery, and your physical therapy requires that you swim every day? For you, the most important parameter is a house with a swimming pool. Therefore, you want to start with that, initially eliminating all houses that don't have pools. That's the idea of a nonhierarchical parametric search."

When it came to AMP's electrical connectors, according to Kessler, the search engine was designed to provide guidance for customers through various levels of their requirements until they arrive at the part number that meets their needs. He and his team began by surveying their largest customers, "those that provide us with major pieces of revenue on an annual basis—$1 million or more." The research revealed that nearly 50 percent of these customers had registered Internet domains, and 30 percent had established a home page on the World Wide Web. "It was apparent to us that customers responsible for a major piece of our revenue were clearly headed toward routine use of the Internet." By the time he was ready to pilot-test an online catalog, Kessler determined that the percentage of upper-tier customer companies with registered Internet domains exceeded 70 percent, and nearly 60 percent had home pages.

AMP approved an official budget for the project in early 1995. The project hinged on a pilot test with eighteen customer companies from around the world. "Two to three people from each company were involved," Kessler says. "We had them use the catalog for a period of time, then we'd get their feedback, tune the interface and other elements, then ask them to look again."

Simultaneously, the company was analyzing existing catalogs and building a database of products that could be searched with the engine. "Our target was to make sure that when we turned the system on, the online catalog would cover the part numbers responsible for 80 percent of AMP's current revenue from catalog parts." (Some parts manufactured for proprietary use—such as those that are the sole property of BMW, Ford, and Chrysler—are never included in catalogs.) The overall total of part numbers was estimated at 30,000. "So by the end of 1995, we had to have those 30,000 part numbers out there." But not just "out there." The parts and all related information had to be fully searchable on the Web *in five languages*: English, French, Italian, German, and Spanish. "When the site finally launched, it had 32,000 part numbers available in the Web-based catalog. Kessler hopes to get 100,000 part numbers online in the near future.

AMP cautiously introduced the system to the twelve test companies. Participants included IBM, Hewlett-Packard, and BMW. "That gave us a chance to see how the system would respond under an increasing load," Kessler says. "AMP is a very conservative company in a lot of respects, and we didn't want to be embarrassed by having the system fail when a lot of people started to use it."

Finally, the company held a cyber ribbon-cutting ceremony with announcements to the company's customer base, sales force, and its internal organization. The AMP electronic product catalog was open to the public.

Users are required to register, then enter a login name and a password. AMP doesn't restrict access, nor does it use the registration information it gathers for hard-sell marketing. "We did it for a number of reasons," Kessler says of requiring registration. "To begin with, every page you see is built dynamically as a result of your last mouse click as well as your language and country of delivery preference. In order to know those preferences, we needed some interaction with our customers."

The registration process also allows Kessler to track who is using the site. He can tell which of the visitors to the site are actual customers. (He can tell when competitors are checking out the site as well.) "That's helped us in two major ways," he says. "It helps our sales staff identify our customers' interests, and it helps the product management teams understand the level of interest that may exist in a product family. We're building a tremendously valuable marketing analysis database." Kessler doesn't use the database to print reports for anybody. "We just capture the data and advise different groups how they can use it if they want to."

Has the site been effective? "We're servicing 180,000 hits a day, and the feedback has been 99 percent outstanding for both product and customer interest," Kessler says.

But is it affecting AMP's bottom line? "The Web site has only recently been commerce-enabled, but clearly the activity registered to date shows strong potential," according to Kessler.

But AMP's program overall *has* eliminated a significant amount of the cost associated with printing paper catalogs. "Last year we produced what we hope will be our last telephone book-thick product guide for the Americas and the United States," Kessler says. "The delivery of paper alone to print that catalog was a $1 million expense. That doesn't include graphics, layout, printing, and distribution—*just the paper*. You print 60,000 of those, then put them into storage. The next day a product manager calls and says he didn't get around to reviewing the last set of bluelines and needs to make a change." Now, Kessler says, AMP can print a limited number of catalogs on demand for trade shows or other needs without producing a complete run available for all customers. "And the catalog will point people back to the Internet," he adds.

The printing savings don't represent the greatest advantage, however. "The possibility of eliminating the printing of paper to some extent didn't stick as a big number. The possibility of eliminating some of our fax-back telephone expense was another piece."

The honor for the greatest advantage that the site presents is reserved for the opportunity AMP now has to connect more closely with its customers at the highest level. "We're able to multiply ten- or fifteen-fold the number of opportunities we have on a daily basis to interact with someone designing a piece of equipment, to have our products at their fingertips," Kessler says. "Because of the Internet, companies like Hewlett-Packard and Allen-Bradley don't even have to bookmark the 'Welcome' or 'Index' pages of our catalog site. They can bookmark the subset of product information they need, and as a result they can get instantly into the raw data they need."

He admits he isn't measuring the revenue-generating capability of the Web site. "I believe it's reaching new customers every day," he notes. "From a utilization point of view, I know 200,000 people have registered, how many are real customers, and how many come back. The reuse numbers have been growing every day since the catalog has been out there. Out of 10,000 registered users, we see queries every day from 10,000 to 15,000 users.

"We see that people from an average of eighty countries per day are being serviced by the site. We've had registrations from 152 countries. We don't have offices in that many countries," Kessler says. "I believe that justifies the investment. So does senior management."

Conclusion

Your Internet presence can be far more than merely being in cyber-space, yet you do not need to record a dollar received for a product sold in order to assess the bottom-line impact of the Internet on your communications efforts. Set measurable objectives at the outset, then record the impact of the Internet against those objectives. Use any of the categories of measurement described above—or any others that are pertinent to your organization—as a starting point for setting and meeting measurable objectives.

Appendixes

Appendix A
Working With IT Staff

Who controls the intranet or the Web site in your organization? In a surprisingly high number of companies, that is a bone of contention. Communicators naturally believe they should be in charge, since the intranet and the Web are communications devices. Information technology (IT) professionals think the intranet and Web are in their jurisdiction, because they are computer networks.

Who owns the intranet or the Web site? The *company* does: It is a resource to be leveraged to the organization's greatest possible benefit. It is, in fact, a conceit that communicators view these systems as strictly communications tools. Many intranets also serve as an infrastructure, facilitating everything from expense reporting and performance evaluations to supply purchases and benefits enrollments. These are hardly the province of the communications department, yet they are entirely appropriate for intranets. As for the Web, electronic commerce falls in the marketing/sales jurisdiction. While communicators can play a role in both these areas, it is highly unusual to expect *traditional, non-Web* performance evaluation processes and sales transactions to be housed within the communications department.

The fact that intranet ownership is an issue indicates that the real problem is the relationship between the communications department and IT. It is a relationship that needs to improve if the two departments are going to work together to produce and maintain a topflight system. And work together they must. Neither department can do it alone, and neither should be subservient to the other.

Resolving the conflict begins with understanding how the problem emerged in the first place. After all, it wasn't all that long ago that the relationship between the communications department and IT was limited to getting new computers installed and configured.

At fault, fundamentally, is the unprecedented speed with which the World Wide Web has become a computing standard. Previous technologies took years to roll out, according to Brad Whitworth, communications manager at Hewlett-Packard in Palo Alto, California. "But the Web wasn't developed because companies determined they needed it," says Whitworth. "It was already there, and people started to bring it in." The more people began using it, the greater the demand for it in order to solve problems that no other technology could address. "It came upon people so quickly because it answered so many concerns."

Who Are These Guys?

The importance of the IT department has grown in tandem with businesses' expanded reliance on computer systems. Overall, investment in IT has grown from 3 to 5 percent of a company's capital budget in the mid-1980s to about 17 to 25 percent today. With so many millions of dollars at stake, it's no surprise that management has sharpened its focus on the IT department's role.

In general, IT's charter in the company includes the following elements:

• *Establish standards.* It is easier for a company to get work done as a team if everybody is using the same system, the same software, the same file types. If you have ever worked for a company with multiple incompatible e-mail systems, you know how frustrating a lack of standards can be.

• *Manage companywide systems.* Given the increasing reliance on systems, there is more work for the IT department to do. Members have to keep the existing systems working, back them up, keep them upgraded, analyze prospective enhancements and replacements, and maintain a smooth-working digital operation.

• *Address systems integration.* In an environment characterized by mergers and acquisitions, there always seem to be divergent systems that need to be incorporated into the workplace.

• *Watch the horizon.* An effective network comprised of the most appropriate tools for the organization can represent one of a company's most significant competitive advantages. Companies cannot afford to be caught with their pants down as competitors embrace a new technology that erodes that advantage. IT is responsible for ensuring that the company is prepared to acquire and assimilate the latest offerings and that it functions within the standards of an increasingly networked marketplace.

• *Live with budget constraints.* The IT department has to work within a budget, no differently than any other department.

• *Solve the Year 2000 problem.* In many organizations, IT resources have been strained beyond reason by the need to make all systems compliant with standards necessitated by the Year 2000 problem.

Learning the Lingo

One source of conflict between IT and communications is the jargon IT professionals seem to bandy about with arrogant supremacy. Much of the language seems contrived to confound all outsiders. In fact, the jargon is simply the language of computers and networking. It's really no different, in terms of how difficult it is to learn, from the jargon associated with printing. Most communicators would have no difficulty understanding the following sentence: *"I'm going four-up on a sheet-fed, two-over-four with spot varnish, a die cut, and the whole thing's gonna be perfect-bound."* Yet few communicators are qualified offset press operators. As professionals, communicators have simply learned enough of the technical side of printing as necessary in order to work with printers to get the required results.

IT professionals are the printers of the digital, networked world. Just as we did with printers, we need to learn enough about computers and networks to be able to work with the IT staff in order to get the same results. (See the Glossary for help in learning IT jargon.)

What Is "Content?"

Often, the friction between IT and communications arises over who is to manage content. Just as frequently, there would be no disagreement at all if the two departments defined what they meant by "content." As communicators, we define content as *subject matter*. It is the material we craft in order to achieve communications objectives. It is the key message, the approach taken to the message, and the message's positioning within the communications vehicle.

When IT staffers talk about content, on the other hand, they are usually talking about file types. An AVI animation file, for example, is content from the IT perspective. So is a WAV sound file or a Java applet. These are a concern to IT, which may be nursing a network along that is bursting at its limited-bandwidth seams.

Sometimes, a communicator may want to use a file type that is incompatible with the existing system. Do all employees in the company have an Adobe Acrobat reader on their computers? If not, it doesn't make much sense to load Acrobat PDF files onto the server. Of course, you could argue that Acrobat files would increase the value of the network and provide a substantial return on investment to the organization. Making that business case could lead IT to agree to install Acrobat readers on every desktop. It is that kind of discussion that helps the two departments move beyond the discord stage. Engaging in such discussions begins with making a mutual commitment to work together in the best interests of the organization.

Mutual Commitment Through Teamwork

Sit down with your IT counterparts and discuss your objectives. IT needs to understand what you are trying to accomplish on the company's behalf and how the intranet and/or the Web figure into the equation. Listen to IT's objectives. With all your cards on the table, take that next big step: Agree to work together to provide the solutions that the organization needs in order to be successful and competitive.

Now, you can build a cross-functional team with mutual responsibility for the success of the Web or the intranet. The team should take ownership of responsibility for the intranet or Web site, which is better than having one department retain control while the other is subservient. Teams establish their own set of objectives, separate from those on which the members are evaluated within the context of their departmental jobs. Once the team has established its objectives, each member works toward those common goals.

Further, teams identify the strengths each member brings to the table. Ownership ceases to be such an important issue. Instead, the focus is on results. Few communicators would want to be responsible for wiring routers, writing interactive programs in C + + or Perl, physically increasing network bandwidth, selecting operating platforms, or installing software on every desktop in the entire organization. Conversely, few IT professionals would claim expertise in setting communications objectives, identifying target audiences, or measuring the effectiveness of communications efforts.

But when the team is committed to the best organizational results, the objectives come first, then the discussion about how best to achieve them. IT can begin to propose technical solutions to problems that might never have surfaced in a different, more confrontational environment.

Appendix B

Promoting Your Online Efforts

The best online communications programs imaginable do you little good if nobody knows they exist. Too many of the current promotion methods are limited to registering Web sites with search engines. While this is a valid tactic, by itself it is far too confined and lets you reach only a fragment of the total audience for whom your messages were assembled. For instance, I have long been a fan of the Ragu spaghetti sauce site (on the Web at *www.ragu.com* or *www.eat.com*). It is highly interactive and entertaining and does a good job of establishing the brand. However how many people jump onto the World Wide Web to get information on spaghetti sauce? Yet there is little outside the Web to draw prospective customers to the Ragu site.

As in promoting any other public relations message, you should plan to use a variety of media and methods in order to reach the widest possible audience. Here is a review of the most common means of promoting online communications.

Online Promotion

While it is important to incorporate other media and methods into your plans to draw audiences to the Internet-based elements of your communications campaign, you also have to account for those people who are already online pulling information suited to their particular interests. Let's examine the ways you can draw those who are on the Net, invoking the "pull" model.

Search Engines and Meta Tags

Different search utilities exist on the Internet. One, the meta-search utility, is simply a collection of other search sites or a means by which you submit a query simultaneously to multiple search sites. The next type of utility is a search engine (or index), such as HotBot (at *www.hotbot.com*) and AltaVista (at *www.altavista.digital.com*). Engines send automated agents, or spiders, onto the World Wide Web, Usenet newsgroups, and other portions of the Internet, collecting every scrap of information they can find. A Web page is added to the engine by dividing the words it contains into an index; each word is attached to the location of the page from which it came. When you enter a query, the engine searches the index and returns every page that satisfies the query. As a result, the more detailed your query, the more likely you will retrieve a listing of sites that meet your needs.

Among the ways search engines rank sites in response to a query is (1) through the multiple occurrences of the key words submitted for the search, (2) by examining the page title, and (3) by cataloging the site's meta tags, which you can create as a part of your site, even though visitors to your site won't see them.

Meta tags are a component of HTML that appears in the heading portion of the code. Meta tags exist solely to assist search engines in their cataloging of Web sites. The two types of meta tags most commonly used are description meta tags and key words meta tags. The description tag is a place to write a one-line boilerplatelike description of the site. A description meta tag would look like this:

```
<meta NAME = "description" CONTENT = "Acme's media
relations Web site offers press releases, transcripts,
print-ready photos, and other resources for working
journalists.">
```

The key word meta tag allows you to introduce every word you can think of that might be entered in a search engine query field by someone you hope will find your site. Here's how a key word tag looks:

```
<meta NAME = "keywords" CONTENT = "media, media relations,
journalist, reporter, editor, newspaper, news, press,
press release, press conference, transripts, speeches,
filings">
```

> **Tip: Don't Overdo It When Writing Tags**
> You can anger many Web surfers if you throw too many
> words into the meta tag, leading people to find your site
> even if it doesn't contain a thing that matches their needs.
> Far too many meta tags are littered with dozens, even hun-
> dreds, of words in an effort to ensure that the site appears
> near the top of every search that may have even the most
> tangential relation to the topic. Limit your meta tag key
> words to those that are genuinely relevant to the site.

Search Directories and Site Registration Services

Search engines are fully automated. Search directories, on the other
hand, are managed through human intervention. Just as the Dewey dec-
imal system was devised to help categorize books in libraries, search
indexes try to catalog the contents of the World Wide Web, placing
sites into categories, subcategories, subsubcategories, and so on. If you
know just what you're looking for, you can begin to drill with relative
ease through a well-planned search index. Yahoo! (at *www.yahoo.com*)
is the best known search directory. Others include InfoSeek (at
www.infoseek.com) and Lycos (at *www.lycos.com*). A typical category
set might look like this (taken from the Yahoo! site):

```
Computers and Internet: Internet: World Wide Web:
Searching the Web: Search Engines
```

Most of the directories include a feature for site owners and managers to submit their sites for inclusion on the index. Figure B-1 shows
a Yahoo! screen that allows you to suggest a site to add to its collection.

There are literally hundreds of directories of various kinds that
permit you to add your site to their list. You might think to submit your
site to Yahoo!, which is so well known, but would you know that you
can also submit it to the Online Marketers Resource Locator? If you
are a public relations consultant, would you know to add your site to
the International Consultants Yellow Pages?

To ensure that you get the greatest possible exposure on the pleth-
ora of directories, services have been created that for a fee handle submission for you. It can be well worth the modest cost to make sure
your site is listed with every pertinent directory. Check into Submit It!
(at *www.submit-it.com*). There are also free submission utilities, which

Figure B-1. A Yahoo! screen that allows you to suggest a site.

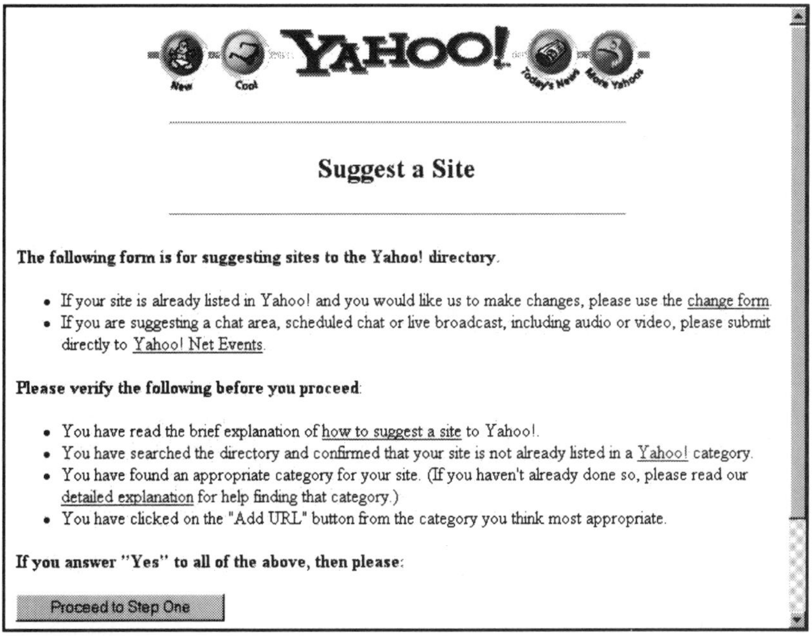

Text and artwork © 1998 by YAHOO! Inc. All rights reserved. YAHOO! and the YAHOO! logo are trademarks of YAHOO! Inc.

get your name to some of the larger directories. Try Add It! (at *www. liquidimaging.com/submit/*) or 123Add It (at *www.123add-it.com*).

Tip: Decide if You Want to Pay a Submission Service

The free utilities are great for getting your site listed in the top search engines in a few simple steps. The fee-based services tend to offer greater flexibility in addition to access to less well-known directories, such as business-specific directories. Assess the audience you are seeking for your site to determine whether the top directories will do or if you need exposure in the more targeted directories. Services like Submit It! provide lists of the directories they handle submissions to, so be sure to see if there are directories to which you would want to be added and if it's worth your while to have Submit It! do it all at once. Otherwise, you would have to visit each directory yourself to submit the URL.

Cross-Linking Agreements

The many-to-many nature of the Internet has led to the practice of cross-linking agreements, in which you agree to include a link to my site if I build a link to yours. Find sites that are related to your business or issue, then send an e-mail to the site owner suggesting the relationship. Don't limit your e-mail to a request ("I saw your site today. If I create a link to it on my site, will you do the same on yours?"). Instead, be sure to articulate why the relationship would be beneficial and where the synergies lie.

For example, if your organization is offering a series of new education-oriented grants, you might contact managers of sites that attract local teachers and school administrators. Adding your link adds value to the content of the site, since many of its visitors may want to submit grant requests. You benefit by contacting the teachers and administrators who might otherwise never have found out about the new grants.

Banner Ads

Given adequate budgets, you may want to develop an online banner advertisement and buy space on sites that are likely to attract your core audiences. For example, Yahoo! sells banner ad space on its various directory pages. If you search for public relations agencies on Yahoo!, the results page includes a banner ad purchased by an agency interested in creating a prominent image for those who may be looking for an agency. There are, of course, many other types of pages that may be suitable for your ad. If you have developed a new investor relations site, for example, you could buy ad space on investor-oriented sites, such as The Motley Fool (at *www.motleyfool.com*).

E-Mail and Discussion Groups

To tell people that your site exists or new content has been added to it, use existing mailing lists of individuals who have asked to be notified of relevant information. You can also make brief announcements about your site in relevant Usenet newsgroups, listserv mailing lists to which you subscribe, and other discussion forums, politely alerting group participants that your online material is available. Be sure to address (in one or two sentences) how the participants in that particular virtual community can benefit from your offering.

Integration With Other Media

So far, we have reviewed ways to get information across about your Internet communications using the Internet itself. These techniques are fine for the members of your target publics who are already online. What about those who aren't online or who are not looking for anything related to your message—even though they would be interested in it if only they knew it was there? The following approaches can be applied to non-Internet communications as a means of luring your audiences to your online materials.

Company Materials

Your organization produces reams of print materials as a matter of routine. Pertinent online information should become a standard part of everything from business cards and letterhead to institutional brochures and press kit folders. Include the company's top-level URL on general materials. Department-specific materials should feature both the general URL *and* any targeted URLs. For example, the vice-president of investor relations should have a business card with the URLs of the company's Web site *and* investor relations site. Business cards also should include e-mail addresses.

URLs can be put on a variety of other promotional items, including pencils and pens, T-shirts, notepads, and pocket calculators.

Related Campaign Elements

When creating an integrated communications effort, you evaluate each media component and use it to its best advantage. Here are some ways to mesh traditional and Internet media in a total public relations endeavor:

• In print materials that form the crux of your communication, point readers to your Web site, where they can get additional information on elements of the print material that especially interest them. This allows you to go into greater detail on these topics, affording the opportunity to exercise influence over individuals with highly targeted interests.

• Offer full text online of materials that appear in print. For example, if your printed bulletin or newsletter includes quotes from an executive speech, refer interested readers to the Web site for the complete text (and even an audio file) of the speech. If a mailing seeking support for construction of a new facility includes segments of an environmental impact report, archive the entire report on your Web site.

• Include a list of e-mail addresses, each of which is managed by an auto-responder. Those who wish more information on a particular subject can send e-mail to the address in question to receive a response that provides details on that issue. E-mail auto-responders do not provide material that is as graphically appealing as a Web site, but far more people have access to e-mail than the Web, making it a resource that can be accessed by larger portions of your target audience.

• State that updates to the material you have produced in print will be available on your Web site as soon as they become available, enticing audience members to visit the site to see if new information has been posted.

• Offer access to interactive materials associated with the information you provide in print. If you are promoting your company's stock as a sound investment, for example, you can incorporate an investment calculator into your investor relations Web site. Current shareholders can calculate the increase in value of their stock since purchasing it. You can promote the site in your annual and quarterly reports.

Advertising

All of your advertising efforts should refer to your Web site URL. Everything from display ads in magazines and newspapers to television commercials and billboards can include a reference to your Web site (and, even better, to specific sections of your site that relate directly to the focus of the ad).

Time magazine once had a display ad for Pentel pens. At the bottom of the ad, the URL for the company's Web site was listed. Why, I wondered, would I want to visit the Web to look at pens? Curious, I visited the site, and I found a wealth of information. For example, there was an illustrated, step-by-step guide to unjamming a mechanical pencil. I don't know if I'll ever need to retrieve that information, but if I do, I know where it resides on the Internet. And my opinion of Pentel has elevated based on the value-added information it has posted to its Web site.

Announcements

When you launch a Web site, a new feature on a Web site, a discussion group, or any other Internet-based service, widely publicize it. Distribute press releases and press kits (including printable screen shots), invite reporters to call in for an online "guided tour," and pitch unique elements of the launch to targeted media. Get as much press coverage as you can for your site. If the site is part of a larger campaign, be sure to use the same logos, letterheads, and other identifiers to link the site to the brand you are communicating through other means.

Appendix C
Writing for the Computer Screen

Writing is at the core of good public relations. The other skills—strategic planning, negotiation, research, etc.—that are needed by a well-rounded communications professional are all but worthless if he lacks writing skills.

When it comes to the Internet, many communicators believe that good writing is good writing, and the medium is not a factor. Evidence supports the contrary. One study showed that material rewritten to incorporate the principles of good *online* writing made a document nearly 125 percent more usable to the reader.

Chapter 4 reviewed some characteristics of reading computer screens that make the process dramatically different from reading anything printed on paper. These include:

- *Physical characteristics.* Online, material is not linear or three-dimensional. It is, however, interactive and multimedia.
- *Physiological impact.* Eyestrain is induced by reading light (which reduces the blink rate) and by having to adjust to type size that is beyond producer control. Scrolling induces nausea.

The consequence of these factors is that people do not read written material on computer screens. Research conducted by Sun Microsystems suggests instead that people *scan* the material they retrieve. Their eyes bounce around a screen in random patterns, seeking out key words that signify that the page contains the information they were seeking. (Refer to Chapter 4 for details about these factors.)

In a world where people are not inclined to read what you have written, even as they rely on the Internet to find information they need, writers face a variety of challenges to get readers to pay attention to their copy. Attention, in fact, is a currency in the information economy. Some argue that *information* is itself the information economy's currency, but any economist will tell you that currency is derived from that which has value *and is scarce* within the economy. Information is far from scarce. If anything, now that everybody has the ability to produce information, we are drowning in it. Attention, on the other hand, *is* scarce. People can pay attention to only one thing at a time. The fact that you are reading this book means you're not listening to an advertisement on the radio, catching a public service announcement on television, or paying much attention to what somebody might be saying in the next room. You're certainly not reading another book or magazine. The trick, then, is getting people to pay attention to what *your organization* has to say. And when they won't read your carefully crafted prose, you need to adopt different writing strategies in order to capture your share of the available attention that exists in your targeted marketplace.

Your Role as a Writer

As a writer whose job is to make sure your audience gets the message you have to deliver, your role in the online world is considerably more expanded than it is in the paper world. Of course, you *still* have the power of your words, but you have much more to take into consideration:

• *The context.* You need to consider context for each chunk or page or file of information to ensure that the reader understands what you're trying to say, regardless of where in your online document she starts.

• *The design.* In print, the writer generally hands finished text to a designer, who makes it look good and enhances its meaning. Online, the design of the page needs to happen simultaneously as *part* of the writing process.

• *The audience.* In print, all audiences get your written work in the same format. The special needs of subaudiences are irrelevant; each must extract what is relevant to him from the same document that other subaudiences are using. Online, however, different audiences can view your work different ways; they can approach the information from different paths. Thus, special attention needs to be paid to who the readers are.

• *Related information.* In print, you can include a bibliography at the back of the work. Online, you need to be aware of related information available at the click of a mouse. Will readers be able to find contradictory documents? Are there documents online that already cover what you want to cover, to which you can link? Are there sites on the intranet or Internet to which you can guide your readers to support or enhance your words?

• *The multimedia options.* Will an audio or video clip, an animation, an interactive tutorial, or some other multimedia tool be beneficial?

• *Interactivity.* Are you accommodating the reader's expectation that your material will be interactive?

• *Navigation.* Are you making it easy for the reader to move effortlessly through your document and to find what he's looking for?

Tip: Understand What Readers Want and Need

Readers *want* control, but they *need* direction! Be sure to add elements that help the visitor to your site find just what she is looking for. These elements can range from navigation tools to sophisticated database applications that personalize information on the page based on what you know about the individual visitor based on previous visits or transactions.

Your job as the writer of the online document is to help the reader identify what she is seeing so she can make a quick decision about its value to her, then be able to move quickly and effortlessly to the next element in your document (or to some other realm of the Internet, should that be her choice).

The New Models and Their Implications for Writing

Chapter 2 explored the four new models of communication that have evolved from the electronic communications revolution: many-to-many, receiver-driven, access-driven, and the market sample of one. Each of these models has implications for the approach you take to writing a document for online presentation.

Many-to-Many

- *Think beyond the page.* A written work is self-contained between its covers. By its very nature, an online work is connected to other online elements. You need to consider which of those elements relate to your work.

- *Realize that your writing is ongoing.* In print, your work is complete once it comes off the press. Online, you need to continually revise, update, and correct your work in response to feedback from the online community of readers.

- *Incorporate links.* The material posted by others, along with the discussion groups related to your subject, may serve your document well. Consider linking to them. You may even want to develop a dedicated discussion capability as *part* of the material you are producing. For instance, if you are writing about benefits enrollment, providing an online forum where employees can discuss the various options gives you some control over the many-to-many nature of the Web.

Receiver-Driven

- *Produce nonlinear writing.* Your writing must, in most instances, be produced in a nonlinear fashion. That is, while you use an outline or structure for your work, each component part must make sense in its own right, and the reader must be able to both find and use it.

Write in chunks. Rather than write in a steady flow, you must write in chunks, each one containing a contextual element of the whole. When repurposing material for the Web, you need to identify the elements that contain a single unit of information—a single notion, concept, or thought—and recast it as a stand-alone element of information that works in its own context in addition to the overall context of the larger piece.

- *Learn to use hyperlinks.* Hyperlinks are the cognitive language of the Web that allow people to find the information they want. They are not an afterthought but a fundamental, integral part of the writing process.

• *Select the right medium for key messages.* If some of your information *must* be seen by every reader, how do you overcome the receiver-driven nature of the Web? When people pull only the information they want and customize their environments to screen out material of no interest, how can you ensure your material will be absorbed? You need to consider using more *push*-oriented tools—such as e-mail—and procuring space on the top-level home page that everybody sees for such messages. You may even need to decide whether the online environment is appropriate for such information.

Access-Driven

• *Understand your audience.* You need to know the audience you are targeting with your information and how its members are most likely to be able to receive it.

• *Prepare text in multiple formats.* Of course, not *every* audience has access to the Web environment (at least, not for a while). As a result, communicators may need to produce multiple versions of their material to accommodate *different* preferred access points.

• *Use the primary medium as the foundation.* If most of your readers are online, the online document becomes the primary document and should be used as the source for producing secondary (e.g., print) documents.

Market Sample of One

• *Link from related sites.* Part of the writing process involves identifying related sites and knowing how to establish links from them to the information you are producing. You should also explore the notion of banner ads as a means of advertising the presence of your information on the system.

• *Develop Frequently Asked Questions.* By establishing a list of FAQs, you accomplish several things. First, you provide material that is easily captured in a search engine's index, making it easy to find. Second, you can provide links to related information. Third, you can have the content owners of other sites create simple links from their sites to your FAQs.

General Guidelines for On-Screen Copy

Some general guidelines apply to writing on-screen copy. (There are also specific guidelines for the various types of online communication, which are covered later.)

Length

- The shorter the better. Generally, you want to fill only *one screen.*
- Do not use more than two "page-downs."
- Offer links to related information to keep the length down and make it easier for a reader to get just the information she wants.
- Don't get carried away with hyperlinks. Too many of them disrupt the flow of the document.

Style

- The writer's "voice" is important, regardless of the document's nature. A conversational style is preferred by online readers.
- Use lists and bullet points.
- If you employ a narrative approach, use short sentences. Use emphasis (italics and boldface) sparingly and only to help the reader in her efforts to scan the page.

Navigation

Writing a document for the screen *must* include the incorporation of navigation tools (buttons, icons, text). Navigation needs to guide readers to:

- The beginning of the document
- The previous chunk of information
- The next chunk of information
- Any indexes or tables of contents
- Search engines that help the reader find the information he is looking for within the document
- The home page of which the document is a part

Writing Electronic Newsletters

E-mail newsletters are those that are distributed to your audience via e-mail. Most e-mail newsletters are distributed as actual e-mail messages, generally limited in scope to ASCII text. However, there are some e-mail newsletters that have more capabilities. But they all share some common traits:

- Readers have to retrieve them as e-mail, so the larger they are, the longer they take to download.
- Readers have to read through them to find what's important to them, along with the messages in all the rest of their e-mail.

When writing e-mail newsletters, stick to just the facts. Avoid featurelike elements, and adopt a newspaper-lead approach as the style for the entire article. If additional information or levels of detail are available, point readers to where they can be found. Don't assume every reader is interested in every detail.

Use short, spartan sentences.

If you are producing your newsletter in ASCII—that is, it uses only the characters you can see on your keyboard, ensuring its compatibility with absolutely *any* e-mail software application—you should abide by the following guidelines:

- Put a listing of all the headlines or subject lines at the top of your message. In this way, readers can browse quickly through the list to see if any of the articles are of interest.
- Keep articles to one or two paragraphs.
- Separate articles with a line of nonletter characters, like these:

Of course, you are not constrained to delivering newsletters produced only in ASCII. There are a variety of ways to distribute newsletters that incorporate graphics and design elements. You can use an application file such as Word (if all members of your audience have

Word), a dedicated e-mail newsletter application such as E*News, or portable document programs such as Acrobat, Envoy, or Common Ground.

Hold each article to a single screen. The formats allow you to use hyperlinks, and you should take advantage of them so that a reader can move easily between and among articles. You also should avoid redesigning your publication each issue or overdesigning it. Instead, develop a template and stick with it.

Writing for the World Wide Web

Overall Structure

Just as you do with a document to be printed, begin with the *structure* of the document when writing for the Web. In fact, it is even *more* important, since that structure becomes the basis for hyperlinks, chunking of text, navigation, and other elements the reader uses to take advantage of the document you have produced.

When preparing an online document, think in terms of an information *tree,* in which your main information is on the trunk, key levels of information are on branches, secondary levels of information are on branches sprouting from the key-level branches, and so forth.

In addition to using the tree as the intuitive guide for your writing, adapt it as an outline of links for your reader, like this:

```
Health and Welfare Plans
    Introduction to Plans
    Medical Plans
        HMOs
        PPO
        EPO
        Indemnity Plan
    Dental Plans
        Indemnity Plan
        Dental HMO
    Vision Plans
        Vision Service Plan (VSP)
```

Of course, you can provide even deeper levels of links. For example, under each of the Medical Plans, you can include links to such things as the categories of coverage, the claims-filing process, and eligibility. These links do not need to appear on one page. For instance, clicking on HMOs can take you to a list of more links regarding HMOs.

Be sure to consider your audiences as you map out and then write your document. You could have more than one type of audience viewing the same document. Consider, for example, a document designed to provide information on a 401(k) investment plan. Part of your audience may be individuals who have never before invested in a 401(k) or never been part of a company that offered one. These novices require information that walks them through the particulars of a 401(k). On the other hand, many of your readers may have been investors for years and do not need to be held by the hand in order to understand the material. Instead, they just want to know specific information, like the five-year history of the high-risk/high-yield foreign stock fund. Ultimately, the document contains the same information for both. The only question is how each audience gets to the information.

Figure C-1 offers a simplified explanation of how different audiences use the same "chunks." The novice is able to move logically and linearly through the document, learning what he needs to know about 401(k) plans, ultimately getting to the section in which he learns about investment options. The experienced user, on the other hand, is able to select either an alphabetical or functional listing in order to quickly find the specific plan in which he is interested.

Another example might be a medical plan. In order to help make an enrollment decision, one employee may want to know about the hospitalization benefits under various plans. In this case, it makes sense to offer links to the various benefits available under each plan for comparison purposes. Another employee, however, has a child who just broke his arm. She wants to know what coverage applies. She might begin on a chronological life-events listing, click on "Dependent Accidents," then click on "HMO" because that's the plan her son is in, then click on "Emergency Hospitalization." Ultimately, the information on HMO hospitalization is the same—it's even *the same file*—but two different employees took two different paths to get to it.

The Written Word

The actual writing of text for the computer screen encompasses a variety of elements that require thinking different from that for paper and

Figure C-1. The parallel paths that different audiences use to get to the same information.

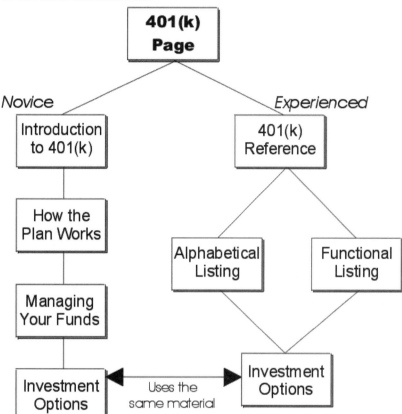

print. This section reviews each of the key elements of writing for online consumption.

Reduce Your Text to Chunks

In many cases, the best approach to writing for the screen is to reduce your text to the smallest component chunk. The best instance in which to do this is when there is so much information that producing it in a linear, one-document fashion would overwhelm readers with information and make it difficult for them to find just the information they are looking for.

A chunk of information should contain a well-defined concept that stands on its own—that is, it makes sense in its own context. The idea contained in the chunk should be clear and should flow smoothly.

The size of the chunk itself should be determined based on:

- How much text is required to convey the full message, idea, or concept?
- How long does it take to download the file that contains the chunk?
- How difficult is it to scroll or page-down through the document?
- What is the trade-off between either scrolling/paging-down or clicking and waiting for hyperlinked pages to appear?

A reasonable rule of thumb is to avoid exceeding two page-downs in order to read through the entire page.

One of the advantages of chunking information is that you can avoid rekeystroking information. For example, you may have disclaimer language or other legalese that appears throughout a printed document. In a hypertext, online document, that disclaimer needs to exist only once on the server. At the end of the document, you can provide a link to the disclaimer rather than type it into different HTML pages over and over again.

Write About Your Subject

Because it is so new, many writers writing for the Web tend to get distracted by the medium itself. You should concentrate on the subject at hand and avoid references to the Web (or using it), which will distract readers from the message you are trying to send. Besides, most readers are savvy enough about the Web that they don't need you to tell them to "click" or "point your cursor" or take any other action that is about the medium. After all, on paper, you wouldn't say, "Put the corner of the page between your thumb and forefinger and flip it so it turns to the next page." "Click here" probably appears more than any other two-word combination on the Web. Don't let it appear on *your* site!

Try not to mention the environment in which you are writing unless it is specifically relevant. Don't talk about the intranet, the Internet, or the Web if you can avoid it. Also avoid references to archives, files, directories, and other terms that refer to the medium instead of your message's key subject.

Don't Write About Writing

Your readers are interested in your subject, not the tools you are using to write about it. Avoid references to the mechanics of your writing. Also, it doesn't pay to get flowery or expressive. Just offer the information and keep it as short as possible. Avoid language like, "Following is a list. . . ." Your reader *knows* it's a list when she sees it. Online, it's almost a point of pride to show that you have figured out how to use HTML to make a list. But such extra writing is just that much more text to distract the reader's eye away from key messages during the process of scanning.

Listen to Your Links and Your Document

Listening to the elements of your document means listening to the signals they send and the reactions they create. Listen first to your links. Are there so many that they distract the reader from the main message? Will too many links invite the reader to leave the document and go somewhere else? Each link is an invitation to a choice for the reader: He is forced to decide whether to click on the link and go where it takes him or stay with the document he is reading.

Next, listen to the document itself. Based on the paths you created to get there, does the document make sense? Does it provide the proper context? Are the links offering information that is consistent with what the reader is expecting from the page?

Limit Distracting Elements

Boldface and italic type, used in print to create emphasis, have a different effect on the screen. When a reader scans a screen, anything that jumps out as different draws the eye. If the boldface or italic type does not contain the key element of your message, it *will* serve as a distraction, making it more difficult for the reader to absorb that key point. Try to establish rules for the use of boldface or italic type.

The same principles apply to horizontal lines, an HTML element that serves to divide one part of a Web page from another. Too many lines make it difficult to scan and can frustrate the reader. Guidelines that help you use horizontal lines according to a scheme make it easier for the reader to understand how they help him use the information on the page.

Document Elements

When you write a Web document, you need to include several elements. These are:

1. *The title.* This is the text that appears at the very top of the screen, in the band of color that begins with the name of the application (e.g., Netscape Navigator, Internet Explorer). Your title should not address the specific context of the material on the page but rather should be a brief description of the topic.

2. *The main headline.* In HTML parlance, this is Head Level 1. This is the headline that tells the reader what this particular page is about. Keep it short.

3. *Subheads.* You may not like the way Head Level 2 looks under Head Level 1 or how Head Level 3 looks under Head Level 2. But the text was designed to make it easy for readers to distinguish between levels, so resist any temptation to use the head level settings for design purposes. Stick with the approach as it is written. Subheads should summarize the topic of the material under them.

In addition, each document (one long page or a collection of chunked pages) should contain a table of contents and a link back to the table of contents, so readers can quickly get to the information they need. You might want to include an index as well, particularly if there is a lot of material with a lot of key words. The table of contents should appear *at the beginning* of the document. The index, on the other hand, should be accessible only if a reader clicks on the link to see it.

Credibility

When your words go out into the world between the pages of a magazine, they get credibility from the fact that the magazine is recognizable as a product of an organization (along with the obvious implication that the organization had enough money to print and distribute it). But there is so much online that such credibility is called into question.

There are several steps you can take in the preparation of your document to ensure that the audience views it as credible. These include:

- The name of the sponsor (the department, division, unit, or team under whose authority the information was produced)
- The name of the author
- An e-mail link to the author, such as:

```
<A HREF = "mailto:john@doe.com">John Smith</A>
```

- The date the document was distributed
- The date(s) the document was revised
- Any other information you can provide to reflect how current the document is

Hyperlinks

There are several types of hyperlinks:

- Links within the same document
- Headlines at the top that link down to the text to which they refer
- Links within text to glossary definitions, footnotes, and other descriptive text
- Links to other documents on different Web pages

When linking to another document, it is best *not* to set your links within the body of your text. This is not a hard-and-fast rule, and a lot of Web page writers don't follow it. But many readers are surprised when they click on a word in the middle of a paragraph and find themselves suddenly transported to another Web site. The flow of the text they were reading has been lost. It is better to set your off-site links at the bottom of the page, using buttons, icons, or textual links. In any case, make sure the links you are providing are relevant, and don't overdo it. A page loaded with outside links (other than a page that is *designated* as an index of links) can be frustrating and hard to read.

When linking within the text, make sure you are using only the links from headlines to text and back to the table of contents, or to brief footnotes or glossary definitions. You should avoid using in-text links to take readers to a new thread of narrative.

When wording your links, watch the vocabulary you use. Avoid:

- "The next thing we consider is . . ." *(What was the* last *thing?)*
- "The solution to this problem is . . ." *(What problem?)*
- "Previous page" *(But I beamed in from the Dilbert Zone.)*
- "Next page" *(Next? Something's next?)*

Also, provide navigation hints at the top or bottom of the document, things like "Up to PPO choices" and "Part of Benefits Guide").

Considering the Need for Hard Copy

While the Web is growing at an unprecedented pace, there are many individuals without access to the computers that contain the Web page. There are blue-collar and factory workers, field representatives, drivers, agents, and a host of other individuals who still need to receive material in print.

That doesn't mean that you, as a communicator, need to handle that distribution. You can make a hard copy available *online* and let supervisors be responsible for providing access to the hard-copy version. They can be expected to print out a hard copy for employees without access, photocopy it, and distribute it. The same method works for employees who need to take hard copies of material home.

Use the online document as the basis for the single-file hard copy. This approach argues even more against referencing Web actions or online mechanics in the text. "Click here" won't mean anything to an individual reading a hard-copy printout of the document!

Make sure the hard-copy version is available as a link at the top of the first page of the online version of the document. You could use the Web and its hyperlinking capabilities to review the online version of the report. Or one click could lead you to a download of a Microsoft Word version that you could print out and read the old-fashioned way.

Creating Text With a Word Processor

Many people create text directly in ASCII (along with their HTML code) or directly in their Web authoring program (such as HotDog, Microsoft FrontPage, or HoTMetaL Pro). While writing for the Web does involve many mechanics of the medium in which the text is to be used, it is still advisable to write in a program designed for writing, then transfer the text to a program where you can manipulate the Web elements.

However, there are some cautions when using a word processor for text destined for the Web:

- Don't use style sheets that come with the word processor. The styles do not translate to the Web.
- Avoid smart quotes and special characters (such as © and ™). On the Web, such items must be created using special code, and the Web does not recognize the special characters from your word processor.
- Turn off auto-hyphenation. If your word processor creates hyphenated text, it could result in nonstandard hyphenation when transferred to the Web.

Appendix D
Online Resources

The Internet provides a wealth of resources to you in your efforts to communicate with your various audiences. One bit of warning: Web sites come and go. Most of the resources listed here are likely to be around for some time, but you can never be sure. This list of resources is maintained in a version that is routinely updated on the author's Web site at *www.holtz.com.*

Public Relations Tools

Communication Arts Magazine
www.commarts.com
The Web site of the best print magazine on graphic design includes exhibits, contest winners, and other sources of ideas for your own foray into print presentation.

Global Prepress Center
www.ledet.com/prepress/
Resources for those involved in desktop publishing, graphic arts, prepress, and printing.

LithoQuoter
www.lithoquoter.com
A resource for putting your print jobs out to bid through a national network of printers. Submit the specs and get the bids back online.

Customizeable News Sources

CRAYON (CReAte Your Own Newspaper)
www.crayon.net
A clever use of the Web that allows you to create your own customized listing of news, columns, and features, which you store on your hard drive. Whenever you load it, it automatically pulls in the latest updated information.

My NewsPage
www.newspage.com
Customize your own NewsPage, which retrieves stories based on categories of interest to you.

NewsHound
www.newshound.com
From the *San Jose Mercury News,* create various profiles and retrieve information on the Web, via e-mail, or both.

Professional Public Relations and Communications Associations

British Association of Communicators in Business
www.bachb.org
Representing European business communicators.

Canadian Public Relations Society (CPRS)
www.cprs.ca/index2.htm
The Canadian equivalent of the Public Relations Society of America.

Communicators Roundtable
www.roundtable.org
An organization representing twenty-four communications, public relations, marketing, graphics, advertising, and information technology organizations, with nearly 7,000 members.

International Association of Business Communicators (IABC)
www.iabc.com
One of the two leading communications associations (the other is PRSA). IABC tends to attract communicators who work inside corpo-

rations or for agencies that handle corporate (or institutional) public relations. The Web site includes a discussion forum where various communications issues are discussed. IABC also maintains a discussion group on CompuServe's Public Relations & Marketing Forum, which is available via the Web at *www.csi.com/forums.*

National Association of Government Communicators
www.nagc.com
Membership covers writers, graphic and video artists, editors, broadcasters, photographers, public information officers—anyone involved in any field that has anything to do with disseminating information within and outside government.

National Investor Relations Institute
www.niri.org
A U.S.-based organization that is tightly focused on investor relations and financial communications. The site includes a treasure trove of links to investor relations sites elsewhere on the Web.

Public Relations Society of America (PRSA)
www.prsa.org
The other major communications association, PRSA, is focused more on marketing-oriented public relations, although the organization certainly addresses corporate PR, investor relations, and a host of other topics. Members tend to be agency employees (or PR counselors) engaged in account management. PRSA also maintains a discussion group on the CompuServe Public Relations & Marketing Forum at *www.csi.com/forums.*

Society for Technical Communication
www.stc.org
Membership includes writers, editors, illustrators, printers, publishers, educators, students, engineers, and scientists employed in a variety of technological fields.

Public Relations Resources

American Demographic Magazine
www.demographics.com
Since demographics are such an important part of traditional communications, this magazine can come in handy—particularly since you

can search its archives for information related to your current communications undertaking.

Business Wire

www.businesswire.com
The online home of one of the premier news distribution services.

Holtz Communication + Technology

www.holtz.com
The author's Web site includes links to other resources, a collection of essays on the application of technology to strategic communication, a knowledge base of online public relations tools, and a variety of other resources.

Internet Wire

www.gina.com
A resource for getting your news release out over the Internet.

Investor Relations Information Network

www.irin.com
Billing itself as the World Wide Data Bank of Annual Reports, this site features some outstanding examples of online annual reports and other investor relations-oriented material.

Marketing 1 to 1

www.marketing1to1.com
A consulting firm that offers plenty of free resources to help develop a greater understanding of the one-to-one marketing concept. Sign up to receive a weekly newsletter or participate in discussions online.

National PR Network

www.usprnet.com
An attempt at a virtual community of public relations counselors and suppliers, this features regular industry updates, employment news, and additional resources.

NewsPlace

www.niu.edu/newsplace
A collection of resources for journalists and other writers conducting research.

Parrot Media Network
www.parrotmedia.com/pmn.html
Television, radio, cable, and newspaper directories.

PR Central
www.prcentral.com
The Web site of the publishers of *Inside PR* and *Reputation Management*. A library of case histories highlights the site.

PR Direct
www.pionews.com
Distributes your press releases to online information services.

PR Newswire
www.prnewswire.com
A leading international electronic distributor of news releases, photos, and other material destined for the media and financial markets.

Pressline
www.us.pressline.com/tmp/
A place on the Web to post your press releases.

Principles of Interactive Media Audience Measurement
www.commercepark.com/AAAA/bc/casie/guide.html
CASIE—the Coalition for Advertising Supported Information and Entertainment—supplies recommended guidelines for providing valid audience measurement of interactive media.

Profnet
www.profnet.com
The Internet is put to a unique use with this service, which accepts submissions from journalists looking for sources for their stories. Businesses subscribe to the e-mail distribution of reporter needs, then offer their own experts as quotable subjects for interviews. Reporters participate free; businesses pay the freight.

Public Relations Agency Web Listing
www.impulse-research.com/impulse/prlist.html
A comprehensive listing of public relations agencies in the United States and abroad that maintain Web sites.

RaganWeb
www.ragan.com
The site of Lawrence Ragan Communications, Inc., which publishes
PR-oriented newsletters and manuals and hosts conferences and work-
shops. The site includes regular updates on PR-related issues, an archive of articles from Ragan newsletters, and a discussion forum.

Who's Marketing Online?
www.wmo.com
An online magazine that focuses on the best and worst cases of online
marketing.

Public Relations Discussion Forums

PRFORUM
www.prforum.com
A public relations practitioner and enthusiast, Carl Carter, created this
space specifically so others in the field would have an online place
to discuss the profession. Topics range from current issues to crisis
management and media relations in general.

Public Relations Mailing Lists

ACR-L
A list to discuss the topic of consumer research. It serves as a bulletin
board for researchers, practitioners, and graduate students working in
this interdisciplinary field. To subscribe, send the words *SUBSCRIBE
ACR-L YOUR_FULL_NAME* to the e-mail address *listserv@listserv.
okstate.edu.*

Direct Marketing Digest
An unmoderated mailing list focused on direct marketing and relationship marketing. For general information, send e-mail to *dm-
intro@argo-navis.com.* For subscription information, send e-mail to
dm-info@argo-navis.com.

Electronic Marketing Digest

A place for marketers and communicators to trade war stories about their online experiences. Subscribe via the World Wide Web at *www.webbers.com/emark/subscrib.html.*

EventWeb

Interactive marketing guidance to those who produce meetings, conferences, and trade shows. Subscribe on the Web site at *www.eventweb.com.*

HTMARCOM

The High-Tech Marketing Communications mailing list maintained by Kim Bayne, who has achieved star status as an online marketer. Everything you need to know about the list is on Bayne's Web site at *www.wolfbayne.com/wolfBayne/htmarcom/.* Bayne also keeps a comprehensive and exhaustive list of other mailing lists on her site. Find it at *www.bayne.com/lists/default.html.*

PRFORUM

About 1,000 public relations practitioners, academics, and students participate in this discussion group. Quality of content varies, but there are enough nuggets to make it worthwhile. To subscribe, send the words *SUBSCRIBE YOUR_FULL_NAME PRFORUM* to the e-mail address *listserv@listserv.iupui.edu.*

Crisis Communications

Avoiding Corporate Crises
www.brobeck.com/sslitplg/15.htm
The legal point of view, prepared by two members of a law firm.

The Crisis Coalition
www2.crisiscoalition.com/crisis/
An affiliation of leading public relations and public affairs companies and consultancies working on prevention, management, and control of organizational crises.

Resources on Writing and Designing for the Web

Applying Writing Guidelines to Web Pages
www.useit.com/papers/webwriting/rewriting.html
Jakob Nielsen, distinguished engineer at Sun Microsystems, is the co-author of this site, which presents research results from a study conducted by the senior scientist at Sun Microsystems on Web readability. An earlier document, still of tremendous value, is at *www.Useit.com/papers/webwriting/writing.html.*

Journal of Computer Mediated Communications
209.130.1.169/jcmc/
From the University of Southern California's Annenberg School of Communication, the *Journal* offers an academic take on the impact and influence of online communication, including but not limited to the World Wide Web.

Journal of Electronic Publishing
www.press.umich.edu/jep/
This quarterly from the University of Michigan offers useful insights, research results, and other proprietary information.

PRSA Technology Section
www.tech.prsa.org
The Public Relations Society of America divides its activities into sections, and the Technology section has assembled a vast array of resources on its Web site.

Tim Berners-Lee's Style Guide for Online Hypertext
www.w3.org/Provider/Style/Overview.html
Berners-Lee invented the World Wide Web and currently chairs the World Wide Web Consortium, so he should know! The site advises on hypertext structure and elements to include in each document.

What Is Good Hypertext Writing?
www.usouthal.edu/usa/business/iems/jutta1.htm
Jutta Degener writes and teaches in Germany but has used outstanding English to promote notions of what makes for good online copy. The

associated list of "dangerous words" is a winner, too, warning writers of onscreen text to avoid everything from "click" to "hot."

General Internet Information

All About the Internet
www.isoc.org/internet-history/
A brief history of the Internet, including an Internet timeline, from the official Internet Society.

Cyberatlas
www.cyberatlas.com
A compendium of Internet statistics and research focusing on demographics and use of the Internet and its various components. Well maintained and up-to-date.

DejaNews
www.dejanews.com
A utility that allows you to find Usenet newsgroup postings that contain words that match your query.

Internet Index
www.openmarket.com/intindex/
Interesting facts about the Internet, updated regularly.

Newsgroups on the Net
www.internetdatabase.com/usenet.htm
A collection of resources about Usenet, including a listing of active newsgroups, links to newsgroup FAQs, and a master list of Usenet hierarchies.

HTML Information and Tutorials

A Beginner's Guide to HTML
www.ncsa.uiuc.edu/General/Internet?WWW/HTMLPrimer.html
Widely acclaimed as the best beginner's guide to HTML, this tutorial from the National Center for Supercomputing Applications walks you

through the various stages and elements of Web page and site development.

Creating Killer Web Sites
www.killersites.com
A companion site to the book by David Siegel, which includes sites that meet the author's criteria.

Elements of HTML Style
www.book.uci.edu/Staff/StyleGuide.html
A brief and elementary—but useful—overview of basic rules for good Web pages.

Spinster's Guide to Writing for the Web
www.bc.edu/bc_org/avp/ulib/sys/html/spin.html
From Boston College's library, this guide offers ideas for improving Web site readability and design.

Web Pages That Suck
www.webpagesthatsuck.com
Learn good design by looking at bad design.

Webmaster Reference Library
www.webreference.com
An electronic magazine coupled with a variety of resources.

Yale Web Style Guide
info.med.yale.edu/caim/manual/contents.html
Covers interface design, site design, page design, Web graphics, multimedia, and animation.

Search Engines and Directories

AltaVista
www.altavista.digital.com
One of the early search engines, from Digital Equipment Corporation.

HotBot
www.hotbot.com
The author's favorite search engine.

InfoSeek
www.infoseek.com
A combination index and engine, allowing you to scour Usenet newsgroups, the news, and companies.

Lycos
www.lycos.com
A combination index and engine.

Search.Com
www.search.com
An all-in-one index of search engines and indexes.

Yahoo!
www.yahoo.com
The best of the search indexes, featuring a variety of other elements,
including news, weather, and maps.

General Writing Resources

Bartlett's Familiar Quotations
www.columbia.edu/acis/bartleby/bartlett/
If you need a quote quickly, visit this site, type in a search term, and
you'll have plenty of options from which to choose.

Grammar and Style Notes
www.english.upenn.edu/~jlynch/Grammar/
A good resource for style and grammar. List owner Jack Lynch even
responds to queries about grammar and style.

Strunk & White's Elements of Style
www.columbia.edu/acis/bartleby/strunk/
The generally accepted bible of writing style, online for quick reference.

Copyright, Trademark, and Other Online Legal Issues

Cyberspace Law for Non-Lawyers

www.ssrn.com/update/lsn/cyberspace/csl_lessons.html

Lectures from a mailing list that provides a compendium of legal issues related to the Internet and the online world, from copyright and privacy to libel and contract law. Fascinating and easy to digest. The site includes a discussion area where you can raise a question and get a genuine legal opinion. It's an invaluable resource.

Appendix E
Recommended Reading

A wealth of literature exists that can help you conduct public relations and communications campaigns, understand the Internet and the World Wide Web, and use the Internet and the Web for your marketing-oriented communications efforts. This list of recommended readings is by no means comprehensive. I recommend them based on having read them or known the authors. Most of these books *are* available for purchase via the Internet, either by visiting Amazon Books (at *www.amazon.com*) or from the author's Web site, (*www.holtz.com*), which provides links directly to the Amazon listing for each title.

Public Relations and Communications

Barton, Laurence, *Crisis in Organizations: Managing and Communicating in the Heat of Chaos* (South-Western, 1992).
  Detailed research on hundreds of strategic challenges facing organizations such as Coca-Cola, Chrysler, and AT&T. Prepare for the unexpected by examining possible crises, including product recalls, industrial accidents, boycotts, hostile takeovers, and strikes.

Bivins, Thomas H., *Handbook for Public Relations Writing* (NTC Business Books, 1996).
  Writing guidelines for the traditional tools of public relations, including press releases, newsletters, annual reports, and speeches.

Caywood, Clarke L., ed., *The Handbook of Strategic Public Relations and Integrated Communications* (McGraw-Hill, 1997).

Forty-five authors contributed to this book, which reviews the study and practice of strategic public relations.

Degan, Clara, *Communicator's Guide to Marketing* (Sheffield Publishing Company, 1987).
A classic review of the role of communications in product and service marketing.

Dilenschneider, Robert, ed., *Dartnell's Public Relations Handbook* (Dartnell, 1996).
Dilenschneider headed Hill & Knowlton, one of the world's largest public relations firms, for several years. He has assembled a book that provides a solid overview of the essential elements of corporate, crisis, and product public relations.

Dougherty, Devon, *Crisis Communications: What Every Executive Needs to Know* (Walker, 1992).
Actions to take before, during, and after a crisis hits a corporation.

Dozier, David M., *Manager's Guide to Excellence in Public Relations and Communication Management* (Lawrence Erlbaum Associates, 1995).
A narrative guide to a major study funded by the Research Foundation of the International Association of Business Communicators, this book offers an easy-to-use set of principles for the management of effective, results-oriented communications.

Grunig, James E., ed., *Excellence in Public Relations and Communication Management* (Lawrence Erlbaum Associates, 1992).
The first result of a major study funded by the Research Foundation of the International Association of Business Communicators, this exhaustive academic tome lays the groundwork for a definition of excellence in public relations and communications management. This is the work that established the foundation of two-way symmetrical communication that is at the core of this book.

Howard, Carole M., and Wilma K. Mathews, *On Deadline: Managing Media Relations* (Waveland Press, 1994).

One of the best books on managing media relations, written by two women who have been there and done that.

Jackson, Patrick, *Public Relations Practices* (Prentice Hall, 1995).
A public relations casebook for teachers, students, and practitioners.

Seitel, Fraser P., *The Practice of Public Relations* (Prentice Hall, 1998).
Seitel, a columnist for the communications industry weekly newsletter *Ragan Report,* is always controversial and intriguing. This book, in its sixth edition, focuses on the practical aspects of conducting public relations efforts and includes forty new case studies.

Introduction to the Internet

Kent, Peter, *The Complete Idiot's Guide to the Internet* (Que, 1997).
If you really need one of these books, that is the one to get.

Krol, Ed, and Paula Ferguson, *The Whole Internet User's Guide & Catalog* (O'Reilly & Associates, 1995).
A down-to-earth explanation of the Internet and all its various components, explained so a complete novice can understand it without being talked down to. An edition was produced to address the Internet capabilities of Windows 95.

Pomeroy, Brian, *Beginnernet: A Beginner's Guide to the Internet and the World Wide Web* (Slack, 1997).
Get online fast and begin using e-mail, newsgroups, the Web, mailing lists, and other Internet tools.

Writing HTML

Lemay, Laura, *Teach Yourself Web Publishing with HTML 4 in 14 Days* (Sams, 1997).
Lemay is the undisputed queen of HTML self-teaching books, and this is the comprehensive guide to the latest version of HTML with

easy-to-follow lessons. There's a seven-day version of the book as well, along with one that is nonversion-specific.

Morris, Mary E. S., *HTML for Fun and Profit* (Prentice Hall Computer Books, 1998).
Another comprehensive guide by a well-regarded author.

Web Design

Sather, Andrew, ed., *Creating Killer Interactive Web Sites: The Art of Integrating Interactivity and Design* (Hayden, 1997).
A walk through the process of designing a Web site for a client, from brainstorming to consultation to delivery and management.

Siegel, David, *Designing Killer Web Sites: The Art of Third Generation Site Design* (Hayden, 1996).
A technical approach from a graphic designer who understands the evolution of the Web from the perspective of both users and designers.

Wilson, Steve, *World Wide Web Design Guide* (Hayden, 1995).
Too old to incorporate new technologies and advances in HTML, this book still covers fundamentals every site designer should keep in mind.

The Internet, Business, and Culture

Frenza, J. P., and Michelle Szabo, *Web & New Media Pricing Guide* (Hayden, 1996).
Configuring prices, creating or analyzing proposals, setting up budgets, dealing with intellectual property rights and copyright issues, and maintaining client relations.

Hagel, John III, and Arthur G. Armstrong, *NetGain: Expanding Markets Through Virtual Communities* (Harvard Business, 1997).
Two McKinsey & Company consultants talk about the future of

virtual communities as a driving force for business and commerce. Compelling.

Janal, Daniel S., *Protect Your Business From Being Stalked, Conned, or Blackmailed on the Web* (John Wiley & Sons, 1998).

Keen, Peter G. W., *Online Profits: A Manager's Guide to Electronic Commerce* (Harvard Business, 1997).
The risks and rewards of doing business online, presented as a primer for managers who still consider themselves clueless.

Norton, Bob, et al., *Understanding Business on the Internet* (Barrons, 1997).
The business publisher's perspective on the impact the Internet is having on business.

Rheingold, Howard, *The Virtual Community: Homesteading on the Electronic Frontier* (Harper Perennial, 1994).
The best book to help you understand the nature of online communities by an author who has himself become an Internet cultural icon.

Schulman, Martin A., et al., *The Internet Strategic Plan: A Step-by-Step Guide for Connecting Your Company* (John Wiley & Sons, 1997).
Checklists, flowcharts, and worksheets for setting up an Internet business plan for your company or client.

Internet Law

Lee, Lewis, ed., *Intellectual Property for the Internet* (Wiley Law Publications, 1997).
This book's steep price of $155 may reflect lawyers' hourly rates, but it covers just about every aspect of the Internet as it relates to legal issues.

Rosenoer, Jonathon, *Cyberlaw: The Law of the Internet* (Springer-Verlag, 1996).
Easy-to-read guide for businesspeople, not lawyers.

Marketing on the Internet

Ellsworth, Jill H., and Matthew V. Ellsworth, *Marketing on the Internet* (John Wiley & Sons, 1996). Somewhat technical in nature, this book reviews the applications of new and emerging technologies as tools for marketing and promotion.

Janal, Daniel S., *The Online Marketing Handbook: How to Promote, Advertise and Sell Your Products and Services on the Internet* (John Wiley & Sons, 1998).

One of the best overviews of how to market products and services online, written in an engaging and entertaining manner by one of the best speakers on the subject.

O'Keefe, Steve, *Publicity on the Internet: Creating Successful Publicity Campaigns on the Internet and the Commercial Online Services* (John Wiley & Sons, 1996).

Getting the word out on using the Internet and other online tools. Includes specific places to go and steps to take in order to get mentioned by various sites and services.

Settles, Craig, *Cybermarketing: Essentials for Success* (Ziff-Davis, 1995).

Settles's company, Successful Marketing, designed Symantec's media relations Web site when the Norton computer software line for Windows 95 was launched. His book provides insight based on experience.

Sherwin, Gregory R., and Emily N. Avila, *Connecting Online: Creating a Successful Image on the Internet* (Oasis, 1998).

An Internet overview for public relations professionals. A focus on the tools brings PR practitioners up to speed on what's available, along with tips on how to get Internet and Web elements built. More here on evaluating Unix or NT than building online campaigns, but it's useful stuff if you want to get a handle on the technology as it applies to your work in a hurry.

Glossary

To deal with a printer, public relations practitioners need a working knowledge of printing lingo. Working with the professionals who produce your online efforts requires the same degree of competence in their lingo. Following are key terms you are likely to encounter as you manage the production of online communications efforts.

access   Getting what you need, usually with permission, from whoever holds it. Access to the Web or the Internet generally refers to a connection through an access provider (also known as an Internet service provider) or a commercial online service (such as CompuServe).

access log   See *log*.

access provider   See *ISP*.

Acrobat   Produced by Adobe Systems Incorporated, this software allows you to capture a document with all of its original formatting—regardless of the software application used to produce it—and let others view it on their computers, regardless of the platform they use. The file Acrobat produces is known as a PDF (portable document format). You need an Acrobat reader to view the document, which is available free from Adobe or anybody with the software to produce a PDF file. PDF has become a *de facto* format on the Internet and works as a plugin to most current Web browsers. Thus, if you create a Web page with a link to a PDF file, the file automatically appears with all original formatting directly on the Web page.

ActiveX   A Microsoft standard for programs that can run in Windows, Macintosh, or Web environments. These programs give you the ability to build interactivity into Web pages that go beyond the limits of HTML. ActiveX "components" can do many of the same things Java can do, and ActiveX also can work in tandem with Java.

address   One of three things: (1) **Internet address**, the domain or associated name that you use to get to a host computer; (2) **home page address**, or URL, of a particular Web site; or (3) **e-mail address**, which you use to send e-mail to an individual.

agent (or **intelligent agent**)   A program that gathers information or performs a service based on parameters you establish, but on a schedule and without your direct involvement.

algorithm   A formula or procedure that solves a problem.

animated GIF   A graphic image made up of independent graphic files that combine to create movement on a Web page.

applet   Small application programs, generally associated with the Java programming language. Java applications that run on Web pages are known as applets.

application   Short for **application program.** Microsoft Word, Corel Draw, and FileMaker Pro are all applications.

article   In the online world, a message that is posted to a Usenet discussion group.

ASCII   American Standard Code for Information Interchange. In general, these are the characters that you see on your keyboard. ASCII is the most common format for text files in computers and on the Internet.

asynchronous   From the Greek, meaning "not at the same time." Discussion forums are asynchronous because participants don't all need to be participating at the same time. Rather, one person can post a message and leave; others can log on later, read the message, and respond. The original contributor comes back at his leisure to view responses.

auto-responder   Software used to generate a prepared message and send it as e-mail in response to e-mail you receive. Any message delivered to a specific address automatically generates the response from the software. Many organizations establish an e-mail address with the name "info" (as in *info@acme.com*) and invite people to send e-mail to the address in order to get more information about the company or its products or services.

avatar   A digital representation of an individual to be used in an online environment. In some 3D worlds, for example, you can pick a fish, a chess piece, or some other character to represent you to other avatars, each of which stands in for the real, live individual sitting at her computer.

back end   An application or program that supports an application or program an individual is using. This application or program usually resides close to where the required resource resides. See also *front end.*

backbone   A larger transmission path into and from which smaller lines feed. On the Internet, local and regional telecommunications networks connect to a backbone in order to send traffic generated locally over long distances.

bandwidth   How much stuff you can send at once. A system with low bandwidth is one that cannot handle the transmission of too much information at any given time. This type of network would be an unlikely candidate for audio and video streams, for example. High bandwidth, on the other hand, means there's plenty of room for many people to grab big files at the same time. Bandwidth is proportional to digital speed. A modem that connects at 28,800 bits per second (bps) has only half the bandwidth of one that connects at 57,600 bps.

banner   A graphic image on a Web site. Banners, generally horizontal strips, are used as a graphic identity for a Web site or as an advertisement (as in banner ads).

baud   Still used but not accurately as a unit of measure for data transmission capacity. It has been replaced by *bits per second* (bps), which is frequently mistakenly referred to as *bauds per second.*

BBS   Bulletin board system (or service). A computer that can be reached by phone or telnet for the purpose of sharing information, exchanging messages, and uploading and downloading files. Computers configured to function as a BBS must contain BBS software. Most BBSs are focused on special interests, such as political discussion, local communities, or games. There are more than 40,000 BBSs active worldwide, each run by a sysop (or system operator), many of whom run their own BBSs from their bedrooms or garages.

beta   Software in the second phase of testing. In this phase, software is generally distributed to a group of volunteer testers from outside the developing organization. These beta testers provide feedback that is used to correct bugs and improve the software before releasing it for sale to the public.

bit   From a combination of *binary digit.* In digital terms, the smallest unit of information. Bits have just one binary value—either a zero or a one. Combinations of bits, which are stored in memory and used to execute instructions, are called bytes. Generally, there are eight bits in a byte.

BitNet   Because It's Time Network, a network of educational sites separate from the Internet, but from which e-mail is freely exchanged on the Internet.

bookmark   As a noun, stored links to your favorite sites. Most World Wide Web browsers allow you to store links. Some browsers give them other names. Microsoft Internet Explorer, for instance, refers to them as favorites.

Microsoft uses the term *bookmark* in its FrontPage Web authoring program as a synonym for internal page anchors (hyperlinks within a single page). As a verb, bookmark refers to the act of storing a site's URL in the browser's bookmark section (as in, "I visited a really great site yesterday, so I bookmarked it").

Boolean   A type of search terminology, named for the English mathematician George Boole. Searching for information on the Web and in other online archives (such as the Lexis-Nexis database) requires the use of Boolean searching, which employs "operators," words such as *and* and *or* that connect to other words and provide the instructions used to complete a search.

boot   To start your computer or, more technically, to load an operating system into your computer (an automatic function on most workstations that occurs when you turn the computer on). It comes from the nontechnical phrase "pull yourself up by your bootstraps."

browser   A program that serves as a graphical interface to the World Wide Web. Mosaic was the original browser; the two most commonly used browsers today are Netscape Navigator and Microsoft Internet Explorer. Browsers "parse" HTML files, converting the instructions contained in the code into the text, formatting, images, interactivity, and multimedia the page author intended you to see.

bulletin board system   See *BBS*.

byte   An eight bit-long string that represents a character, letter, or symbol on the computer.

C and C++   Programming languages that are widely used in the programming community.

cascading style sheet (CSS)   A means of instructing a Web browser how to display certain graphical elements of a Web page. Cascading style sheets were introduced in 1997 and provide desktop publishing-like control over type in Web pages.

CDF   See *Channel Definition Format.*

certificate (or **security certificate**)   A file sent to you identifying the source of a program or other item you are about to receive on your computer. Used to ensure that you that you are receiving the information or file from a valid source.

certificate authority   An issuer of security certificates.

CGI   Common gateway interface, the usual method for a Web server to pass control to an application program and receive data back when it's done. For example, if you complete a form online, the data you submit are passed by

CGI to an application that resides on the server, where they are processed, and the results returned to you on your computer screen. Most of the code that is written for CGI scripts is completed in either the PERL or TCL programming languages.

cgi-bin The most common name of a directory on a Web server in which CGI scripts are stored. The *bin* part of the directory name is short for "binary."

Channel Definition Format (CDF) The "push" technology developed by Microsoft for incorporation in its Internet Explorer Web browser. See also *Netcaster.*

chat To type back and forth with other people on the Internet (or another online service) in real time. The biggest venue for chat is on an Internet service called Internet Relay Chat (IRC).

click To press a mouse button, usually over a hyperlink, in order initiate an action on a Web page.

click rate The frequency with which visitors to a Web site click on an advertisement (such as a banner ad) that is displayed on the page.

click stream The sequence a Web site visitor uses to navigate through a site or from site to site. You start on a given page, then follow a link to another page, then another link to a different page, and so on. The total route you took is your click stream.

client The requesting program or user in a client-server relationship. When you type a URL into a Web browser, you and your browser are the client, making a request of the server that contains the information you wish to retrieve.

co-location A server that belongs to one person or group that is physically located on an Internet-connected network that belongs to another person or group. Many companies make a living by providing a network on which you can co-locate your server, saving you the expense of acquiring your own Internet connection.

common gateway interface See *CGI.*

compression The reduction of the size of data in order to save space or transmission time. Most audio and video that you retrieve over the Web was compressed in order to allow you to retrieve it in a reasonable amount of time.

cookie A file that is placed on your computer hard drive by a Web site you have visited. The next time you visit that particular site, it looks for the cookie, which helps the site remember who you are, what you've done on the site before, and any other information you may have stored. Contrary to popular misconception, cookies cannot read your hard drive, gather files from your computer, damage your data, or provide anybody with access to your system.

counter   A program on a Web site that counts the number of people who have visited the site. Many counters look like speedometers.

CSS   See *cascading style sheet.*

cyber   A prefix attached to just about any noun in order to couch something as part of the computer or online age. Thus, cyberspace is the online world, cyberfiction is fiction published online, and cyberculture is the culture adopted by people who inhabit cyberspace.

CyberCash   Digital money that exists on your computer. The total value of your CyberCash is reduced each time you use it to buy something. There are no standards yet for CyberCash, although several companies offer competing methods.

cyberspace   The virtual space in which computer-mediated communication takes place. Originally coined by science-fiction author William Gibson in his novel *Neuromancer.*

data   Information that exists in digital form, usually on a computer.

data mining   The analysis of data in order to uncover information or relationships that may not have been evident before.

database   A collection of data—usually by a program designed to facilitate the collection—making it easy to access, manage, update, change, and query the information. Most database applications on the market are relational databases, which allow you to reorganize information in a variety of ways.

desktop   A computer display that provides you with graphical metaphors for the same tools you might use in an office—documents, writing tools, project folders, etc.

digital camera   A camera that records and stores the images it has photographed in digital format so they can be displayed or transmitted by a computer. No film is used in a digital camera.

digizine   A magazine delivered in digital form, such as on CD-ROM or a Web page. See also *eZine.*

directory   A Web site that attempts to catalog the contents of the World Wide Web. Unlike search engines, with which they are sometimes mistaken, directories apply human decision making in the process of placing sites into categories. Yahoo! is a search directory.

discussion group A catchall phrase for any bulletin board where you can leave messages to which others can respond asynchronously. Discussion groups exist on the Internet in a system called Usenet, on commercial on-line services, and on Web pages, as well as on privately run BBSs.

disintermediation Giving an individual direct access to information or resources that usually would require a mediator, filter, or third party.

display The visual interface through which you interact with a computer, usually the monitor. Display modes are the levels of clarity with which you view information on the monitor. There are four general display modes: CGA (Color Graphics Adapter, the earliest of the color display systems introduced by IBM), EGA (Enhanced Graphics Adapter, which allowed viewing of up to sixteen colors), VGA (Video Graphics Array, the accepted minimum standard for current computers, which allows you to see between sixteen and 256 colors), and SVGA (Super Video Graphics Array, which can display up to 16 million colors).

distributed Said of information that is spread out over a network.

dithering A computer program's attempt to approximate a color from a mixture of available colors that is undertaken when the desired color is not available. Netscape Navigator, for example, offers a palette of colors. If a color you present on a Web page is not one of the palette colors, Navigator dithers a color from those colors that are available in an attempt to come as close as possible to the color you wanted.

domain Generally, a set of network addresses organized by hierarchy. The top-level hierarchy specifies the purpose of the domain (e.g., *.com* is a commercial domain). The next level identifies a unique place within the top-level domain (equivalent to an IP address). On the Internet, domain refers to a name with which a name server can associate a record. A domain name locates an organization on the Internet. For example, *www.amacom.org* locates an Internet address for AMACOM Publishing. The domain name system (DNS) takes the name you entered into a Web browser and translates it into a numeric IP address that the Internet understands.

download Transmission of a file from one computer (usually a server) to another (usually an individual workstation). On the Internet, you usually download a file when you request it from a Web site.

dynamic HTML New Hypertext Markup Language tags, options, style sheets, and programming that allow you to create Web pages that are more animated and responsive to user interaction than was available with the last iteration of HTML (version 3.2).

EDI Electronic Data Interchange, a standard format for the exchange of business data, including online financial transactions.

Electronic Data Interchange   See *EDI.*

e-mail   The exchange of messages by computer.

emoticon   See *smiley.*

encryption   The conversion of data into a format that cannot be deciphered by anybody other than the individual(s) for whom the data were intended. The format into which data are converted is known as a cipher.

end user   The individual at a workstation who uses the information, software, or hardware you have produced. The individual for whom the information, software, or hardware is designed.

engine   A program that performs an essential function. On the Internet, a search engine is a program that uses an algorithm to search an index of words from Web sites, newsgroups, or FTP archives based on a specific query or search argument.

enterprise   An organization or institution that uses computers as an integral part of its business.

environment   The combination of hardware and software in a computer (as in an "operating system environment") or on a computer network (as in "the intranet environment").

ethernet   A protocol that makes it possible to run a local area network (LAN).

extranet   A collaborative network based on Internet technology (i.e., TCP/IP protocols) that links an organization with key audiences. Extranets are different from Web sites because audiences (including customers, suppliers, and strategic partners) have access to proprietary information, such as inventory and account status. Audiences also can submit information that can be sent directly into proprietary company databases. Often, an extranet is conditional access to selected portions of a company's intranet.

ezine   A magazine that exists online. Short for "electronic magazine," ezines can be independent online publications or the digital versions of print publications. See also *digizine.*

FAQs   Frequently Asked Questions, lists of questions and answers that provide people with basic information on a given topic or site. FAQs originated in Usenet newsgroups, where newcomers would pepper the existing community with questions that already had been repeatedly addressed. FAQs evolved so newcomers could get answers without bothering those who have been part of the community, keeping the online discussions more focused on new and emerging issues. FAQs now exist on Web sites and mailing lists as well.

file A single unit of data saved under a name. These can be executable files (those that launch a program), data files (something you created and saved in an application), or support files (those that interact with a program to make it work).

file format Usually a three-letter extension appended to the name of a file. That extension determines its format. For example, *exe* is an executable file, *doc* is a Microsoft Word file, *wp5* is a WordPerfect file, and *bak* is a backup file.

file sharing The process of making files available to others on a computer network. Networks allow you to establish various levels of access, so some people may have the ability to work with your files, some may be able only to view them, and others may not be able to see them at all.

File Transfer Protocol See *FTP*.

finger A program you can use through your Internet service provider to get information on another user (such as the user's name, the Internet service provider he uses, the last time he was logged on, and other information he may choose to make available).

firewall A combination of hardware and software that is used to isolate a computer network from intrusion by the outside world, usually users of other networks.

flame An e-mail or newsgroup message that is the online equivalent of hysterical yelling and screaming. Flames often attack individuals for their ideas, the way they expressed themselves, or their online behavior.

flame war An online discussion that has degenerated into a series of personal attacks.

flamebait A message posted to a newsgroup that is deliberately provocative, designed to elicit strong responses, or flames.

forum A virtual discussion venue hosted by a non-Usenet service. See also *newsgroup*.

frame A separate section of a Web page that you can control independently of other sections. Frames are created in HTML, resulting in an effect that establishes separate windows within the Web browser. For example, an index of a site could exist in a narrow frame on the left side of the browser; clicking on each entry opens up a new page in the larger frame that occupies most of the browser to the right of the index frame.

freeware Software that is given away at no charge, usually made available for downloading.

Frequently Asked Questions See *FAQs*.

front end An application or interface with which the user interacts directly. See also *back end*.

FTP   File Transfer Protocol, the TCP/IP protocol that enables the transfer of files from a server to a user's computer.

gateway   The entrance to a network.

GIF   Graphics Interchange Format, a standard graphical file format, originally developed by CompuServe, that is the predominant format used on the World Wide Web. See also *JPEG*.

gigabyte   About 1,000 megabytes, or about a billion bytes.

Gopher   An Internet-based system for storing files in a hierarchical format. Gopher (developed at the University of Minnesota) predates the World Wide Web as a means of finding information made available for public retrieval. Most of the material on Gopher servers is getting outdated as the Internet migrates to the Web; however, many academic institutions still rely on it.

gopherspace   All of the information contained on all of the Gopher servers across the entire Internet.

graphical user interface   See *GUI*.

Graphics Interchange Format   See *GIF*.

groupware   Software designed to run on a network that allows groups of people to work together in a collaborative fashion regardless of their physical proximity to one another. Lotus Notes is groupware.

GUI   Graphical user interface, the graphical, visual metaphors on a computer screen that a user uses in order to work with the information the computer contains. Windows 95 and the Mac OS are GUIs. DOS, which is text-based, is *not*.

helper application   A small program that works in tandem with a Web browser in order to complete an action or an effect. When a link on a Web page is associated with a file that runs on a helper application, the browser automatically launches that application, and the file runs in the application's separate window. This is different from a plugin, which runs as part of the browser window. See also *plugin*.

hit   A means of measuring the number of files downloaded, requested from your server. Each hit represents a request for a single file. If your Web page has two graphics and a Java applet, four hits are recorded each time that page is accessed: one for the page itself, one for each of the graphics, and one for the applet.

home page   The entryway or starting point for a World Wide Web (or intranet) site. The first page someone sees when visiting your site is generally named *index.html* and is almost always the home page.

host A computer that has full two-way access to other computers on the Internet. Hosts are assigned IP (Internet Protocol) addresses made up of a local number and the network number.

HTML Hypertext Markup Language, the scripting code used to create Web pages. HTML is supposed to be a standard code—that is, the script produced for any Web page produces similar results in any browser. That standardization is addressed by the World Wide Web Consortium. However, in their competitive efforts, Microsoft and Netscape continually add new features as elements of new browser versions, hoping to have the features incorporated into the next official standard iteration of HTML.

HTTP Hypertext Transfer Protocol, the TCP/IP protocol that makes the World Wide Web work on the Internet. HTTP governs the treatment of files—including graphic, text, sound, and video—between Web servers and browsers.

hyperlink Text produced in HTML that is tagged to be presented as a link to another element. Hyperlinks (shortened from the original "hypertext link") can take you to another part of the same page, another page on the same site, another page on another Web site, a non-Web document (such as a word-processor file), or a multimedia element. Links that go to a multimedia element are often referred to as hypermedia.

Hypertext Markup Language See *HTML.*
Hypertext Transfer Protocol See *HTTP.*

imagemap Enables you to click on a part of a graphic on a Web page hotspot that is hyperlinked to another destination. Imagemaps designate the coordinates of the hotspots and incorporate the links themselves. There are two kinds of imagemaps. Client-side imagemaps are built into the HTML code and are enacted directly by the browser. Server-side imagemaps are more complex, requiring a separate file with hotspot coordinates to be stored on the server.

impression Each time an HTML page is requested from a server. Different from hits, which record only individual files requested from a server, impressions are more valuable to communicators who need to know how many times a page has been viewed.

information technology See *IT.*
Integrated Services Digital Network See *ISDN.*
intelligent agent See *agent.*
Interactive Voice Response See *IVR.*

interactivity The exchange between a computer and the individual using it. Various programs and applications have varying degrees of interactivity, with games at the high end and productivity tools like word processors at the low end. The World Wide Web is popular in large part because it provides tremendous levels of interactivity to users.

interface   As a noun, the various elements on the computer screen (including text, buttons, and other tools) that allow you to interact with the program or application you are using. As a verb, to interact or communicate with someone or something.

Internet   The global network of computer networks that are interconnected using the TCP/IP suite of protocols.

Internet Protocol   See *IP.*

Internet Relay Chat   See *IRC.*

Internet service provider   See *ISP.*

Internet telephony   The use of the Internet for voice telephone calls, faxes, and other activities generally associated with the telephone. Since a connection to the Internet is almost always a local call, long-distance charges evaporate when you use the Internet. However, you sacrifice sound clarity and usually experience a very short delay when the party at the other end speaks.

intranet   The principles and protocols of the Internet applied to a private network within an organization for the exclusive use of employees (and, in some cases, other select audiences, such as suppliers and strategic partners).

IP   Internet Protocol, the set of rules responsible for the address of each packet of information sent from one computer to another on the Internet.

IP address   A thirty-two-bit number that identifies each sender and/or receiver of information that is sent in packets across the Internet.

IRC   Internet Relay Chat, the system for real-time dialogue between people on the Internet. IRC allows individuals to establish chat rooms with names that identify the topic under discussion. Individuals "enter" the room and engage in real-time chat by typing back and forth to one another.

ISDN   Integrated Services Digital Network, a means of sending data over regular phone lines at speeds higher than possible using ordinary standards. If you have an ISDN line, you also need a terminal adapter or a router to convert the data to information you can view on your computer screen.

ISP   Internet service provider, a business that provides access to the Internet for individuals and businesses. You would use an ISP if your organization does not have its own point of presence on the Internet. When you dial a number to connect to the Internet, you are dialing one of your ISP's modem numbers. ISPs provide a range of services, including hosting Web sites.

IT Information technology, a common acronym for the departments within organizations that are responsible for computer-related activities. The term also relates to any technology used to create, store, exchange, and use information.

IVR Interactive Voice Response, a computerized system that walks callers through a series of prompts in order to obtain information from recordings over the telephone.

Java A programming language developed by Sun Microsystems that can be executed on a Web browser by any computer regardless of the platform it uses. The programs developed in Java are called applets and run directly in the browser window. Java applets can produce animation, interactivity, and a number of other Web programs.

Java Development Kit See *JDK.*

JavaScript A scripting language developed by Netscape that can be incorporated into Web pages. Not to be confused with Java, JavaScript is used to create functionality on Web pages that ranges from images that change when you roll a cursor over them to automatically changing pages (such as changing to the current date).

JDK Java Development Kit, a software development package from Sun Microsystems that implements the basic set of tools needed to write, test, and debug Java applications and applets.

Joint Photographic Experts Group See *JPEG.*

JPEG Joint Photographic Experts Group, a format for displaying graphic images on Web pages. JPEG files (which have the extension *jpg*) are better for photographs than GIF, which is better for clip art.

Jughead A tool used for searching gopherspace. This search utility is similar to Veronica, another search facility. Both are named after characters from the Archie comic book series.

junk e-mail Also known as spam, unsolicited e-mail that comes to your inbox, usually trying to sell you something. See also *spam.*

KB Kilobyte, about 1,000 bytes.

kbps Kilobits (or thousands of bits) per second. A measure of bandwidth. A 28.8 modem transmits data from the Internet to your computer at 28,800 kbps.

killer app Killer application, an application or program that becomes so popular, useful, or necessary that it induces people to buy computers and install networks in order to use it. Many people have bought computers in order to exchange e-mail, making e-mail the killer app of the Internet.

kilobit   A thousand bits. See also *kbps*.

kilobyte   See *KB*.

kiosk   A common location for a computer, keyboard, and monitor where people can access information. Kiosks are generally perceived as high-tech structures, such as those found at entrances to malls, hospitals, and high-rise buildings. However, a kiosk can just as well be a table or a cubicle containing a computer. The only requirement to qualify as a kiosk is that the system be available to groups of people who are in physical proximity to the kiosk.

kludge   A patchwork solution to a technology problem.

K-12   Kindergarten through 12th grade. A designation used to identify the purpose of a Web page or other online resource (as in, "This site is an ideal K-12 resource").

LAN   Local area network, a network of computers connected to a single server that exists within a small geographic space. Individuals on the same floor or in the same building might be on a LAN.

leased line   A phone line that is rented for exclusive use, twenty-four hours a day, seven days a week, from one location to another location. Required for the highest-speed data connections.

legacy   Applications and data that were produced for the last technology but still exist within the enterprise. IT departments are routinely challenged to keep legacy data useful even though the technology used to store and use the data has changed.

listserv   As a proper noun, a program that is used to manage e-mail mailing lists. As a common noun, a generic name for all programs that manage e-mail mailing lists. In both cases, users subscribe to the list by sending an e-mail message to the listserv. Subsequently, any messages sent to the mailing list are distributed by the listserv to all subscribers.

livecam   A computer attached directly to another computer and linked (usually) to a Web site in order to display a current image. Also known as Webcams, these cameras are used to show progress on a construction project or how a particular landmark looks at any given moment.

local area network   See *LAN*.

log (or **access log**)   A file that records each individual request for a file that a server has received.

login   As a noun, the account name used to gain access to a computer system. As a verb, the act of logging in to a computer system.

lurk   To read posts in a discussion group (such as a Usenet newsgroup) without posting an article of your own. Lurking gives you the opportunity to get the lay of the land, learn the culture of the group, and find out who the influential participants are. As long as you don't post a message, nobody knows you visited.

mail bomb   The practice of sending huge amounts of e-mail to a person or address with the sole intent of punishing somebody, usually for sending spam (unsolicited e-mail) or breeching netiquette. Mail bombs can cause entire servers to crash, affecting everybody who uses the server, not just the offending party.

mailing list   A list of people who subscribe to a listserv. See also *listserv.*

mainframe   A large computer that handles the heavy-duty computing activities of businesses.

markup   Characters inserted into text files that are interpreted by a program in order to determine how the text (and other elements) should be displayed. The characters that constitute the markup are called tags. In HTML, the markup language that gives World Wide Web pages their appearance, <b> is a tag that designates type should appear in boldface. Thus, the following line would appear in boldface on a Web browser: <b>This is boldface type.</b>

Mbone   A portion of the Internet that has been reserved for the distribution of audio or video files to multiple users at the same time. The technical term for the distribution is IP multicasting.

mbps   Megabytes (or millions of bytes) per second. A measure of bandwidth.

megabit   A million bits.

megabyte   About a million bytes. See also *mbps.*

megahertz   Also shown as Mhz and MHz, a million cycles of electromagnetic currency alteration per second. The "clock speeds" of computer microprocessors are designated by their megaherz rating. An Intel Pentium II 200-Mhz computer chip handles 200 million cycles per second.

meme   Taken from the biological notion introduced by Richard Dawkins, a meme is an adaptive mechanism that permits humans to pass ideas from one generation to the next. On the Internet, a meme is a statement that becomes accepted as fact and takes on a life of its own despite dedicated efforts to correct inaccuracies. For example, the urban myth of the Good Times virus, which is a hoax, has become a meme; it keeps cropping up despite the fact that the hoax has been soundly discredited.

mirror site   A Web site that has been copied and placed on another server in order to reduce traffic to the original server and make files available from a server located geographically closer to the individuals who might want to access them.

modem   A device that interprets analog data transmitted over a regular phone line into information that can be viewed on the computer. The word comes from "modulator demodulator," since the modem demodulates the analog signal and converts it to a digital signal the computer can understand, and modulates a digital signal from the computer, converting it into an analog signal in order to send it to somebody else via modem.

MOO   An object-oriented MUD. See also *MUD*.

Moore's Law   Posited by Gordon Moore, founder of Intel, it suggests that the amount of storage possible on a microchip doubles every eighteen months. Moore's Law is the basis for the speed with which state-of-the-art computer technology becomes obsolete.

Mosaic   The first World Wide Web browser, distributed in late 1993 by a graduate student team at the National Center for Supercomputing Applications at the University of Illinois. The team was led by Marc Andreesen, who later became a senior executive at Netscape.

mouseover   The act of rolling your mouse over an object on the computer screen, resulting in the image changing. You can create the mouseover effect using JavaScript. See also *JavaScript*.

Moving Picture Experts Group   See *MPEG*.

MPEG   Moving Picture Experts Group, the format for compressing video for transmission over the Internet.

MSIE   Microsoft Internet Explorer, Microsoft's Web browser.

MUD   Multi-user dungeon, a text-based virtual environment that provides a social environment on the Internet. The structure of a MUD can allow its builders to create multiple rooms with objects in them that can be occupied by people who visit the MUD. The metaphors employed can be as widely varied as a conference facility or a medieval castle. Those who visit the MUD can interact with each other as well as the objects that have been created and placed in the MUD's various rooms.

multicast   Data that are transmitted from one point to many points simultaneously. Used for video and audio transmissions, as well as routine updates, such as a sales staff's database. See also *Mbone*.

multimedia   Multiple media employed in a single presentation. A Web site that uses graphic images, text, and sound is a multimedia Web site.

multitasking   Doing more than one thing at a time. In computing terms, multitasking is a function of a computer that can be engaged simultaneously in multiple tasks. For example, you can receive a fax and work on a spreadsheet at the same time.

multi-user dungeon   See *MUD*.

multi-user simulated environment   See *MUSE*.

MUSE   Multi-user simulated environment, a version of a MUD. See also *MUD*.

Native   Original.

NC   Network computer, a computer designed to be linked to a network. The NC contains few elements of its own, such as a hard disk, CD-ROM, or disk drive. Instead, it is managed from the server to which it is connected, and any applications that run are downloaded from the server. Designed to be inexpensive (under $500), NCs were initially introduced by Oracle and Sun as an alternative to Microsoft's Windows operating system.

Netcaster   The "push" technology adopted by Netscape for its Navigator Web browser. See also *Channel Definition Format*.

netiquette   Standards of behavior established for the Internet, applied generally to newsgroup communities and e-mail. A combination of "network" and "etiquette."

netizen   A member of the Internet community, notably one who participates in general discussions about the Internet and its governance. Also refers to people on the Internet who use the network as a means of engaging in political debate and decision making. A combination of "network" and "citizen."

Netscape   Netscape Communications Corporation, the company that makes and sells the Navigator Web browser. Navigator is often called Netscape, but the word specifically refers to the company, not the browser. Netscape also makes server software and other related products.

network   Computers or other networks connected to one another, or combinations of computers and networks connected to one another.

network computer   See *NC*.

Network News Transfer Protocol   See *NNTP*.

newbie   Somebody who is new to the Internet. Also refers to any new user of any technology. Experienced users often grow impatient with newbies and their seemingly endless flow of questions and refer to them as clueless newbies.

newsgroup   A virtual community facilitated by the Usenet system, comprised of individuals who share an interest in a specific topic. The Usenet hierarchy starts with a broad description of the kinds of topics included, such as *rec* (recreational), *soc* (societal), and *sci* (scientific). Descending levels of the hierarchy are used to identify the specific topic under discussion (such as *soc.culture.pakistan.history*, where interested participants can discuss the cultural history of Pakistan).

NNTP   Network News Transfer Protocol, the protocol that governs Usenet newsgroups on the Internet.

node   A connection point on the Internet.

object-oriented   A form of computer programming that focuses on data objects and their relationships instead of on procedures that operate on the data.

online service (or **proprietary service**)   A service that provides access to the Internet through its own proprietary interface, and often offers its own content. Examples are CompuServe, America Online, and the Microsoft Network.

open   A system for which the underlying code has been made publicly available. Anybody can develop applications for the system, and (in many cases) it is standardized. The Internet is an open system. Lotus Notes is not; it is proprietary, because IBM (which owns Lotus) retains the source code and only authorized institutions can develop Notes applications.

operating system   The program that makes a computer work. DOS, Windows, Unix, Linux, and Mac OS are examples of operating systems. The operating system (abbreviated OS) manages the operations of all other programs on a computer.

packet   A unit of data that is sent from a computer to another point. Generally, when a file is sent over a packet switching-based network, the file is deconstructed into small (thirty-two-bit) units of data, each of which is an individual packet. Each packet takes the fastest route at the instant it is sent. When the packets arrive at their destination, they are reassembled with other packets so the recipient can view the entire file.

page   A single HTML file on the Web. A Web site is made up of multiple pages.

palette   The colors that a Web browser is designed to display. Colors included in images that do not match these colors are dithered in order to approximate the desired color as closely as possible.

password   A code used to gain access to a secure system.

PGP   Pretty Good Privacy, a tool for encrypting messages that can be decrypted only by the individual for whom it was intended.

Pixel   The unit of measure for computer screens. Screen resolution is defined as the number of pixels that appear horizontally and vertically on the screen. The standard resolution of 640 by 480 means that 640 pixels fit on the screen horizontally, and 480 fit vertically. The pixel is the smallest unit on the screen. Color images are made up of pixels, each of which contains only one color.

plain old telephone service   See *POTS*.

platform   The system that makes a computer work. Platforms are comprised of an operating system (such as Windows 95) and a microprocessor (such as the Intel Pentium II). The Mac OS does not work on the Intel Pentium II, just as Windows 95 does not work on the Motorola chip that powers Macintosh computers. The Windows/Intel platform has come to be known as Wintel.

plugin (or **plug-in**)   A small program that is executed as part of a Web browser (as opposed to a helper application, which runs in a separate window).

point of presence   See *POP*.

Point-to-Point Protocol   See *PPP*.

POP   Point of presence, a point of access to the Internet. Each POP has a unique IP address.

POP3   Post Office Protocol 3, the standard protocol for receiving e-mail. (SMTP—Simple Mail Transfer Protocol—is the protocol for *sending* e-mail.) Not to be confused with POP.

port 80   The default port (the place on a computer that is connected to another device) on a Web server that receives requests from browsers.

Post Office Protocol 3   See *POP3*.

posting (or **post**)   A single message added to a discussion group.

POTS   Plain old telephone service, the standard phone service, as opposed to newer technologies, such as ISDN.

PPP   Point-to-Point Protocol, a protocol that allows two computers to communicate with one another. Your Internet service provider (ISP) may use PPP to establish a connection between you and the ISP, so the ISP can pass your requests on to the Internet, then pass the responses back to you. See also *SLIP*.

presence   What you are said to possess when you have a Web site dedicated to your organization, a product, an issue, or any other particular topic.

Pretty Good Privacy   See *PGP*.

proprietary service   See *online service*.

protocol   Rules that govern the means by which data are transmitted across a network. TCP/IP is the suite of protocols that governs the Internet. Protocols that are part of the suite govern e-mail, network news, the Web, and other elements of the Net.

proxy   A device that resides on a firewall or gateway that handles requests for information. The proxy server operates based on customized instructions that determine what kind of information is to be allowed in and out of the network. Companies use proxy servers to restrict access to objectionable or nonwork-related Web sites, for example.

push   Technology that allows Web-based information to be delivered to you without your having initiated a request for the information. In general, "push" is the model that characterizes e-mail, while the Web encourages you to "pull" information. However, technologies continue to be introduced that help information providers push their Web-based information, often after users have signified their interest in having the information pushed to them.

Quicktime   A process developed by Apple Computer for viewing audio/ video/animation on a computer screen. Quicktime has been incorporated into the Web as a means of integrating video clips into a Web page.

RealAudio   Streaming audio and video technology developed by Progressive Networks. It is the *de facto* streaming technology on the Web. See also *streaming.*

router   A combination of hardware and software on the Internet that determines where a packet should be sent next.

scalability   The ability of a computer system to function well when it grows or shrinks.

search engine   A utility that allows you to search the contents of the World Wide Web, Usenet newsgroups, and other Internet data, based on a query you construct. There are two kinds of search engines. One is a directory, in which people intervene to categorize Web sites. (If you want information on how to get a passport, you would start with the "Government" category and drill down.) The other is an engine, which scours the Web, gathering all the pages it can find and indexing the words on each page. When you search an engine, the utility searches for all pages that contain the word or words you request. (Finding information on how to get a passport on an engine would involve conducting a search based on a string of words like "passport obtain new.")

Secure Sockets Layer (SSL)   A protocol designed by Netscape Communications that enables encrypted, authenticated communications to move across the Internet.

security certificate See *certificate*.

Serial Line Internet Protocol See *SLIP*.

server A combination of hardware and software that responds to requests from clients. Servers are configured to serve up Web pages, e-mail, newsgroups, and other elements.

shareware Software that is available to download so you can try it before you buy it. Most shareware works on the honor system; if you continue to use it, you are expected to pay for it, but if you don't pay, you are able to continue to use it. Recently, some shareware programs have been equipped with time-out functions that render them useless after a specified trial period (usually thirty days).

Shockwave A Web plugin that allows you to view multimedia files developed in Macromedia Director. Shockwave is commonly used for combinations of animation and sound, but it also allows the user to manipulate the image. Thus, Shockwave is popular for games that can be played directly from a Web page.

shovelware Content that is converted to HTML without any change to its structure or substance, and simply "shoveled" onto the Web.

Simple Mail Transfer Protocol See *SMTP*.

site A self-contained collection of Web pages, comprising the total "book" on a given topic. A collection of pages that address a company's lines of business is a company Web site.

SLIP Serial Line Internet Protocol, a set of rules that govern the connection between two computers, usually an individual workstation and an Internet service provider. The other popular protocol for this purpose is PPP, which has become more popular than SLIP because of its improved reliability. See also *PPP*.

smiley (or **emoticon**) ASCII text characters used to convey an emotion. Used in e-mail and in newsgroups as a substitute for facial expressions. Smileys are viewed sideways. The most common smiley is a smiling face used to connote happiness or joy: :-) If you tilt your head to the left, you see the colon is the eyes, the dash is the nose, and the close-parenthesis is the smiling mouth. Smileys were very popular as the Internet grew but have been used less and less as people have learned to express themselves in e-mail.

SMTP Simple Mail Transfer Protocol, the protocol for sending e-mail.

spam Unsolicited e-mail sent in bulk to many e-mail addresses, usually for advertising purposes. The name comes from a Monty Python routine, in which a waiter describing the restaurant's offerings increasingly adds the word "spam" to the listing until the entire description is nothing but spam.

splash screen   The first Web page you see when you go to a site when the page is designed to capture your attention. This page often introduces the site, then automatically loads the actual home page. In other instances, you see the splash page that contains a link to the home page.

SQL   Structured Query Language, a standard language for using a database in a network environment.

SSL   See *Secure Sockets Layer.*

streaming   A format for sending video and audio files over the Internet in real time. When you retrieve a video or audio stream, you see or hear the file as it reaches your computer, without having to wait for the entire file to download first.

Structured Query Language   See *SQL.*

style sheet   A definition of the characteristics of type that appears on the page, inserted into HTML code. See also *cascading style sheet.*

surf   The act of following hyperlinks from one Web page to another. Adapted from "channel surfing," which is the act of clicking through television stations with a remote control device. Surfing suggests a random approach to viewing pages as opposed to a structured search for specific information.

sysop   System operator, an individual who runs a computer server, although the term is generally associated with the individual responsible for a privately operated bulletin board system. Individuals who manage discussion forums on CompuServe are also known as sysops.

system   A collection of computer elements (e.g., hardware, software, connectivity tools) that combine to serve a common purpose.

system operator   See *sysop.*

T1, T3   A phone company-provided line that delivers Internet data directly to your building, eliminating the need for an Internet service provider, and requiring you to obtain and configure the hardware and software to essentially become an ISP for your own employees. T1 lines transmit data at 1.544 mbps and T3 lines at 44.736 mbps.

tag   Text that is used in markup to define how text should be treated. See also *hyperlink, HTML.*

TCP   Transmission Control Protocol, the protocol that tracks the packets of data that move across the Internet.

TCP/IP   Transmission Control Protocol/Internet Protocol, generally used to designate the family of protocols that define the various functions of the Internet.

telnet   A method by which you gain entry into another (host) computer on the Internet.

terabyte   About 1,000 gigabytes.

thread   The elements of an online discussion (in a newsgroup or forum), in the order in which they were added. Threaded discussion outlines show each post along with the responses, usually by indenting responses. In this way, you can determine the levels of the discussion.

TIF (or **TIFF**)   A graphics file format, very common for high-resolution graphic images but not viewable on a standard Web browser.

Transmission Control Protocol   See *TCP*.

Transmission Control Protocol/Internet Protocol   See *TCP/IP*.

uniform resource locator   See *URL*.

Unix   A computer operating system with the TCP/IP protocols built in. Many servers running on the Internet use Unix as their operating system.

URL   Uniform resource locator, the address you type into a Web browser in order to retrieve a page from a server.

Usenet   The system of asynchronous discussion groups on the Internet. See also *NNTP*.

vaporware   Software that a company has described and promised but that has not yet been produced. Many software companies float the idea of a software package in order to assess its viability in the marketplace. Vaporware also is used to describe software that has not been released by the official release date.

Veronica   A utility for searching gopherspace. It is similar to Jughead, another search facility. Both were named after characters from the Archie comic book series.

videoconference   A conference in which parties in different cities interact with one another by viewing each other on a television or computer screen. Videoconferences can involve groups or individuals. The Internet has led to the development of computer-based videoconferencing that is comparatively inexpensive, compared with previously expensive television-based systems.

virtual   Said of the computer instead of "real." A virtual meeting would be one that took place over the computer (such as a videoconference) instead of in person in a conference room.

Virtual private network (VPN)   A private network that runs using public systems, including the Internet. If you run a VPN, you save your organization the cost of having to install a "real" private network.

Virtual Reality Markup Language   See *VRML*.

virus   A program that "infects" your computer. Viruses are generally attached to other programs you might download or obtain from an infected disk. When they are activated, they launch activities that range from the harmless (such as displaying a message) to the devastating (like wiping out your hard drive). You can prevent most viruses from infecting your computer by installing an antivirus program and keeping it updated with current virus definitions.

VPN   See *virtual private network*.

VRML   Virtual Reality Modeling Language, a scripting language that allows you to create three-dimensional environments that run on the World Wide Web.

WAIS   Wide Area Information System, a commercial software package that allows indexing of vast quantities of information and then making the package searchable across networks like the Internet.

WAN   Wide area network, a collection of local area networks (LANs) that are interconnected, providing each LAN with access to the others. A WAN also can be a collection of private networks that are linked together.

Web site   A collection of Web pages that combine to form a complete entity. As the pages of a book form the entire book, so the pages of a Web site make up the entire site.

Webcam   See *livecam*.

Webcast   The delivery of a broadcast (live or delayed) over the World Wide Web.

Webcasting   The scheduled updating of news or information accomplished by pushing the information to your desktop via the World Wide Web. See also *push*.

Webmaster   A nebulous term that has little meaning but generally describes the individual with responsibility for a Web site or server. It can also mean the individual responsible for content, infrastructure, or both.

Wide Area Information System   See *WAIS*.

wide area network   See *WAN*.

wireless   Access to online or telecommunications services through signals carried over the air, rather than through wires.

workstation   A computer for individual use.

World Wide Web   The universe of resources on the Internet available using the HTTP protocol. See also *HTTP*.

zine See *ezine*.

zip A format for compressing data in order to reduce the size before transmission over a network. Reducing the size of a file means it can be transmitted more quickly, and the recipient can download it faster. When you retrieve a file that has been zipped, you need to unzip it using software designed for that purpose.

Index

(Page numbers followed by the letter *"n"* refer to footnotes.)